LITERATURE AND LANGUAGE DIVISION
THE CHICAGO PUBLIC LIBRARY
400 SOUTH STATE STREET
CHICAGO, ILLINOIS 60605

D0204714

R0000871728

REF.

FORM 125M

Literature & Philosophy Div.

The Chicago Public Library

Received_____

Chicago Public Library

REFERENCE

Form 178 rev. 1-94

THE SOUL OF WIT

A Study of John Donne

MURRAY ROSTON

OXFORD
AT THE CLARENDON PRESS
1974

Oxford University Press, Ely House, London W. 1

GLASGOW NEW YORK TORONTO MELBOURNE WELLINGTON
CAPE TOWN IBADAN NAIROBI DAR ES SALAAM LUSAKA ADDIS ABABA
DELHI BOMBAY CALCUTTA MADRAS KARACHI LAHORE DACCA
KUALA LUMPUR SINGAPORE HONG KONG TOKYO

ISBN 0 19 812053 2

© *Oxford University Press 1974*

All rights reserved. No part of this publication may be reproduced, stored in a retrieval system, or transmitted, in any form or by any means, electronic, mechanical, photocopying, recording, or otherwise, without the prior permission of Oxford University Press

REF
PR
2248
.R58

*Printed in Great Britain
at the University Press, Oxford
by Vivian Ridler
Printer to the University*

Roooo8 71728

LITERATURE AND LANGUAGE DIVISION
THE CHICAGO PUBLIC LIBRARY
400 SOUTH STATE STREET
CHICAGO, ILLINOIS 60605

16.00

PREFACE

I T will be apparent from the following pages how indebted I am to the scholarly writings of Dame Helen Gardner, Louis L. Martz, Hiram Haydn, and many others. Specific sources have been acknowledged in the notes, but I welcome this opportunity of expressing my more general appreciation of the contribution they have made to our understanding of Donne and his era. Dame Helen has recently deepened my debt significantly by her personal interest in this study, and by a number of valuable suggestions which I was able to incorporate in the text.

The final checking of the manuscript required access to larger libraries than are available in Israel. This problem was happily solved when Stanford University invited me once again to spend a sabbatical year as a visiting professor in its English department, and I am most grateful to the chairman of the department, Professor Bliss Carnochan, and to his colleagues for the warm hospitality and friendship they have always extended to me.

On a more personal note, it is a pleasure to record my gratitude to my wife Faith who, with her usual affection and quiet humour, encouraged me to find time for the writing of this book in the midst of other duties.

M.R.

Bar-Ilan University
Ramat Gan, Israel

CONTENTS

LIST OF PLATES

I

THE TWO WORLDS

DONNE'S literary reputation has proved as inconstant as the mistresses of his verse. Acclaimed in his day as the Monarch of Wit, as in some respects 'the first poet in the World', he had become by Dryden's generation a sad object-lesson of potential ability spoilt by careless diction and abstruse speculation; and although in subsequent years he retained a small coterie of distinguished admirers, he remained a minor figure, of interest to the literary historian or biographer, but almost unknown outside those circles.

The revival of his reputation in the early part of this century was dramatic. After generations of neglect, every student seemed suddenly to have his lines by heart, and there was a new excitement in the air as love and poetry, soulfulness and wit, science and the imagination became recharged by the fresh integrative vitality of his verse. Critical theory, which had with rare exceptions so long excluded Donne from the higher reaches of Parnassus, now used him as the standard of excellence against which other poets were to be measured, on the universal assumption that here at last was a poet whose literary achievement was beyond question. He was seen as encompassing within his poetic range the entire orbit of human experience, ingeniously displaying within his verse the resourcefulness of a virtuoso in linking the seemingly incongruous and incompatible to create a new poetic unity.

For his admirers in the nineteen-twenties, he was the gay rake, irreverently overthrowing all moral convention for the sake of immediate sensual pleasure; yet at the next moment posing as the saint or martyr of love, delighting in the rare purity of a refined and sacred union. The *personae* of his verse wittily assumed the antithetical roles of sceptic and mystic, of impudent philanderer and grief-stricken lover, of lay alchemist and medieval scholiast—at times alternating the parts, at others blending them into a complex personality which assimilated with apparent ease the diverse worlds of Augustine and Montaigne, of Petrarch and Loyola, of the Neoplatonic Ficino and the astronomer Kepler. The very extravagance of these unlikely combinations was, it was felt, intended to leave some teasing, residual suspicion of his own seriousness. The final commitment was left deliberately in doubt as he darted away in pursuit of new game, the dramatic realism of his monologue carrying with it the ironic hint that he might, after all, be merely playing a part, adopting a temporary disguise which he will discard in a moment. Above all, he was seen by his new admirers as daringly extending the previous limits of the 'poetic' by psychologically projecting himself into a wide variety of roles with a casual and even sceptical disregard for personal consistency of viewpoint.

Attractive as it may be, there is a danger in this twentieth-century reading of his poetry. We tend in every era to recreate the literary figures of the past in our own image or to fasten upon them our own deepest concerns. In a widely admired study of Hamlet, for example, Jan Knott has recently transformed him into an existentialist member of the Polish underground protesting against a totalitarian regime; and at a time of civil-rights interest and sexual permissiveness, Leslie Fiedler presented us with a Huck Finn symbolizing the suppressed homosexual guilt feelings of the American White Protestant.[1] There is in such continued reinterpretation a healthy sign that literature has contemporary relevance for us, touching upon and illuminating our own immediate concerns; but this search for relevance carries with it the risk of critical distortion, as shifts in emphasis and selectivity in reading may modify a character to suit our own predilections.

The task of identifying the specific predilections which dictated the twentieth-century response to Donne is eased to some extent by our knowledge of its historical source. Whatever increased respect may have been quietly fermenting among scholars, it was T. S. Eliot's celebrated essay on the metaphysical poets, the review welcoming Grierson's anthology in 1921, which swept Donne into fashion as a major figure in English poetry.[2] In it there appeared a passage which was to prove seminal for subsequent criticism, since it reversed traditional standards, singling out for especial praise that very quality which Dr. Johnson had condemned so disparagingly, Donne's flair for unifying in poetry the apparently heterogeneous and disconnected splinters of human sensibility:

When a poet's mind is perfectly equipped for its work, it is constantly amalgamating disparate experience; the ordinary man's experience is chaotic, irregular, fragmentary. The latter falls in love, or reads Spinoza, and these two experiences have nothing to do with each other, or with the noise of a typewriter or the smell of cooking; in the mind of the poet these experiences are always forming new wholes.[3]

As we can now appreciate with the hindsight which time affords, Eliot's critical assessment was prompted to no small extent by a personal need, his search for a poetic model from the past on whose authority the range of contemporary poetic imagery and subject matter could be broadened beyond the self-imposed limits prevalent in the established poetry of his day. His interest was therefore directed primarily to the literary implications of Donne's rehabilitation—at least on the conscious level—so that his focus here is on the nature of a *poet's* mind. But the enthusiasm with which Donne was received by the wider public points to an attraction for the nineteen-twenties which outstripped the technicalities of imagery, important as they may have been for the creative artist. The inordinate impact produced by Eliot's brief statement that a 'dissociation of sensibility' had set in after the metaphysical school suggests that in fact Donne came to symbolize in a much more profound sense a unification of experience sorely needed at that time. With the rich harvest of twentieth-century poetry before us, it is easy to forget that in the first decades of this century writers were experiencing a sense of paralysis and futility which boded ill for the future of all artistic creativity. The principles of analytical systematization were being extended to areas of human thought and behaviour which had previously been regarded as sacrosanct, and which were suddenly being exposed to a new and withering scrutiny. The very relevance of poetry and drama to the mechanism of the scientific world was being questioned. Joseph Wood Krutch, writing in the twenties, despairingly predicted the disappearance of all tragedy from the literary scene, perhaps even the disappearance

of love itself, as man's intuitive faith in a moral order faded before
the vision of the cold immensities of space, where his own life had
no more meaning '. . . than the life of the humblest insect that
crawls from one annihilation to another'.[4] What was worse, the poet
found himself intellectually sterilized as the objective conclusions
reached by empirical means seemed irrefutable even to himself, and
as he saw his own most cherished aspirations formulated in psychological phrases which left him powerless to resist, pinned and wrig-
gling on the wall. Beneath the apparently self-assured, satirical tone
of Aldous Huxley's *Point Counter Point*, for example, lies the tragic
impasse of the sensitive artist who sees all aesthetic achievement
reduced to prosaic, mechanical components, and who can find no
convincing answer to the growing accumulation of evidence that
all art, music, and poetry are no more than a psychological illusion,
a delusive titillation of man's physical responses. The splendour of
Bach, symbolizing the acme of all aesthetic endeavour, ludicrously
disintegrates as it is dissected in modern terminology into its
physically verifiable elements:

Pongileoni's blowing and the scraping of the anonymous fiddlers
had shaken the air in the great hall, had set the glass of the windows
looking on to it vibrating; and this in turn had shaken the air in Lord
Edward's apartment on the further side. The shaking air rattled
Lord Edward's *membrana tympani*; the interlocked *malleus*, *incus*, and
stirrup bones were set in motion so as to agitate the membrane of the
oval window and raise an infinitesimal storm in the fluid of the
labyrinth. The hairy endings of the auditory nerve shuddered like
weeds in a rough sea; a vast number of obscure miracles were
performed in the brain, and Lord Edward ecstatically whispered
'Bach!'[5]

The passage is amusing, intellectually supercilious, but the deeper
spiritual concern reaches its crescendo towards the end of the novel
when Spandrell, in a passage obviously paralleling this description
of Bach, is driven to despair. Compelled to admit that even the
magnificent slow movement of Beethoven's A Minor Quartet, with
its vision of supreme loveliness, cannot be regarded in the new
empirically based world as evidence of a divinely created and harmonious universe, he goes deliberately to his death, unable to

endure the knowledge that beauty is merely an illusion created by the nervous system of the body.

We are, I think, justified in setting against this background the contemporary admiration of Donne as a rare personality from the past who seemed to have succeeded in reconciling science and humanism during a similar period of pragmatic scepticism, by creating a poetry which, so far from ignoring the discoveries of cosmographers, alchemists, and physicians, had invested such scientific innovations with poetic vitality and delightedly incorporated them into his imaginative world. A thought, as Eliot put it, was for Donne an expression which *modified* his sensibility; it did not cancel it out. The intellectual and the emotional response could satisfactorily coexist within the poetic self without proving mutually exclusive, as they had for so many of Eliot's generation. This was the association of sensibility which proved so attractive to the age, not so much as a literary technique as in the expression Donne gave thereby to his ability to live in a divided world.

Accordingly, it was the vividness of Donne's poetic response to the scientific universe which fascinated his new admirers rather than the ascetic meditation of his religious writings. His talk of compasses, limbecks, and elliptical orbits to image forth his excursions into love, as well as his almost empirical exploration of love's varieties excited his readers with a new sense of the relevance of poetry to life, even in an age awed by research laboratories, industrial mechanization, and the theory of relativity. It was the gay, impudent, often indecent Donne of the love poems who formed the focus of attention, the youthful man-about-town joining, as Grierson put it, 'the band of reckless and raffish young men who sailed with Essex to Cadiz and the Islands'. And Helen Gardner has recorded how, for her own student generation in the twenties and thirties, he had come to be thought of popularly '. . . as a kind of early D. H. Lawrence, boldly adumbrating a modern sexual ethic'.[6] He was seen anew as the typical Renaissance sceptic whose libertinism closely paralleled the naturalism of Montaigne; and Louis Bredvold concluded an article on the libertine Donne with a sideglance at its connection with the twentieth-century predicament, arguing that such a study could offer insights into '. . . the adequacy of the naturalistic philosophy which is widely current even in our own day'.[7] Donne's relationship to the New Philosophy, the seventeenth-century version of modern science, became the fashionable object of critical interest, and while his religious poems were not ignored, they were set on one side as the product of his later, ecclesiastical years when financial privation, domestic tragedy, and the frustration of his hopes for court preferment had driven him reluctantly into holy orders.

There is much in this picture of Donne that remains undeniably true. The early poetry testifies to his contempt for prudery, to his fund of ready wit, and to his joy in the outrageous inversion or parody of accepted moral as well as literary norms. But this is not the full picture, even for the early years, and the easy distinction between the profligate Jack Donne of the *Elegies* and the sober Dr. John Donne of St. Paul's has been rightly exposed, notably by J. B. Leishman, as a dangerous oversimplification.[8] The distinction is, it is true, Donne's own. However, in the passage on which the phrase is based he was referring not to any sharp break in his life-pattern but, more specifically, to the new responsibilities of ecclesiastical office. His controversial defence of suicide, *Biathanatos*, written when he was a layman, ought not, he felt, to be published now that its author was an ordained member of the Anglican clergy; although even then he did not repudiate its contents. He writes to Sir Robert Ker in 1619:

> Keep it, I pray, with the same jealousie; let any that your discretion admits to the sight of it, know the date of it; and that it is a Book written by *Jack Donne*, and not by D. *Donne*: Reserve it for me, if I live, and if I die, I only forbid it the Presse, and the Fire: publish it not, but yet burn it not; and between those, do what you will with it.

It is, for example, a little difficult to reconcile with the conventional picture of Donne as a youthful libertine Walton's account of him during this period of his life as closeted in his room each morning during the early hours from 4.00 till 10.00 studying the theological distinctions between the Reformed and the Roman Church. If we distrust Walton's account as being retrospectively biased by Donne's later fame as a preacher, we have Donne's own recollection of that early period when, in his *Pseudo-martyr* he rejects the charge that his religious conclusions were reached hastily, insisting that in his youth he refrained from any

> violent and sudden determination, till I had, to the measure of my poore wit and judgement, survayed and digested the whole body of Divinity, controverted betweene ours and the Roman Church. In which search and disquisition, that God which awakened me then, and hath never forsaken me in that industry, as he is the Author of that purpose, so is he a witnes of this protestation; that I behaved my selfe and proceeded therein with humility, and diffidence in my selfe; and by that, which by his grace, I tooke to be that ordinary meanes, which is frequent prayer, and equall and indifferent affections.[9]

This is a powerful passage to set against the view of Donne predominant during the upsurge in his reputation forty or fifty years ago. It does not cancel out the insolent, often ribald Donne of whom we catch glimpses behind the masks of his *personae* in the earlier poems, but it does suggest the need for caution in making any sharp distinction between youthful rake and solemn dean.

Whether in fact he lived licentiously in his youth it is impossible to determine on the basis of the meagre biographical evidence which has survived. With all due allowance for Donne's brilliance in projecting himself psychologically into the dramatic situation of his speakers, it would, I suspect, be naïve to imagine that the often crude eroticism of the *Elegies* was based on knowledge acquired at second hand (even though he himself remarked of his poetry that 'I did best when I had least truth for my subjects').[10] Moreover, when Morton urged him to take holy orders, Donne himself expressed a fear that the widely publicized 'irregularities' of his past life might, despite his subsequent repentance, bring discredit on the Church were he to be formally ordained, and we may assume that such irregularities included more than the incident of his secret marriage.[11]

All this is mere conjecture, and largely irrelevant to the poetry itself; but the evidence in hand, though it may not settle the question of his behaviour in his youth, does point firmly towards one fact which is highly relevant—that even in his most sceptical and satirical phase he was deeply preoccupied by a search for religious truth. It has been suggested by some that his youthful religious interest may have been an exclusively intellectual pursuit, like the dabbling in philosophy fashionable among students of his day; but this theory too is belied by the passage just quoted from the *Pseudo-martyr*. There he calls God on oath to witness that these theological inquiries had been conducted with humility and diffidence and were accompanied by frequent prayer—phrases that scarcely accord with mere intellectual curiosity. And whatever sins may be laid at Donne's door, he has never been charged with attempting to whitewash his own faults and weaknesses. Elsewhere he records how a hankering after the world to come occupied his thoughts even in his youth, before the financial troubles following on his marriage provided any tangible justification.

> I have often suspected my self to be overtaken . . . with a desire of the next life: which though I know it is not merely out of a wearinesse of this, *because I had the same desires when I went with the tide, and enjoyed fairer hopes than now*: yet I doubt worldly encombrances have increased it.[12]

On Donne's own evidence, then, it would appear that his secular and religious concerns were more intimately related than has generally been assumed. It has been tempting, for example, for those critics preferring to divorce the impertinent libertine from the grave dean to explain away his tendency to sanctify love in religious terms or to celebrate divine union in blatantly sexual metaphor on the grounds of Donne's irrepressible desire to shock, even at the risk of blasphemy. His impudent wit, it was argued, carried over even into his ecclesiastical period. Such an explanation, however, fails to account for that tender ethereality which marks his most distinguished love poetry or for the religious passion which dwarfs the overt sexuality of image in the holy sonnets. In such secular poems as 'The Extasie', 'The Canonization', or 'A Valediction: forbidding Mourning', the purity of spiritual love becomes idealized as a rare, almost divine phenomenon, soaring beyond the level of terrestrial 'lay' lovers, fettered as they are to their bodily senses:

> Dull sublunary lovers love
> (Whose soul is sense) cannot admit

Absence, because it doth remove
Those things which elemented it.

But we by a love, so much refin'd,
That our selves know not what it is,
Inter-assured of the mind,
Care lesse, eyes, lips, and hands to misse.

Is this so far removed in ambience or theme from the devotional poems, where the soul, yearning for divine fulfilment, struggles to divorce itself from that same fettering to earthly desires?

Donne's tendency to pose, to overthrow his own arguments just when they appear most convincing, to dart from one vantage point to another in order to question the validity of any single criterion, seems only to confirm the impression that until the later religious phase of his life, his dominant mood was irresponsible and iconoclastic. As a result, the incongruity of visualizing death in terms of the ravishing of the human soul or love in terms of revered sainthood has led generations of critics to stress the preposterous extravagance of his conceits rather than their ultimate assertions of a genuinely held belief. This distinctly metaphysical characteristic has provoked in one era Dr. Johnson's stricture that such *discordia concors* was mere 'perverseness of industry' and in our own age the encomia of critics delighting in the audacity of Donne's more sacrilegious allusions. Yet whether the response to this audacity be approving or not, the tone of insouciant irreverence in his secular poems should never be allowed to obscure the substratum of seriousness which transforms his conceits from the casual literary exercises of a gallant into poetry touching upon the most intimate and at the same time the most universal concerns of man. The irony and humour performed a valuable function over and above their contribution to the literary form by protecting him from the dangers of a solemn sententiousness; but they in no sense vitiate the serious underlying assumption visible even within the early poems, that the material and immaterial worlds were inextricably connected, and that there existed some profound force unifying all experience despite its apparent diversity. If his poetry appears at times casual and facetious, Donne needed no one to inform him of the agonizingly cathartic function

of poetic creativity which transforms into art the innermost search-
ings of the soul:

> Then as th'earths inward narrow crooked lanes
> Do purge sea waters fretfull salt away,
>   I thought, if I could draw my paines,
> Through Rimes vexation, I should them allay,
> Griefe brought to numbers cannot be so fierce,
> For, he tames it, that fetters it in verse.[13]

The specific form of Donne's wit, his provocative drawing together of opposites, can perhaps be best appreciated by comparing
it for a moment with the wit of the eighteenth century. Neo-
classical poets also employ at times the technique of an initially
incongruous juxtaposition, but they elicit a totally different response
from the reader. They carefully evoke a surface and momentary
delight in an amused pretence which is then immediately resolved,
in contrast to Donne's revelation of an authentic and lasting paradox. Pope describes how on Belinda's dressing-table

> The Tortoise here and Elephant unite,
> Transform'd to Combs, the speckled and the white.

The Gargantuan image suggested in the first line of a grotesque
coupling between elephant and tortoise is at once restored to
normal, comfortable perspective by the explanation that we are
speaking merely of tortoise-shell combs inlaid with ivory. Like the
teasing rococo ornamentation on the cool rectangular panels of a
Louis XV salon, or the mildly surprising 'ha-ha' in the landscape
gardening of Capability Brown, the surface incongruity only
momentarily disturbs the confident, underlying rationalism of the
age. In contrast, the purpose of the heterogeneity in Donne is to
jolt us into a realization that the only true validity lies in meaningful
paradox, and that any attempt to separate human experience into
neatly divided categories is both arbitrary and false. Of the Crucifixion scene he writes:

> There I should see a Sunne, by rising set,
> And by that setting endlesse day beget;

In its context the paradox of the sun rising as it sets is not surface word-play leading to a rational, Popean resolution. On the contrary, for the Christian reader its strength lies in the vision of a religious truth outreaching the physical laws of nature in a moment of cosmic revelation.

The same holds true for much of the amatory verse too, despite the tendency of critics to divorce the two areas of his poetry. In an analysis of 'The Canonization' which was to become a model for the New Critical school, Cleanth Brooks maintained (what is now common knowledge) that the love–religion equation was no cynical or bawdy parody but a serious recognition of the complex inter-relationships existing in man's universe. The parallel between the lovers and the religious anchorite may appear far-fetched, he argues, but it rests on their renunciation of the unseemly scrambling for personal advancement at court in favour of '. . . the more intense world' of love. Brooks saw the final message of the poem as an asser-tion in paradigm form of the paradoxical quality of the creative imagination; the well-wrought urn functions internally as a symbol for the poem itself, which achieves, by the subtlety of its artistic form, what a prosaic 'half-acre tomb' could not hope to attain. In this respect his analysis marked a notable advance over previous attempts; but it stops too short.

At a certain level it is true that Donne's response to the complex-ity of imaginative experience here supports the Empsonian valida-tion of ambiguity in poetry; but this is surely only a side product of the rich experience offered by the poem in totality. The final impact of 'The Canonization' has little to do with Donne's theory of the poetic imagination, or even with his dialectically justifying the paradoxical equation of lovers with anchorites. It is rather the gradual initiation of the reader into a mystery which he has been privileged to share. In Brooks's analysis, this sacramental element has evaporated. In the following stanza, for example, which he recognizes as of central significance in the poem, he focuses attention upon the classical Phoenix image of death and rebirth:

> We are Tapers too, and at our owne cost die,
> And wee in us finde the Eagle and the Dove,
> The Phoenix ridle hath more wit
> By us, we two being one, are it,

> So, to one neutrall thing both sexes fit.
> Wee dye and rise the same, and prove
> Mysterious by this love.

Reminding us, quite rightly, of the sexual connotation of 'dye' in seventeenth-century usage, he assumes that Donne means in this stanza '. . . because our love can outlast its consummation, we are a minor miracle, we are love's saints'. However, by restricting his commentary exclusively to the plane of their physical relationship, he misses its deeper resonance. We are offered in his commentary a mildly ludicrous picture of the lovers patting themselves on the back for their degree of sexual prowess which has enabled their love even to survive orgasm, and their canonization is attributed by him to the fact that '. . . Their love is not exhausted in mere lust'.[14] But what, we may ask, has happened to the Christian implications of death and resurrection in the phrase which serves as the stepping-stone to the pulsating mystery of the final line?

> Wee dye and rise the same, and prove
> Mysterious by this love.

'Dye' here certainly carries a sexual connotation, but it points backwards to the means of the ascent, and from this point on it is the resurrective element which finally triumphs, elevating the lovers to the sainthood of an ethereal rapture which will prove the envy of all future generations.

Is it pedantic to quarrel on so small a point, or is it possible that this symbolizes much of Donne criticism during this century? If Donne's speaker is not emotionally committed, then the poem is no more than an amusing exercise in Neoplatonism, with the Phoenix and the Christian martyr functioning as witty surface metaphors.[15] If, however, as I propose to argue, his poetry is seen as expressing a whimsical dissatisfaction with the actuality of physical experience in order to reach beyond to a more permanent reality, then the initial incongruity of the image suddenly swings round to become deeply meaningful. The tone is, at certain moments in the poem, ludicrous and exaggerated, as is the equation with the Christian martyr if taken too literally. But the ethereality of love's experience at the highest level, and the purity of the relationship it creates, emerge from the poem as resonant truths.

In brief, the terminology so widely applied to Donne since T. S. Eliot's essay needs to be readjusted. We have tended since then to regard Donne's art as the poetic *amalgamation* of disparate experience, as though he were joining two equally valid worlds, the factual and the emotional, to create the poetic artefact. His poetry, however, constitutes rather a *transmutation* of the actual, as its spiritual significance is perceived. It is as though physical reality, whether of the flesh or of alchemical experiment, becomes true only at that moment when it touches upon the ethereal, and partakes of eternity. Hence the importance of *ecstasy* in Donne's poetry, both in the religious and the amatory sense, when the soul has almost separated from the body for a momentary glimpse of the divine before it returns to the confines of the flesh or achieves its final separation in death.

Such a claim, in the truncated fashion of its presentation within these brief introductory pages, may well appear tendentious, ignoring those facetious, libertine poems in the collection of the *Songs and Sonets* upon which so much of Donne's reputation rests. Before exploring this deeper concern more closely, therefore, and attempting to identify the cultural source to which it can be traced, it may prove helpful to examine a typical example of such apparently light-hearted amorousness in order to suggest that even there the levity and wit may conceal a more serious undercurrent. 'The Sunne Rising' has usually been read as a typical piece of humorous bravado, representing, as one critic put it, '. . . the exultant brag of a young lover after a night of love'.[16] Deserting the normal mood of the *aubade*, in which the waking lover glories in the joys of the past night and laments the inevitable need to rise, Donne's speaker is irritable and peremptory, berating the sun for daring to disturb the privacy of his love by squinting like some Peeping Tom through the crevices of the window blinds:

> Busie old foole, unruly Sunne,
> Why dost thou thus,
> Through windowes, and through curtaines call on us?

Taken out of its cultural and historical context the poem is indeed no more than an amusingly exultant brag. But placed within it, it is a *tour de force*.

At the turn of the century, the man-centred universe appeared to have been discredited for ever by the new cosmology. The revolutionary theory of Copernicus had posited a vast mechanistic universe in which the earth orbited subserviently about the majestically central sun; and the theory was confirmed empirically in Donne's day when Galileo gazed through a telescope to identify satellites orbiting about Jupiter in defiance of the Ptolemaically conceived universe. The implications were obvious enough, and man now appeared to have shrunk to the status of an infinitesimally tiny creature crawling on the surface of a minor planet, in a vast heliocentric system. Against that background 'The Sunne Rising', while remaining a genuine love poem, is at the same time ranging much further in purpose. For it constitutes a challenge to the New Philosophy itself, provocatively reaffirming in the face of all contrary scientific evidence the pre-eminence of man in the cosmic pattern, and the impregnability of his inner experience. It is not, I think, pure chance that the object of Donne's amused scorn in this poem is that newly dignified centre of the Copernican solar system, the 'busie old Sunne'—but here ludicrously stripped of its majesty and reduced to a foolish old busybody. Unawed by the discoveries of the cosmographers, his speaker dismisses as mere impertinence the sun's attempt to impose on true lovers (whose treasured intimacy makes each moment an eternity) those petty, factual divisions of time fit only for the juvenile and the small-minded:

> Must to thy motions lovers seasons run?
> Sawcy pedantique wretch, goe chide
> Late schoole boyes, and sowre prentices . . .

and the stanza concludes with the calmly resonant assertion of love's unchanging splendour, before which the laws of mundane actuality shrivel away to impotence:

> Love, all alike, no season knowes, nor clyme,
> Nor houres, dayes, months, which are the rags of time.

A moment later the poem appears suddenly to admit the reverence of the sun's beams—but it is only a trick, an inversion of normal prose order, designed to puncture that inflated impression. And the couplet leads into a passage which not only constitutes the turning-point of the poem, but in fact presents a recurrent and central motif of Donne's philosophy.

> Thy beames, so reverend, and strong
> Why shouldst thou thinke?
> I could eclipse and cloud them with a winke,
> But that I would not lose her sight so long:

The surface humour here is obvious enough—for all his apparent confidence, the speaker, by closing his eyes in ostrich-like denial of the sun's existence, will not prevent it from shining on the rest of the world. It cannot so easily be eclipsed with a wink. But in the context of the poem, the challenge emerges not as mere braggadocio but as a reassertion of man's centrality in the universe, and above all of the inviolability of his inner being. When the lover closes his eyes, the sun will indeed continue to shine for the rest of the world; but for *him*, the centre of his closed solipsistic universe, it has in fact ceased to exist, and no power will enable it to enter his consciousness. To be noticed by the lover at all, the sun must rely on the beauty of the mistress, who alone entices him to open his eyes. There is an obvious humour of exaggeration here, but the deeper theme continues to stress the sanctity of the isolated, individual self as the lover confidently challenges the sun on its next journey around the earth to search for anything worthy of comparison to their supreme love. When the sun returns with its information tomorrow, he adds, it should come *late*, at a more seemly hour than the disturbingly early call today.

> Looke, and to morrow late, tell mee,
> Whether both the India's of spice and Myne
> Be where thou leftst them, or lie here with mee.
> Aske for those Kings whom thou saw'st yesterday,
> And thou shalt heare, All here in one bed lay.

The argument, presented obliquely until this point, can now be restated with firmer directness. The entire universe shrinks away before the magnificence of their love—'Nothing else is'; and they exclude the world not in ascetic self-denial, but because everything it offers is contained or excelled in their own intimate relationship. It is not fortuitous that this sense of treasured privacy became characteristic of Donne's poetry, for it provided in an amatory as well as a religious setting a symbol of his concern with the rich inner experience of man besides which—for all his delight in the flesh, in alchemy, and in geographical exploration—the tactile, measurable world of reality appeared trivial and mundane:

> She is all States, and all Princes, I,
> Nothing else is.
> Princes doe but play us; compar'd to this,
> All honor's mimique: All wealth alchimie.

By the end of the poem, the supposedly awesome and reverend sun of the new Copernican world has become comically relegated to the status of a tired, elderly servant, longing to be released from his burdensome duties. Moreover, this depiction of the sun as obligated to warm the earth and wake sleepy apprentices draws its authority, and hence its confident humour, from the biblical world-picture which hangs as the backcloth to Donne's validation of man—the order of divine creation as related in Genesis. There God forms the earth first, bestowing upon it the various forms of fruit and vegetation to satisfy man's needs. Only then are the sun and moon placed in the heavens as mere accessories to the earth, their function being to provide its future inhabitants with light and warmth, and to divide night from day so that men might know when to rise from bed and pursue their daily tasks. Such was the traditional world which the New Philosophy had seemed to dislodge and which Donne had so adroitly reinstated.

With their own superiority now assured, the lovers, no longer irritable at the sun's intrusion, can in the final stanza compassionately tolerate its feebleness:

> Thine age askes ease, and since thy duties bee
> To warme the world, that's done in warming us.
> Shine here to us, and thou art every where;
> This bed thy center is, these walls, thy spheare.

The tone is, as usual, impudent, the argument in its surface form extravagant; but in the process of that argument the insignificance of man in the heliocentric world of science has been discarded as no more than a foolish joke. The rich experience of the human spirit has become the centre about which the sun is forced subserviently to revolve, and the triumph of love is validated. In its bravura and its amusing amatory setting, the poem is certainly far removed from the solemnity of Donne's later sermons; yet in its profounder theme, affirming the dominion of man in a universe created specifically to serve his needs, it is a remarkable poetic achievement, foreshadowing the unifying motif of his preaching, his insistence on the preciousness of the human soul besides which all else pales into insignificance:

> For man is not onely a contributary Creature, but a totall Creature; He does not onely make one, but he is all; He is not a piece of the world, but the world it selfe; and next to the glory of God, the reason why there is a world.[17]

This concern with spiritual significance in Donne's poetry, if it has not been entirely ignored in modern criticism, has been seriously underplayed. Clearly, no one can read 'The Extasie' without responding to its sense of wonder at the distillation of love's purity in the disembodied and united souls of the lovers:

> Wee then, who are this new soule, know,
> Of what we are compos'd, and made,
> For, the Atomies of which we grow,
> Are soules, whom no change can invade.

But because of those predilections of the twentieth century discussed above, an undue emphasis has been placed on Donne's supposed detachment, his sceptical refusal to become fully engaged. It has become customary to speak of the 'ironic pose' which allows him to play with mutually exclusive philosophies of life without expressing any ultimate preference. Basil Willey, in a celebrated definition of metaphysical sensibility, described it as '. . . a capacity to live in divided and distinguished worlds, and to pass freely to and fro between one and another', and he adds that those divided worlds are held together in loose synthesis as the poet establishes analogies and correspondences between them. The main point he makes (and the italics are his) is that the poet explores those divided worlds

'. . . not being *finally committed* to any one'.[18] Such a definition is
patently inapplicable to Donne's devotional poetry, with its repeated prayer that no worldly thought should distract him even
momentarily from his task of spiritual self-renewal; and no one, I
believe, has questioned the fully metaphysical quality of the holy
sonnets, or of the 'Hymne to God my God, in my Sicknesse'. The
definition is, therefore, already partially disqualified. In the same
way, it seems to me unsatisfactory to speak of Donne's finest secular
poems—'The Relique', 'A Nocturnall', 'Sweetest Love', or even so
audacious a poem as 'The Sunne Rising'—as playfully uncommitted
to either world. On the contrary, there is a very marked commitment to the world of the spirit and it is, I think, that very commitment which creates the specifically metaphysical quality of the
poems.

I have no intention of transforming the delightfully witty lover
of these amatory poems into a soulful religionist by reading back
into that period the ascetic yearnings of his ecclesiastical years.
That would be a travesty of literary criticism. In fact, so far from
detracting from their importance, I propose to argue that the lively
humour, the overt flippancy, the teasing reversals of argument, and
the brash impudence of his libertine posing fulfil a central function
in expressing with subtle tangentialism his own dissatisfaction with
the scientism of his day. In brief, the wit itself will be regarded in
this study as a key to the underlying unity of the early and later
Donne.

If our own age has tended to emphasize those elements in Donne
which accorded with its own immediate needs, we may perhaps
best restore the balance by replacing him firmly within the historical and cultural context within which he wrote and which in part
determined the motifs of his verse. One of those cultural elements
which can prove particularly enlightening for an understanding of
his poetry is the much-abused art of the Counter-Reformation—the
painting and architecture of the contemporary Jesuit movement
which expressed in visual form the spiritual concerns of the era in
which he lived. It should, however, be made clear at the outset that
such comparisons are in no sense aimed at the establishing of
parallels between art and literature for its own sake. This is a

specifically *literary* quest, and those readers (there are, I am told, still many) who resent in principle the drawing of any such comparisons between the arts, are invited, if they wish, to ignore the following chapter and proceed directly to the literary discussion which follows. There are, however, two reasons for my including it here. The first is that my own conclusions about Donne were reached initially through an interest in mannerist painting, or rather through my annoyance at what I felt to be its misrepresentation. The literary application followed later, and the more closely I examined the parallels, the more illuminating such application appeared. There seemed no reason why I should not share that process of discovery with the reader. Secondly, I believe with Mario Praz that those literary critics who proclaim the impropriety of comparing the literary and the plastic arts sound a little like the aerodynamic experts who argue that the tiny wing-space of a bumble-bee is technically incapable of lifting its unwieldy body. Theoretically they are no doubt correct; yet the bumble-bee flies none the less.[19] Literature is not composed in a cultural vacuum, and it is surely no chance phenomenon that has, for example, produced in our own day a Theatre of the Absurd to reflect the fragmented or grotesque images of man in the canvases of Picasso and Francis Bacon. No self-respecting English department would today permit a student to engage in research on Wordsworth without a knowledge of the philosophical theories of Locke and Godwin (despite an initial hesitation when the possibility of such investigation was first suggested),[20] nor on the rise of the novel without an acquaintance with the economic and sociological changes of the eighteenth century. Yet departments often remain suspicious of the suggestion that a familiarity with the rococo may prove helpful for an understanding of Pope, or with Hogarth for the satirical mode of Fielding. Certainly such art parallels must be handled with care— with, in fact, no less care than those based on contemporary philosophical or sociological patterns; but the need for such circumspection does not automatically disqualify such investigation.

At all events, this is not the place to argue the point. I can only emphasize that the art parallels suggested in this study are offered neither as proof of the literary theory adduced, nor as an attempt to prop up an otherwise shaky argument. My reading of Donne rests exclusively upon the textual analyses of the poems examined, the art analogues serving only to broaden the cultural setting and to intimate that Donne was not alone in the method he chose for responding to the problems and challenges of his day.

II

MANNERIST PERSPECTIVE

THERE is a tradition in art history that the term of abuse levelled at a provocatively new school becomes defiantly adopted by the innovators as the official name of the movement, and gradually sheds its pejorative connotation. In time we are left with a Gothic cathedral free from vandalist associations, or with Impressionism stripped of its originally derogatory intent. Mannerism has formed a rare exception. Neglected for centuries as a minor substream of the baroque, it has, when isolated, been treated almost unanimously as an inferior art form, expressing in idiosyncratic and self-conscious style the collapse of Renaissance values. In a summary typical of this predominant attitude to mannerist art, Germain Bazin recently described it as a '. . . sickness of styles—a sort of neurosis, a symptom of their inability to define themselves which led second-rate artists, overwhelmed by the authority of the great masters, into an extravagance of gesture and expression, an over-lengthening of proportions and unnaturally twisted attitudes in the portrayal of figures'.[1]

Those critics, comparatively few in number, who have been concerned with relating art and literature, have almost invariably adopted this traditional condemnation, using their dislike of mannerist painting to expose the weaknesses of the equivalent literary forms. Helmut Hatzfeld identifies the distinguishing mark of mannerism as 'simply a lack of discipline' symptomatic of post-Renaissance literary decay, and Miss M. M. Mahood, evincing a patent dislike, compares the negating 'frigidity' of mannerism with the more satisfying splendours of the baroque. In the most influential and detailed of such studies, the antipathy is even more clearly marked, for Wylie Sypher throughout his examination of the era repeatedly applies such disparaging terms both to mannerist art and literature, defining them as '. . . a kind of facile learning, an abused ingenuity, a witty affectation, a knowing pose, a distorting through preciosity, or a play with conventional proportions, images and attitudes'.[2] Such a definition certainly holds true for a very small area of mannerism—what genre does not have its less inspired practitioners? It describes adequately the grotesque paintings by Giuseppe Arcimboldo whose strained inventiveness could produce the portrait of a human face constructed exclusively out of gnarled roots, fish, or vegetables (Plate 2); but it will not do as a criterion for Tintoretto's *Miracle of St. Mark*, El Greco's haunting *View of Toledo*, or indeed Donne's 'Canonization' and the holy sonnets. Sypher informs us a little later that the mannerist poet or painter '. . . usually tells the truth in a key pitched so high it is hysteria or ecstasy, or else in a key so low it is nearly inaudible', and we are, I think, entitled to wonder where the hysteria may be found in 'Goodfriday, 1613. Riding Westward' or the ecstatic tone even in 'The Extasie' itself, which preserves a firm intellectual and emotional control throughout, as it delicately manipulates the Platonic, amatory, and religious implications of its title:

> To our bodies turne wee then, that so
> Weake men on love reveal'd may looke;
> Loves mysteries in soules doe grow,
> But yet the body is his booke.
>
> And if some lover, such as wee,
> Have heard this dialogue of one,
> Let him still marke us, he shall see
> Small change, when we are to bodies gone.

This traditional condemnation of mannerism rests upon an outmoded critical assumption—the idea that art flourishes only in eras confident of their ideals and secure in their political and social institutions. It is a relic of the view which used to pervade student anthologies, with their introductory chapters on the 'intrepid explorers' of the High Renaissance. To assume that the troubled and agitated mood of the Counter-Renaissance provided an atmosphere less conducive to literary and artistic accomplishment than the supposedly securer era of Gloriana is to rank the patriotic *Henry V* as dramatically superior to the disturbed self-searchings of *Hamlet* and *Lear*. Moreover, if we turn to the realm of religious poetry, which forms a substantial segment of metaphysical writing, the point remains equally valid. The poem of a confident, untroubled believer assured of his personal salvation is not by virtue of that confidence automatically superior to one acknowledging the author's struggle against despair or his sense of personal unworthiness. Theologically John Keble's prayer is impeccable:

> Only, O Lord, in Thy dear love
> Fit us for perfect Rest above;
> And help us this and every day,
> To live more nearly as we pray.

but few would prefer it as poetry beside the magnificent turbulence of Gerard Manley Hopkins's weary complaint to his God:

> Wert thou my enemy, O thou my friend,
> How wouldst thou worse, I wonder, than thou dost
> Defeat, thwart me?[3]

This is agitated, troubled, distorted in a very real sense; but so far from being invalidated by its emotional distress, the verse derives its poetic vigour and forceful rhythms from that very agitation. It is strange, therefore, that the spiritual insecurity of the Counter-Renaissance should have been so widely and so long regarded as a criterion for disparaging the art it produced.

Like its literary counterpart, mannerist art enjoyed a brief revival in the nineteen-twenties when, disillusioned with traditional values, expressionists and surrealists began to admire the rejection of classical formalism in El Greco; but the revival was little more than a passing fashion, and art criticism soon reverted to the familiar tone of condescension or censure. The literary reinstatement of Donne and Marvell was both more enthusiastic and more permanent, and although Donne's reputation has fluctuated since the Grierson revival, it has never been in danger of reverting to its former state of neglect. After C. S. Lewis's frontal attack on Donne had been rebutted by Joan Bennett, critics settled down to a less committed but by no means less rewarding analysis of his relationship to the intellectual and religious climate of his day. The historical emphasis of Rosemond Tuve and Louis Martz betrayed less of that exhilarated delight in Donne's poetic immediacy than had been visible among their predecessors but they wrote none the less from a firm conviction that he was a poet of stature. On the other hand the attempts to relate him to the artistic milieu of his time, valuable though they have been, have tended to carry across from mannerism the taint of an inferior art form and, what is worse, to use mannerism to explain the weaknesses of Donne's poetry while ignoring the insights it can offer into those very real poetic achievements which have made him so attractive to our age.

In the earliest stages of planning this present study, I had been faced with the intimidating prospect of attempting to reinstate mannerism as an aesthetically valid art form before proceeding to any exploration of its relationship to Donne. But the task has been alleviated, at least in part, by the recent appearance of Arnold Hauser's stimulating study *Mannerism*.[4] Its central thesis that mannerism was the progenitor of modern art leaves me unpersuaded. Whatever parallels may exist between the two eras in the sense of alienation they shared and the collapse of established norms, so complex a mode of art could scarcely have straddled three centuries in its development and retain the relationship of aesthetic progenitor and offspring. His investigation, however, offers a most valuable side product; for the reader, in comparing the art of the sixteenth and twentieth centuries, inevitably perceives that the derogatory terms so widely applied today to the mannerists as a means of disqualifying them artistically could be applied with equal ease and no less inappropriateness to the post-impressionsts, cubists, and surrealists of more recent years. It would be patently absurd today solemnly to charge Braque or Picasso with having 'distorted' reality as if that were a crime against aesthetic morals, or Kandinsky with having failed to achieve artistic integrity because his colours were 'unnatural'. Their distortion of shape and colour was deliberate, and such a charge would have failed to acknowledge that modern art is expressing its rejection of romantic idealization and photographic accuracy in favour of an aesthetic vision transcending the merely factual and turning instead to the geometric and the abstract. Their aim is not identical with that of the mannerists, but the comparison does at least cast doubt upon the criteria whereby the latter have been condemned on the grounds of their 'hysterical foreshortenings' and their supposedly 'freakish', 'frantic', and 'neurotic' disproportions.

The firm perspective of High Renaissance painting and the classical perfection of such statuary as Verrocchio's *Colleone* or Michelangelo's *David* presupposed, as we know, a confidence in the natural world and in man's place within it. Right reason, Hooker could claim, was the star of Universal Law, and out of this conviction was to grow the New Philosophy of the empirical sciences. However, the past few decades have witnessed a growing awareness that at the very moment of such confidence, the Counter-Renaissance (as Hiram Haydn has called it) was already at work, challenging and subverting those assumptions of cosmic order.[5] Tillyard's widely accepted 'world-picture' of an era united by its optimistic faith in the harmony of the universe, with the hierarchical patterns of heaven reflected in the graduated classes of society has been recognized as misleading in its willingness to ignore or underplay the powerful contrary forces undermining that structure; and it is now apparent that those frequently quoted lines from *Troilus and Cressida* about the heavens and this centre observing degree, priority, and place, so far from being the final expression of the Elizabethan world-picture formed merely one aspect of a polymorphous and volatile age.

The far-reaching influence of Machiavelli on sixteenth-century thought, both in his actual writings and in the philosophy of ruthless self-interest which was popularly identified as his, can no longer be conveniently isolated as a 'surprisingly' early instance of seventeenth-century pragmatism. Within the era itself, he challenged the very fundamentals of that cosmic order to which Tillyard and others have pointed, dismissing as irrelevant to the human situation the traditional concept of heavenly justice and of the moral imperatives derived from it. The scepticism of Montaigne was no less antagonistic to this traditional picture of a settled Chain of Being, undercutting as it did the authority of established opinion and demanding in its place an unprejudiced questioning of all accepted beliefs no matter how persuasive their surface appearance and no matter how intimidating their ancestry. He rejected as mere gullibility the common practice whereby '... men's opinions are accepted in the train of ancient beliefs, by authority and on credit, as if they were religion and law. . . . Thus the world is filled and soaked with nonsense and lies. The reason why we doubt hardly anything is that we never test our common impressions. We do not probe the base, where the fault and weakness lies.' But more subversive in its implications even than these revolutionary modes of thought was the changing concept of the universe itself. The collapse of the Ptolemaic universe centred upon man, with its spheres moving in perfect harmonious circles about the earth, cannot be conveniently postponed to Galileo's sighting of Jupiter's four satellites in 1610. Copernicus had enunciated his theory of a heliocentric system more than sixty years earlier. Galileo thus functioned rather as a confirmer of doubts that had been fermenting through most of the previous century, weakening man's confidence in a morally purposive universe and troubling him with thoughts of a vast cosmos indifferent to human affairs.

It is clear, therefore, that concurrent with the Renaissance at the height of its vigour there existed a Counter-Renaissance, undercutting the very ideals to which it consciously aspired, the duality often existing within the philosophy and aspirations of the same individual. In the religious sphere, for example, the Reformation rebellion against an authoritarian Church symbolized, it is true, a new faith in individual liberty, affirming the right of every Christian to read the Scriptures for himself and to construct his personal interpretation of the text. In that respect it reflected the dominant modes of the High Renaissance. Yet in Luther's own writings, quite apart from the literature of his Calvinist successors, it stressed no less the doctrine of predestination, which cancelled out that very self-determination so often regarded as typical of the age, by robbing man of the right to earn the grace of heaven. Where, indeed, in the conventional setting of a renewed faith in human rationality are we to place Calvin's chilling warning that the natural gift of Reason was, at Adam's fall, severely damaged and '. . . being partly weakened and partly corrupted, a shapeless ruin is all that remains'?

Within the realm of art, that same shadow falls across the sixteenth century at the very moment when it appeared to have reached the acme of its secure optimism. Upon the ceiling of the

Sistine Chapel the idealized serenity of the Renaissance achieves its noblest expression in Michelangelo's fresco of *The Creation of Man*. There, a calm, benevolent God gently extends his hand to infuse life into a recumbent but potentially vigorous Adam who gazes unafraid into the eyes of his Creator. There is little to distinguish man from God in size, in form, or in intelligence of expression, and the scene affords a perfect visual expression of the new concept of man: '. . . how noble in reason, how infinite in faculties, in form and moving how express and admirable, in action how like an angel, in apprehension how like a god'. Yet in the altarpiece of that same chapel (as in the continuation of this monologue) the harmonious vision is shattered. In the few years that had elapsed since he painted the ceiling, Michelangelo's mood had darkened, and now the tortured figures in his Day of Judgement writhe in unspeakable horror as their damnation is decreed. What had originally been planned as a painting of the Resurrection, had become transformed into a grimly brooding depiction of the *Dies Irae*, dominated by a powerful and stern Christ whose unwavering condemnation of the sinners forces even the merciful Virgin to turn her head away as though powerless to intercede. Naked figures bloated by gluttony or marked by dissipation and vice are dragged irrevocably downwards to a hell no longer inhabited by the traditional devils of the Middle Ages but by more terrifying shapes—human beings corrupted by their own viciousness and sin. There is no hint of glory in the altarpiece, even for those who rise at the right hand of Jesus; only of a tormented awakening from death, and the entire scene, set in a vast, unframed void suggests an infinite vortex of figures whirling endlessly about the central figure of Christ. The turbulent movement of this scene is reflected in the canvases of Giulio Romano, of Rosso Fiorentino, and of Tintoretto, with their crowded bodies straining and twisting in physical and spiritual agony.

The restless searching and inner dissatisfaction which replaced the serenity of the Renaissance ideal—a restlessness that disturbed the later Raphael and the later Shakespeare before becoming the dominant mode of the era—has generally been identified by that inclusive term 'baroque'. It both extended and contradicted the assumptions of the Renaissance. As in *Hamlet*, it insisted on the splendour of mortal man, infinite in faculty, while it recognized the gloomy implications of a pragmatic philosophy which foretold nothing but decay and putrefaction beyond the grave. The beauty of man's body might excite the imagination with a classical delight in human potential and with a confidence in man's ability to construct new ethical standards and life-styles, but Machiavelli and the revival of Senecan Stoicism brought with them the sobering realization that traditional Christian morality could be surrendered only at a forbidding price. Shakespeare's Edmund is both amusing and attractive in his sardonic superiority to conventional ethics and his contempt for superstitious subservience to the stars above; but for his audience there is always the latent fear that his philosophy may prove ultimately victorious and we need the reassurance of his final repentance and death to reconcile us to life itself. Like Iago, he mesmerizes us by his 'honest' admission to himself of his own ruthless self-interest, but he threatens our very existence with the possibility of a world peopled by the hideous offspring of the new Edmunds and Gonerils.

However, the more closely one examines this baroque mingling of potential splendour and gloom—expressed visually in the new *chiaroscuro* of Parmigianino, Caravaggio, and others, with their dark shadows and contrasting shafts of bright light—the more strange it appears that mannerism and baroque should so long have remained virtually undistinguished. For this Counter-Renaissance art movement was in fact split into two almost diametrically opposed tendencies, sharing a rejection of tranquil harmony but reacting to it from essentially different angles. Both movements find their religious impetus in the Counter-Reformation, epitomized by the protracted sessions of the Council of Trent which sat intermittently from 1545 to 1563 to formulate a Catholic response to the Lutheran rebellion.[6] Yet within the convocations of the Council and in the broader cultural changes outside which both preceded and accompanied the sessions, may be perceived two dominant and almost contradictory strategies—to crush the Reformation revolt by a reassertion of the Catholic church's unquestionable authority and at the same time to correct by a process of self-criticism and self-purification the shortcomings which they had been forced by the

Protestants to acknowledge. Like the lady who insisted that she had never borrowed her neighbour's pots and had in any case already returned them, the church on the one hand maintained its own continued infallibility, while at the same time it implicitly admitted the validity of Luther's strictures on the corruption existent within its walls. The Council, for example, reaffirmed the doctrine of transubstantiation and introduced the official Catechism as a means of strengthening the Pope's monopolistic right to pronounce finally on matters of faith; yet it also quietly abolished the office of *quaestor*, or indulgence-collector, which had been a major target in all Reformation charges of ecclesiastical corruption. While these strategies are too subtly interrelated to be arbitrarily segregated, it is possible, I believe, to see them as the primary motive forces for these two art movements, mannerism finding its fulfilment in self-criticism and in a refined, sensitive spirituality, and the baroque, as has been long recognized, reaffirming through its wealth and splendour the exclusive and unquestionable authority of Rome.

The monumental solidity of the baroque cathedral, the finality of its dogmatic assertion, is achieved primarily by the sense of weight it conveys—not the stable weight of a pyramidal structure, but the energized weight of massive arches supported by clusters of thick, reduplicated columns. The more intimate Renaissance church preceding it had been dominated by a classical restraint, the cool rectangular panels and unified centrality of Brunelleschi's Pazzi Chapel reflecting the current belief in the near-equality of man and God. As in the Italian villas of the sixteenth century where the symmetrically squared front, free of overhanging cornices, offers a flat façade on which the non-functional pilasters are decoratively embossed, so the Renaissance church served as a calm sanctuary to human reason, contemplating no daring flights towards heaven nor threats of cataclysmic wrath from above. The worshipper was not dwarfed by a towering structure but experienced a satisfying sense of his own dignity within the classical orders. The baroque adopted the same classical motifs of triangular pediments resting upon pilasters, but the pediments have suddenly been thrust out from the wall, to be supported by sturdy pillars and pedestals, as in Della Porta's façade to *Il Gesù*. The cornice juts out with an ominous, beetling, top-heavy effect, casting dark shadows below, and a new feeling of gravity and the dynamic interplay of forces —the downward pressure resisted by an upward thrust—has replaced the gentler, almost static quality of Renaissance architecture.

The baroque is imposing in both a literal and metaphorical sense; it presses down upon the viewer with full visual exploitation of its heavy masonry. The late Gothic cathedral had also, of course, been constructed of masonry, but the architect had manipulated the stone to create the illusion of delicate lacework. There the light-coloured fan tracery appears merely to join rather than to support the large translucent windows, and the pointed Gothic arch carries the eye upward with an airy grace. In contrast, every line of the baroque testifies to the ponderous solidity of its structure, from the semicircular barrel-vaulting to the heavily arched recesses darkening the light which filters in from the small windows beyond. The decorative motifs aim to overpower by sheer numbers, suggesting the infinitude of a massed, heavenly choir. Where the tall Gothic windows of King's College Chapel had been placed within the long straight walls of the nave to create a majestic calm, the baroque cathedral overwhelms the viewer with its countless plinths and capitals, its pediments and architraves, its entablatures and moulded friezes. The walls themselves, for all their solidity, are broken up into innumerable doorways and niches, as though orchestrated out of fluted pilasters and contrapuntal recesses to rise in crescendo to the interconnected arches spanning the nave. Dominating them all is the semicircular vault above the transept, symbolizing the heavenly sphere, the culmination of all human striving. While within the cathedral this illuminated vault offers a release from the more sombre plenitude of the interior, it fulfils an almost contrary function from without. There the august dome, the hallmark of the baroque, has replaced the slender spires and pinnacles of the Gothic, and seems to enclose the building from above, visually compressing the structure within earthly bounds (Plate 1). The tapered lantern which surmounts it points heavenward, but suggests that any upward flight must first overcome the gravitational pull of the weighty dome anchoring it to the solid building below.

The implication of this massivity is of central significance in distinguishing the baroque from mannerism. It betokens, for all its ultimate concern with the Judgement Day and the salvation of an after-life, a conviction that the materiality of this world is not to be trifled with. Although the baroque insists, as all Christianity must, on the ephemerality of terrestrial existence, it betrays a post-Renaissance awareness that it is within the physical confines of the tangible world that man must work out his salvation. Through the baroque, the Catholic church was paradoxically reasserting its spiritual force by an intimidating exhibition of earthly power, leaving to its mannerist spokesmen the traditional, medieval call to asceticism and self-abnegation. And it is here that the Protestant Milton makes contact with the Catholic baroque and aesthetically becomes part of it without losing his Reformation roots. For the Protestant, approaching the problem from the opposite direction, is no less concerned with a physical demonstration of divine power. As Max Weber showed us long ago, the Protestant concern with covenant and personal election prompted him to look to the material world for evidence of that divine blessing which would alone assure him that he himself formed one of the elect.[7] The corporeal world thus assumed a new significance for the Protestant, and divine manifestation became less a matter of visionary visitation than of his correctly interpreting the events of this world and more specifically of his own life. His bond with the actuality of the Old Testament covenant where heavenly approval expressed itself in the form of bountiful flocks, herds, and wealth was therefore stronger than with the apocalyptic asceticism of the New. Despite his theological antipathy to an art form inspired by the Catholic church, the Protestant found a strange satisfaction in the impressive assertion of God's magnificence which the baroque displayed, and he readily absorbed and adopted many of its elements.

For this reason, the paradox of a baroque cathedral, employing physical solidity to impress man with his spiritual obligations, finds its counterpart in Milton's *Paradise Lost*. His scenes of heaven and hell conjure up the vision of an infinite universe charged with boundless energy. But the power and energy, for all their infinitude, exist within a physical actuality and are never conveyed in terms of transcendental supernaturalism. The temptation of Adam and Eve upon which the epic pivots, results, it is true, in a spiritual Fall, an act of disobedience against divine prohibition; but in Milton's poem it is described in predominantly fleshly terms, the fruit at once inflaming carnal desire so that Adam and Eve 'Began to cast lascivious Eyes, she him / As wantonly repaid; in Lust they burn'.[8] Moreover, this scene in the Garden of Eden is set against the background of an epic battle between the celestial forces of good and evil, in which the clang of armour and the thunder of cannon reverberate through the vast reaches of space:

> Arms on Armor clashing bray'd
> Horrible discord, and the madding Wheels
> Of brazen Chariots rag'd; dire was the noise
> Of conflict; over head the dismal hiss
> Of fiery Darts in flaming volleys flew,
> And flying vaulted either Host with fire.
> So under fiery Cope together rush'd
> Both Battles main, with ruinous assault
> And indistinguishable rage; all Heav'n
> Resounded, and had Earth been then, all Earth
> Had to her Centre shook. (vi. 209 ff.)

The armaments of divine warfare are formidable in the violence of their irresistible force. The battlefield may be heaven, the participants angels and archangels, but in Milton's epic we are left in no doubt of the awesome massivity of the brazen chariots, the iron globes, and the chained thunderbolts which form the arsenal and weaponry of this titanic struggle. The earthiness of the scene is intensified by the imagery of belching, glutted entrails:

> Immediate in a flame,
> But soon obscur'd with smoke, all Heav'n appear'd,
> From those deep-throated Engines belcht, whose roar
> Embowell'd with outrageous noise the Air,
> And all her entrails tore, disgorging foul
> Thir devilish glut, chain'd Thunderbolts and Hail
> Of Iron Globes, which on the Victor Host

Levell'd, with such impetuous fury smote,
That whom they hit, none on thir feet might stand,
Though standing else as Rocks, but down they fell
By thousands, Angel on Arch-Angel roll'd. (vi. 584 ff.)

Examined in isolation, the physical tangibility of this description may appear less remarkable; a battle is, after all, a battle whether it takes place on earth or in heaven. Yet if we set beside it, as we shall in a moment, the hallucinatory world of religious mannerism, with its disembodied souls in ecstasy, its blending of real with ideal, and the intangible elasticity of its time and space, this specifically baroque delight in the tactile, the monumental, and the solid becomes clearly accentuated.

In expressing infinity in such finite and concrete terms, Milton was not unaware of the theological contradictions involved—the mathematical fallacy, for example, that it should take precisely nine days and nine nights for Satan to fall through the immeasurable vacuity of space. At those moments when he is anxious to remind us of the limitations of man, when the Archangel Raphael relates to mortal Adam the wonders of Creation, he guardedly explains through the angel's lips that such terminology is anthropomorphic in its intent, reducing to human language the otherwise ineffable grandeur of heaven:

. . . what surmounts the reach
Of human sense, I shall delineate so,
By lik'ning spiritual to corporal forms,
As may express them best. (v. 571–4).

But this technique of 'measuring things in Heaven by things on Earth' is in no sense restricted to the enclosed inner narrative. Outside Raphael's account, when the anthropomorphic explanation is no longer relevant, it is still through gravitational pulls and muscular strength that the powerful poetic impact is achieved. The account of Satan's fall from heaven to hell is a poetic *tour de force*; for it translates into sound the enormity of that plunging descent, compelling us, as we read, to descend the voice scale from the lofty 'Him' down to the 'Bottomless perdition' which marks the end of his grim journey. The fall is presented not as a disciplinary exile from the heavenly assembly, but as a terrifying plummeting through space to the weighty chains of imprisonment below:

> Him the Almighty Power
> Hurl'd headlong flaming from th' Ethereal Sky
> With hideous ruin and combustion down
> To Bottomless perdition, there to dwell
> In Adamantine Chains and penal Fire,
> Who durst defy th' Omnipotent to Arms. (i. 44)

In her study of the baroque elements in Milton, Miss Mahood has surprisingly suggested the contrary viewpoint. She argues that in *Paradise Lost* Milton succeeds in transcending the physical laws of dynamics, and is able to '. . . imagine a world in which none of these laws apply, in which untoward levitation suddenly gives way to unexpected gravitational force'.[9] But the sole passage she quotes as evidence would seem to confirm my own view rather than hers, depicting as it does the mechanics of Satan's struggle to overcome the technical problems of his ascent:

> At last his Sail-broad Vans
> He spreads for flight, and in the surging smoke
> Uplifted spurns the ground, thence many a League
> As in a cloudy Chair ascending rides
> Audacious, but that seat soon failing, meets
> A vast vacuity: all unawares
> Flutt'ring his pennons vain plumb down he drops
> Ten thousand fadom deep, and to this hour
> Down had been falling, had not by ill chance
> The strong rebuff of some tumultuous cloud
> Instinct with Fire and Nitre hurried him
> As many miles aloft. (ii. 927 ff.)

The heavens themselves retain here the physical properties and gravitational pulls of this earth. Satan is no sylph-like, gossamer creature but a mighty warrior; he cannot hope for levitation without the use of 'sail-broad' wings with a span large enough to bear his great weight. When he meets a 'vast vacuity' his wings no longer sustain him, for there is nothing against which they can beat, and he plunges earthward, saved only by the strong rebuff of a stormy cloud. Each thrust must be met by a counter-thrust, and Satan himself is obligated to struggle through immense spaces to reach his goal; he cannot, like the conventional angels of other eras (or, in fact, like Donne's) simply materialize at his destination. Weary distances must be traversed, steep battlements scaled, and the weaponry of war resisted. The celestial battle of this epic ranges far beyond mortal confines, but the forces it employs are essentially those of the terrestrial world enlarged to awesome proportions.

Milton's theological inquiry into the nature of matter is perhaps only tangentially relevant to his poetic treatment of it, for his imaginative descriptions of the heavens frequently contradict his own more formal statements. In his prose treatises, he claims that matter, because of its divine origin, is imperishable in the created world, a view which displays in itself a baroque respect for physical reality in accordance with the dominant epic treatment of his theme. His conclusion in the prose tract is unequivocal, that '... if all things are not only from God, but of God, no created thing can be finally annihilated'.[10] On the other hand, even within the epic itself, he visualizes a gradual decrease in substantiality as the scale of creation is ascended, and he draws a graceful analogy from the natural world where the intangible perfume of the topmost blossom represents the angelic spirits on the higher rungs of the cosmic hierarchy:

> . . . more refin'd, more spiritous, and pure,
> As nearer to him plac't or nearer tending
> Each in thir several active Spheres assign'd,
> Till body up to spirit work, in bounds
> Proportion'd to each kind. So from the root
> Springs lighter the green stalk, from thence the leaves
> More aery, last the bright consummate flow'r
> Spirits odorous breathes. (v. 475–82)

Such belief in the spirituality of celestial creatures might appear to nullify any possibility of warfare, physical injury, or material destruction in the heavens themselves, and he does, in fact, at times remind us of the insubstantiality of these airy spirits. The description of Satan's first wound is a passage which Pope was later to parody in his own entertaining account of Belinda's sylph, sliced in half by a pair of scissors, whose airy substance, to our relief, 'soon unites again'. So, in the original duel, Michael's sword:

> . . . met
> The sword of *Satan* with steep force to smite
> Descending, and in half cut sheer, nor stay'd
> But with swift wheel reverse, deep ent'ring shear'd
> All his right side; then *Satan* first knew pain,
> And writh'd him to and fro convolv'd; so sore
> The griding sword with discontinuous wound
> Pass'd through him, but th' Ethereal substance clos'd
> Not long divisible, and from the gash
> A stream of Nectarous humor issuing flow'd
> Sanguine, such as Celestial Spirits may bleed.
>
> (vi. 323–33)

Such comment, partially ironic, flashes out at rare moments to illumine the grotesque futility of angelic warfare and hence of Satan's attempt to overthrow divine authority;[11] but these momentary asides never interrupt for long the overwhelming impression that we are witnessing the corporeal clash of superhuman forces, even though they may be technically disembodied. The poetic power of language and imagery is used deliberately to crush any theological reservations.

In baroque painting, the physical and tactile predominate no less. There is little likelihood that the heavy, buxom nudes of a Rubens canvas will fade into insubstantiality and reveal that they are abstract ideals only temporarily clothed in material form—as occurs in Donne's 'Aire and Angels':

> Still when, to where thou wert, I came,
> Some lovely glorious nothing I did see.
> But since my soule, whose child love is,
> Takes limmes of flesh, and else could nothing doe,
> More subtile than the parent is,
> Love must not be, but take a body too,
> And therefore what thou wert, and who,
> I bid Love aske, and now
> That it assume thy body, I allow,
> And fixe it selfe in thy lip, eye, and brow.

Here the spiritual ideal of love attaches itself lightly to the lip, eye, and brow of the body, as though maintaining only a minimal contact, just sufficient to become visible to the human eye. Rubens's women, on the other hand, are not to be parted from their ample flesh—a flesh in which the artist delights as the essence, not the temporary garb of womanhood. In such scenes of rape as his *Daughters of Leucippus* or *The Sabine Women*, the male captors must unenviably exert all their muscular strength, visibly straining to lift their weighty prizes from the ground. Even in the whirling vigour of his visionary works, the emphasis remains gravitational, with the bodies, as in his *Fall of the Damned*, hurtling down through space to parallel the Miltonic passage on Satan's fall.[12] In such rarer instances as *The Assumption of the Virgin*, where figures do miraculously rise towards heaven, the resistance to the heavy downward pull is powerfully conveyed and the miracle consists not in any supernatural or ethereal release from their control but in their overcoming the ever-present physical laws of nature. The matronly corpulence of his female Junoesque figures is present in Milton's description of Eve, who

> . . . half imbracing lean'd
> On our first Father, half her swelling Breast
> Naked met his under the flowing Gold
> Of her loose tresses hid: hee in delight
> Both of her Beauty and submissive Charms
> Smil'd with superior Love, as *Jupiter*
> On *Juno* smiles, when he impregns the Clouds
> That shed *May* flowers; and press'd her Matron lip.
>
> (iv. 494 ff.)

This firm acceptance of mass, solidity, and weight revealed in the tactile elements of baroque art and poetry is symptomatic of a shift in attitude to the universe at large. The pragmatism of the Renaissance which, for all its idealized harmony, had discovered a new delight in the material as well as the spiritual world, and had reintroduced realistic perspective into its painting and drama, had itself been almost imperceptibly absorbed into the subsequent baroque. Any religious attempt within the baroque to resist the growing mechanistic philosophy of an empirical age began not from a denial of the tangible but from an acknowledgement of its validity. Instead of emphasizing an ascetic Christian withdrawal from life, it found the most impressive instrument for strengthening religious faith in a demonstration of the enormous energy and power within the physical world, which testified *a minori* to the splendour of its divine source. In responding to this baroque movement, the Protestant was inhibited both theologically and temperamentally. He had chosen the plain style both in life and art, identifying the austere with that Christian humility and restraint to which he aspired. Accordingly, the exuberance of baroque plenitude, with its 'idolatrous' images and ostentatious display of material wealth, ought to have been anathema to him. Yet as the dominant artistic mode of the era, militantly asserting the claims of the Church against a rising scientism, its attractions were difficult to resist. Milton, it is true, consigns to the regions of hell the obviously baroque structure of Pandaemonium, but his condemnation is hedged with praise. Its architect Mulciber, he admits, had built in heaven before his fall, and in the closing lines of the description he ungrudgingly acknowledges the magnificence of the building compared with the finest architectural achievements of man:

> . . . out of the earth a Fabric huge
> Rose like an Exhalation with the sound
> Of Dulcet Symphonies and voices sweet.
> Built like a Temple, where *Pilasters* round
> Were set, and Doric pillars overlaid
> With Golden Architrave; nor did there want
> Cornice or Frieze, with bossy Sculptures grav'n;
> The Roof was fretted Gold. Not *Babylon*,
> Nor great *Alcairo* such magnificence
> Equall'd in all their glories . . .   (i. 713)

The new St. Paul's of London, quieter and less ostentatious than its continental counterparts, was an obvious attempt to provide a Protestant rival to St. Peter's, equally imposing in its monumentality.

In absorbing the pragmatism of humanist philosophy, the baroque absorbed too its respect for Reason, the logical process which in the new empiricism connects and systematizes the observable natural phenomena; and it is Reason that serves as the corner-stone of *Paradise Lost*. The supreme task that Milton sets himself in his major epic is to *justify* the ways of God to men, and it is a task of which he never loses sight throughout the multiple ramifications of the poem. For him religious faith can be preserved and defended only if it can be placed within the rational systems of human thought. Strangely enough, Milton's triumph as a poet lies in the very impossibility of his task—the fact that faith can never be finally rationalized. His Christianity would need to be stripped both of its splendour and of its paradox before it could be neatly fitted into the rational chain of being, accepted by the era of Dryden and Pope. In Milton the reasoned defence creates a passionate inner dialectic; at one level he insists on the logical defensibility of the Creation and Fall while at another he recognizes the hopelessness of attempting to compress the vast theological system into any human framework of right and wrong. If knowledge alone can lead to faith, why, we must ask, should the Tree of Knowledge, of all trees in the Garden, have borne the forbidden fruit? And above all, by what strained logic are we to exonerate God for permitting the dread damnation of a Fall in order to demonstrate the mercy of divine Salvation? These are common-places of Miltonic criticism, but it is their implication that concerns us here. Throughout the epic—as throughout the baroque itself—this clash between Rational Will and Instinctive Energy makes the work vibrate with artistic power. Within the baroque cathedral, the splendour of the heavenly scene painted upon the ceiling achieves its emotional impact by the sense of effulgent release it offers from the heavy pressures and dark massivity of the building itself. Without the firm architectural structure darkened by its contrasting shadows and heavy cornices, the soaring magnificence of the vision would be merely ornamental (as it was later to become in the decorative ceilings by James Thornhill at Greenwich Hospital). Within *Paradise Lost*, however, it is the insistence upon Reason, upon intellectual justification within a physically realistic world that provides the heavy structure within which the forces of spiritual energy can be compressed before bursting forth in the cosmic battle for man's soul. This dialectic of vigorous rebellion and omnipotent authority represented by weighty chains thrown off for daring flight till damnation be heaped on Satan once again, creates the tension of concrete forces out of which the poetry draws its imaginative force:

> So stretcht out huge in length the Arch-fiend lay
> Chain'd on the burning Lake, nor ever thence
> Had risen or heav'd his head, but that the will
> And high permission of all-ruling Heaven
> Left him at large to his own dark designs,
> That with reiterated crimes he might
> Heap on himself damnation, while he sought
> Evil to others, and enrag'd might see
> How all his malice serv'd but to bring forth
> Infinite goodness, grace, and mercy shown
> On Man by him seduc't, but on himself
> Treble confusion, wrath and vengeance pour'd.
> Forthwith Upright he rears from off the Pool
> His mighty Stature . . .   (i. 209 ff.)

From phrase to phrase the passage shifts disturbingly between the longing to escape heavenward and the crushing downward forces which prevent Satan from rising. The heaviness of 'Heap . . . damnation', 'Treble confusion', 'wrath', and 'vengeance' offset by the 'goodness', 'grace', and 'mercy' shining above create the spatial dynamics specific to the baroque.

As we turn from the baroque to mannerism, we find ourselves, although still within the framework of religious faith, in an almost totally different world. In mannerist art there can be no such physical battle even in metaphor, because the material world disintegrates at a touch. We gaze at an El Greco painting as into a distorting mirror, with the figures strangely elongated, an eerie light casting a mystical luminosity over the scene, and buildings standing like cardboard façades in some fantastic dream world. Within such a liquescent, dematerialized world there is no framework for vigorous self-assertion—only for spiritual yearning, ecstasy, and self-surrender. Nor is it, of course, the perspective that imposes the mood; they arise interdependently as the emotional and artistic expression of what may be termed the alternative response to the High Renaissance, the introspective and self-critical as opposed to the more externalized and authoritative baroque. Donne's 'Nocturnall upon S. Lucie's Day' is, for example, an extraordinary exploration of human despair, the very reverse of such dogmatic assurance. It conveys a feeling of unfathomable nothingness which reaches far below the nothingness even of the grave. The speaker here becomes metaphorically the quintessence of vacuity and spiritual emptiness, the gloomiest of creatures on this darkest night of the year, the very epitaph of universal winter and death:

> The world's whole sap is sunke:
> The generall balme th' hydroptique earth hath drunk,
> Whither, as to the beds-feet, life is shrunke,
> Dead and enterr'd; yet all these seeme to laugh,
> Compar'd with mee, who am their Epitaph.
>
> Study me then, you who shall lovers bee
> At the next world, that is, at the next Spring:
>   For I am every dead thing,
>   In whom love wrought new Alchimie.
>   For his art did expresse
> A quintessence even from nothingnesse,
> From dull privations, and leane emptinesse:
> He ruin'd mee, and I am re-begot
> Of absence, darknesse, deathe; things which are not.

The entire poem is a negation of actuality, a withdrawal into the inner self as the real world loses its meaning.

This poem is by no means typical of all Donne's writing, but it does represent an element in the mannerist mode which has provoked much adverse criticism. It has been argued that mannerism is merely a reactionary art form, achieving its most dramatic effects by the facile process of inverting or disrupting the natural perspective and idealized serenity established as norms by the Renaissance. The principle of spatial equipoise is repudiated by the huddling of crowded figures into one corner of the canvas, angels swoop down from heaven in disproportionate foreshortening, the subtle blending of harmonious colours is replaced by glaringly discordant pinks, greens, and lurid blues such as are never seen in the waking world, and the superb nudes of an earlier era become skeletal, or violently contorted, often for no apparent reason. Certainly in the Northern Countries which, despite Dürer's visit to Italy, remained comparatively untouched by the High Renaissance, mannerism is almost non-existent, the near-Gothicism of Bosch, Dürer, and Breughel leading smoothly into the full-blooded baroque of Rubens. There, mannerism had no classical tradition on which to sharpen its teeth, no authoritative convention whose repudiation or inversion would startle the viewer.

We should recall, however, that there is nothing inherently invalid in the reactionism of an art form. Wordsworth's 'spontaneous overflow of powerful feeling' was no less a reaction to the rationalist restraint and intellectual decorum of Pope's age, yet it has never been disqualified on that score. The criterion is, in the broadest sense, how effectively the reaction expresses in artistic form the emerging cultural patterns of the time. Moreover, mannerism, though it was reactionary, was by no means a mere instrument for a disgruntled *avant-garde* protesting against the tiresome success of the artistic establishment. As art historians now recognize, it was the outgrowth of stylistic changes appearing within the later works of the leading Renaissance artists who constituted that establishment—Raphael and, even more influentially, Michelangelo who were themselves responding to the changing intellectual climate. The latter's Medici tomb, the Laurentian library, and his fresco *The Conversion of St. Paul* created as great a stir in aesthetic circles as the work which had first established his reputation some thirty or forty years earlier. His sculpture betrays hints of a mannerist tendency as early as 1516, when the anguished *figura serpentinata* of his *Dying Slave* suggested, as yet in embryonic form, a disenchantment with the calm frontality of his own *Pietà* in St. Peter's, and his Florentine *David*. It was as though he realized that their tranquillity reflected only half of life, leaving no room to express those doubts and anxieties which were to oppress his later years. In 1545 *The Conversion of St. Paul* marked the full development of his mannerist period, summarizing the changes he had been gradually introducing into his own work and anticipating the future trends of mannerism at large. The fresco erupts into violent movement, rejecting the harmonic repose which used to underlie Renaissance paintings even when their theme was tempestuous. In the centre the horse rears up wildly, its hindquarters grotesquely dwarfing the rest of its body as naked human figures tumble headlong on either side. Above, the figure of Christ plummets earthward, his outstretched arm with difficulty clearing a path through the crowding angels that block his way. And Paul, whom an earlier school would have placed in a position of centrality, is almost lost in the mass of struggling figures below, where he lies dazed on the ground, his back to the celestial vision, his eyes closed as though mortal sight were superfluous in experiencing the inner turmoil of his spiritual conversion.

Among the lesser luminaries of the era, parallel changes were occurring which, at least in their earlier form, were more indicative of technical experimentation than artistic achievement. It has long been apparent that the graceful but anatomically disproportional *Madonna of the Long Neck* (1535) by Parmigianino was neither a whimsical extravagance nor (as was once argued in connection with El Greco) an unfortunate instance of astigmatism, but a deliberate departure from the repetitively 'perfect' Madonnas of the Renaissance. In the initial stages of the movement a strain of medievalism is discernible, as though the new school, like the later Pre-Raphaelites, were wondering what had been lost, or what price had been paid for the impressive achievements of the Renaissance itself. In Pontormo's *Joseph in Egypt* (1518) we find the same 'expressionist' transgression of chronology as had characterized medieval paintings and pageants. An illustration in the twelfth-century Lambeth Bible, for example, could include within one frame a composite picture containing various biblical scenes—Abraham receiving the angels, the sacrifice of Isaac, and Jacob's dream of a ladder reaching to heaven. The medieval reader needed no footnote to inform him that the three Old Testament events depicted were united and, in a sense, contemporaneous, not in their historical occurrence within the confines of human time and space but in their spiritual significance as prefigurations of the Annunciation, the Crucifixion, and the Resurrection; and the figure of Jesus in the centre of the illustration served as the unifying motif. So in Pontormo's picture we discover two separate scenes within one frame—the arrival of Joseph's brethren to the left, while Jacob blesses Ephraim and Manasseh in the top right-hand corner, even though the viewer would know that the two scenes were not coincidental in time. The physical restrictions of time and space are here ignored as irrelevant.

This transgression of chronological harmony finds its counterpart in the structural composition of the painting which deliberately cuts across the balanced perspective of Renaissance style by means of a staircase curving across the middle of the scene and carrying the eye upwards towards a statue totally unconnected with the subject matter of the painting itself. In Parmigianino's *Madonna*, too, a series of pillars behind her, huddled closely together, support nothing, the figures on her right crowd against her and press out of the frame, destroying tectonic calm, and in the background can be perceived the tiny figure of a prophet—perfectly in proportion (as though to prove that Parmigianino could paint with anatomical precision when he wished) but reduced to the size of a medieval donor, symbolically dwarfed by the more sacred figures. Moreover, in both these paintings, the securer equilibrium of the Renaissance is challenged. The Madonna is half-sitting, half-standing in a posture which suggests that both she and her child are in danger of slipping to the floor; and in Pontormo's painting, though we may eventually work out the peculiar architectural planning of the building, at first sight the staircase appears to lead nowhere, and the precarious absence of a rail is accentuated by the small child with one foot almost over the edge.

Were these the only examples of mannerist art, there would be some justice in the conventional charge that these painters were merely conveying a sense of disturbance and insecurity and in this respect it would, I think, be justifiable to argue that their importance is no more than historical. Without the subsequent changes in mannerist art, the significance of this 'disturbance' would never have been apparent, for there is nothing within the paintings themselves to suggest the nature of their dissatisfaction with the prevailing mode. They lack the energizing quality of their successors. In the work of Tintoretto, however, the religious mannerist philosophy has already matured, and there is no need to move outside the paintings themselves to learn the artistic and more broadly philosophical message they convey. It is not the purpose of this present study to follow in any detail the more general development of mannerist art—the startling angle from which Titian depicts *Abraham's Sacrifice* to lend it dramatic immediacy, or the heavenly figure in Tibaldi's *Conception of St. John* swooping in sharply foreshortened perspective to join the celestial and earthly scenes. Artists had begun experimenting with fragmentation of pictorial unity and the restless movement of crowded figures before Tintoretto began painting, and his early work such as *Vulcan, Venus, and Mars* forms a natural part of this new tradition. The change which he introduced and which epitomized what I shall term *religious mannerism* is not merely the elaboration of a new technique in religious painting. It marks the moment when the technical innovations were transformed into an essentially new artistic vision.

In Titian's *Abraham's Sacrifice* the surprising angle of vision is enormously impressive. The raised arm of Abraham wielding a sharply pointed knife is held back by the angel as if it were about to descend upon us, the spectators, who view the scene from below, as it were beside the woodpile on which Isaac kneels. But it is a Renaissance painting none the less—with the muscular strength, the spatial harmony, and the realistic perspective of an earlier school. Its mannerist quality is restricted to this change in viewpoint. In the series that Tintoretto painted on the theme of St. Mark, however, mannerism entered a new phase in which the shift in viewpoint is no longer a spectacular or theatrical device but has become symptomatic of a cultural shift in perspective. Tintoretto is now the exponent of the Counter-Renaissance itself, questioning the validity of the phenomenal world and seeking reality not within the tangible and visible but beyond them. The laws of perspective and solidity have lost their authority and become subordinated to an ultimate spiritual truth. His artistic techniques may have little direct affinity to medieval art, but he shares with that earlier school the assumption that this world is no more than the anteroom to eternity, and his paintings are intimately conceived as visionary experiences seen with the inner eye of the soul.

In *St. Mark Rescuing the Saracen* (1548) it is clear how far removed we are from the direction to be taken by the baroque proper, with its clash of dynamic and irresistible forces. Against an impressionistically turbulent background of dark storm-clouds and raging sea, in which only the cloud is visually substantial, the Saracen is being gently lifted from a sinking vessel, rising effortlessly at the touch of St. Mark's hands. In the dramatic foreshortening which Tintoretto inherited from his teachers but had now transformed into the focal point of his own painting, the saint himself floats weightlessly above, unsupported by wings and untroubled by the laws of gravity. The radiant light that accompanies him emanates from a point above and behind his body, demonstrating Tintoretto's rejection of any attempt at even illusory support such as we find in Rubens's *Assumption of the Virgin*. Over the entire painting is shed that phosphorescent glow which robs each object of its tactile quality, and it is significant that the one vivid figure, the old man battling the elements in the lower left-hand corner, is holding two poles or oars which fade into the sea, resting unsupported in the water; there is nothing solid against which he can exert his strength, and once again the reality of the physical world has disintegrated. This is not the apocalyptic dream-world of Hieronymus Bosch, where the nightmarish scenes depict grotesque, semi-human creatures undergoing the ingeniously designed tortures and pleasures of the medieval after-life. There, for all the distortion, the Lilliputian figures are clearly delineated, often in vivid caricature, in a disturbingly surrealistic fantasy of post-mortal existence. But for Tintoretto, as for El Greco, it is as though the miraculous event were occurring here on earth, with the concrete world shimmering into insubstantiality through the fervour of the visionary experience.

In his *Removal of the Body of St. Mark* (Plate 3) dark storm-clouds again predominate, but here a new dimension is added; for the flash of lightning in the sky seems literally to electrify the scene, and the tranquillity of the focal group of figures bearing the saint's body contrasts with the tormented or wraith-like shapes stunned by the spiritual impact of their proximity to the sacred corpse, and fleeing in terror. The mannerist 'disturbance' here is not, as has so often been argued, the result of insecurity or loss of direction; nor is it symptomatic of alienation in any twentieth-century sense of the term. Instead, it is the dislodgement of physical reality by a religious faith which finds its satisfaction in the emotional rather than the

1. S. Maria della Salute, Venice

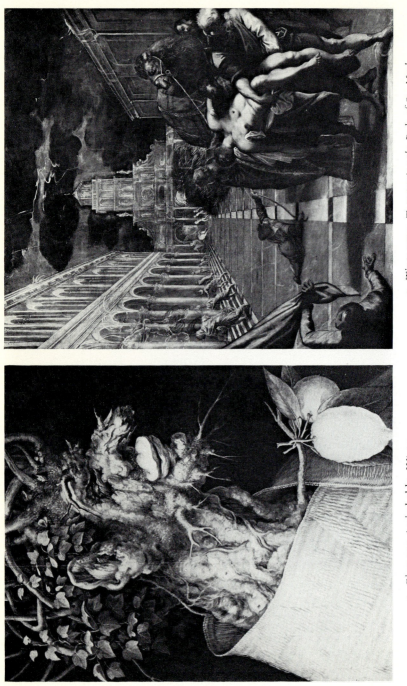

3. Tintoretto, *Transporting the Body of St. Mark*

2. Giuseppe Arcimboldo, *Winter*

4. Bellini, *The Agony in the Garden*

5. El Greco, *The Agony in the Garden*

6. El Greco, *St. Francis with Brother Rufus* (detail)

7. Buontalenti. Altar steps in S. Stefano, Florence

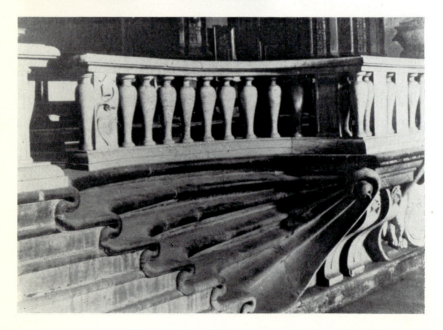

empirical world. In Tintoretto, in El Greco, and, not least, in Donne, there is spiritual agony and self-torture in the struggle to achieve salvation—a struggle demanding troubled introspection and near-despair; but there is never any real doubt that salvation exists for those who can achieve it. In his more cynical moods, as in Satire iii, Donne's speaker will scoff at the squabbling sectarianism of Christianity, dismissing the monopolistic claims of each sect in turn:

> Seeke true religion. O, where? Mirreus
> Thinking her unhous'd here, and fled from us,
> Seekes her at Rome; there, because hee doth know
> That shee was there a thousand yeares agoe,
> He loves her ragges so, as wee here obey
> The statecloth where the Prince sate yesterday.
> Crants to such brave Loves will not be inthrall'd,
> But loves her onely, who at Geneva's call'd
> Religion, plaine, simple, sullen, yong,
> Contemptuous, yet unhansome . . .

But this is all to justify his own temporary wavering between these sects before making that choice which, he maintains, must inevitably be made before life ends:

> Yet strive so, that before age, deaths twilight,
> Thy Soule rest, for none can worke in that night.

Even during his periods of doubt and self-searching he remains strong in his conviction that Truth does stand at the summit, and it is in the light of that conviction that the merely tangible world of empiricism loses its attraction for the religious mannerist. Science would advocate the straight route to the top of the mountain, the shortest distance between two points, but for him the oblique approach is preferable, as he insists in a famous passage in this same poem:

> On a huge hill,
> Cragged and steep, Truth stands, and hee that will
> Reach her, about must, and about must goe;
> And what th' hills suddennes resists, winne so.

There are, as Hauser has argued, some remarkable parallels

between mannerism and our own age of alienation. The two schools
are united in their rejection of that harmony and order assumed by
an earlier era. But he is wrong to ignore a gulf which no other similarities can conceal. Our twentieth-century alienation, perhaps best
typified by the existentialist movement, begins from an awareness
of the death or withdrawal of God from the mechanistic universe;
and even the religious existentialism of Buber and Tillich is an
attempt to bridge the terrifying void that has opened between man
and his Creator. The impulse of religious mannerism, however, is
charged with the unquestioning conviction of the immediate
presence of the divine, besides which the phenomenal world
becomes almost irrelevant. Beckett's Vladimir and Estragon,
symbols of twentieth-century man, half-heartedly attempt suicide
as they wander aimlessly in the faint, almost absurd hope that Godot
may yet come to rescue them from the wasteland of their lives. In
contrast, El Greco's paintings are aflame with the certainty of his
faith. His friend Giulio Clovio recorded in a letter:

Yesterday I visited Greco, thinking to take a walk with him through
the city. It was a most lovely day, with the spring sunshine at its
best and would have given pleasure to anybody. The whole city
was festive. When I went into his studio, I was astonished; the
shades were pulled so completely over the windows that you could
hardly distinguish the objects in the room. Greco was seated in a
chair—neither working nor asleep. He would not go out with me, as
he said *the daylight blinded the light within him*.[13]

His closing of the shutters lest the sunlight disturb the richness of
his inner vision scarcely suggests sterile alienation of self in any
modern sense of the term, nor an admission of the hopeless fragmentation of the universe, but rather a conviction of cosmic purposeful-
ness transcending the merely visible and corporeal. And it is a
distinction which must be borne in mind in any examination of
Donne too, lest, as has so often happened, we unjustifiably project
into his poetry the dilemmas of our own age.

Tintoretto himself betrayed no hint of devotionalism in his outer
life. He was regarded by his contemporaries as eccentric, unscrupu-
lous, and inordinately ambitious. But his canvases are vibrant with
the religious fervour of the Counter-Reformation. His *Last Supper* of

1594 discarded that humanist concern with the drama of Christ's betrayal which had animated Da Vinci's work (as it had Tintoretto's earliest version of the scene). Instead, his interest has shifted to the religious mystery of the Eucharist, the moment symbolizing the transubstantiation of the wafer and wine of the Mass into the flesh and blood of Jesus. He was presenting pictorially the Council of Trent's reaffirmation of the supernatural quality of the Eucharist in the face of Protestant heresy: 'If anyone denies that, in the sacrament of the most holy Eucharist, are contained truly, really, and substantially, the body and blood together with the soul and divinity of our Lord Jesus Christ and consequently the whole Christ; but says that He is only therein as in a sign, or in figure, or virtue; let him be anathema.' Tintoretto's concern with the sacramental miracle is reflected in the stylistic treatment of the scene, which glimmers with an unnatural and almost macabre luminosity. Against the gloom of a *chiaroscuro* background, Christ's head shines with a dazzling light as he offers the food to his disciples, crowding each other along a table which slices the room at a disquieting angle. Each is strangely silhouetted, almost isolated against the incandescence of his own halo. Around a flaming oil lamp suspended from the ceiling swirl ghost-like angels in homage, and the radiating brilliance of both the lamp and Christ's nimbus identify the lamp itself as the pictorial symbol of Christ Risen. There is no attempt at realism here, such as the arch which Da Vinci carefully placed above Christ's head as a naturalistic equivalent of a halo. The miraculous had been reaffirmed.

In El Greco, that yearning for the celestial which characterizes religious mannerism reaches its artistic climax. In terms either of the Renaissance or of the baroque, it is easy enough to dismiss the strange elongation and grotesque colouring of his canvases as an 'overstrained' striving after effect; but in fact his distorted figures form no part of that generally accepted definition of mannerism as a capricious desire to startle by intellectual ingenuity. The latter element is visible in mannerist art at its most trivial level in the cleverly designed grottoes of Buontalenti with their concealed waterspouts ready to drench the unwary visitor, and their sculptured tableaux of nymphs and dolphins emerging unexpectedly from within apparently solid rocks at the turn of a hidden tap.[14] If Buontalenti and El Greco are both mannerist, they stand at such opposite poles of the art form that the co-ordinating term becomes almost meaningless. For in El Greco there is neither caprice nor the desire to startle by novel distortion, but a profoundly serious attempt to transmit through his art his own conviction that the way to salvation lay not in the new-found world of universal, empirical reality, but in the spiritual and emotional experiences of individual men. The corporeal becomes transfigured and de-elemented as the quintessence both of the human and the inanimate is drawn tremblingly upwards towards eternity.

The contrast between Renaissance and mannerist art can perhaps be best illustrated by placing his *Agony in the Garden* beside Bellini's earlier version of the same theme (Plates 4 and 5). They are both remarkably fine paintings in their different styles. In Bellini's the dominant mood is of serenity, with the canvas suffused by a gentle golden glow as the dawn spreads across the horizon. In the centre, Jesus kneels upon a rounded rock, natural in form, yet conveniently shaped to serve as a praying-stool. Beside him the three disciples sleep undisturbed, and in the distance can be seen the soldiers coming to arrest him as they make their way along a path which winds over a small bridge into the fenced garden. The physical topography is rendered in accurate perspective and detail. In the distant sky, a small angel stands on a cloud holding the chalice but in no way disturbing the harmonious scene, reflected in the calm, sweeping curves of the natural landscape. There is no hint of the agony recorded in the Gospel of St. Luke, and Bellini was obviously untroubled by the discrepancy. His interest was in the tranquillity achieved after the agony, the comfort offered by the appearance of the angel; and in the Renaissance tradition, it is in the peacefulness of the scene that he finds his artistic satisfaction.

In contrast, El Greco's painting vibrates with the emotional force of Christ's spiritual agony. His face is calm as he gazes at the angel before him, but around him the landscape trembles in excited tor-ment, as though not yet recovered from the intensity of the vision-ary experience. Behind the central figure of Jesus towers a rock, not rounded as in Bellini, but cragged and steep; and it is a rock such as never existed in nature. It thrusts up out of the ground in a convulsive movement, seeming to fold back upon itself in its eagerness to leap upwards. Beyond it, a pale moon is almost obscured by unreal storm clouds that merge with the rock, creating in pictorial image Donne's vision of chaos:

> Doth not a Tenarif, or higher Hill
> Rise so high like a Rocke, that one might thinke
> The floating Moone would shipwrack there, and sinke?[15]

The iridescent light of the painting, moreover, comes not from the direction of the moon, but against all natural law from directly above, with a mysterious beam emanating from yet another point over the angel's head. At his side sleep the three disciples, but they sleep in a hollow that whirls round them like a maelstrom, accentuating the restless movement of the painting as a whole. The figure of Jesus himself, robed in a weirdly luminous purple and blue that seems to glow in the unnatural light from above, is, like so many of El Greco's martyrs and saints, caught at the moment of rapture. He is poised, his hands held delicately before him as if to recover his balance; but the spasm of the rock behind suggests the surging upward movement of his soul. No path leads from the soldiers visible in the distance to the place at which he kneels, for natural, rational perspective is discarded at the moment of spiritual revelation, and the entire scene is subordinated to the perspective of the inner eye.

The shimmering upward movement of the *Agony* is shared by almost all his religious paintings, conveying with imaginative force the tension of body and soul forcibly united on this earth, but striving to part. The spirit yearns to escape from the trappings of the flesh and to rise in a flamelike surge of ecstasy into the celestial. At times, as in his *St. Bernard of Siena*, the martyr gazes down sadly at the world around him in renunciation of the temporal, this medieval *contemptus mundi* often finding its symbolic representation in the presence of a skull. But more frequently, that perpendicular elongation familiar from Parmigianino's *Madonna of the Long Neck* and the *figura serpentinata* of the later Michelangelo, is transformed into a remarkably effective device for achieving the transcendental, spiritualizing effect at which he aims. The impossibly slender limbs of his ascetic saints seem weightless, as if the soul were stretching the body upwards in an agonized longing to overcome the physical restrictions of terrestrial habitation. It is an effect caught to perfection in Marvell's 'Dialogue Between the Soul and the Body':

Soul: O who shall from this Dungeon, raise
A Soul inslav'd so many wayes?
With bolts of Bones, that fetter'd stands
In Feet; and manacled in Hands.
Here blinded with an Eye; and there
Deaf with the drumming of an Ear.
A Soul hung up, as 'twere, in Chains
Of Nerves and Arteries, and Veins.
Tortur'd, besides each other part,
In a vain Head and double Heart.

Body: O who shall me deliver whole
From bonds of this Tyrannic Soul?
Which stretcht upright, impales me so,
That mine own Precipice I go . . .

Marvell visualizes the soul, like El Greco's tall figure of *St. James the Great* 'fett'rd . . . in Feet'; that is, held back from its natural levitation by its bodily tethering to the earth. In all such paintings the saint's feet are disproportionately small, as if their function were not to support the body's weight which their size makes them incapable of doing, but to retain a minimal contact with the earth until the moment of mortal release. The soul, like the drop of dew to which Marvell compares it elsewhere, 'slights' the earth, scarcely touching the place on which it rests.

How loose and easie hence to go:
How girt and ready to ascend.
Moving but on a point below,
It all about does upward bend.[16]

In the same way, those remarkable images 'Deaf with the drumming of an Ear' and '. . . blinded with an Eye' convey the poet's disdain for the physical instruments of sense which serve merely to drown the still, small voice of conscience or to block the visionary sight of the inner eye. The latter phrase captures in an arresting metaphysical paradox the dilemma of El Greco himself, fleeing to the darkened room in order to see, as the sunlight of Toledo blinds him to the spiritual truths he seeks.

There is clearly some affinity here to the contemporary theme of *King Lear*. Gloucester, too, stumbled when he saw, and only when his eyes were gouged out did he attain to insights paralleling Lear's own progression from self-centred authoritarianism to selfless pity and humility. But we should beware of blurring the distinctions. The insights achieved through their suffering, spiritual though they may be in their moral implications, have no visionary or supernatural quality. They reveal the truths of human behaviour in this world, ripping off the outer robes of office to expose man's hidden sin and corruption:

> *Lear*: What! art mad? A man may see how this world goes with no eyes. Look with thine ears: see how yond justice rails upon yond simple thief. Hark, in thine ear: change places, and handy-dandy, which is the justice, which is the thief? (IV. vi. 151 ff.)

The theme of the play is man's moral blindness in evaluating human actions on this earth, his inability to distinguish flattering tongues in this world from silent but loving hearts; while for the mannerist the obstacle to true perception is the totality of physical experience which hampers or distorts his vision of eternity.

The mannerist emphasis on spirituality is attained, then, primarily by dematerializing the actuality of the world and suggesting in the slender limbs and long, sensitive fingers of his martyrs an unearthly attenuation of the flesh which has all but surrendered to the aspirations of the soul. The vertical straining of the body culminates in the uplifted face, particularly in the eyes which, functioning here as the windows of the soul, draw the spectator's thoughts upwards, away from terrestrial affairs. It is precisely here, however, that many readers familiar with Counter-Reformation art may well shudder at the remembrance of those voluptuous and often gaudy paintings of the era familiarly known as *kitsch*, which represent the besetting sin of this aesthetic mode. Yet it is as unfair to class El Greco and Tintoretto with this more popular art form as it is to identify *Wuthering Heights* with the Gothic novels of Horace Walpole or Mrs. Radcliffe. They grew out of the same literary genre but are aesthetically incomparable. In Murillo's various versions of *The Immaculate Conception*, for example, the less attractive elements of Counter-Reformation art take command. In contrast to the thoughtful, troubled eyes of an El Greco saint caught between the two worlds and yearning for release (Plate 6), the Virgin's upward gaze is that of a typical heroine from contemporary Restoration melodrama complacently assured of her own innocence and piety, and revealing neither anguish nor unsatisfied longing. She floats on a crescent moon, surrounded by admiring cherubs to take her destined place on her heavenly throne. Where a Raphael Madonna, for example, displays an outgoing maternal tenderness towards the children playing at her feet, Murillo's Virgin is enclosed within the consciousness of her own purity; and if the over-all picture achieves a certain decorative charm, it inspires in many viewers a distaste for its overt sentimentality.[17] El Greco's *Mary Magdalen Repentant* is almost alone among his works in its hint of conscious piety, perhaps because the artist found it more difficult to enter into the female experience; but the eyes of his male saints reveal the introspection not of a narcissist caught up in admiration or obsession with his own inner self,[18] but rather of an inquirer into the human condition, endeavouring to discover by his own self-scrutiny, the predicament of all mankind of which he forms a part. There is in his portraits, as in Donne's holy sonnets, an artistic control which the works of Dolci and others merely vulgarize.

In fact, one of the dangers in evaluating mannerist art and poetry is the tendency to associate Donne with Crashaw, and El Greco with Murillo when they are artistically, if not historically, poles apart. They share, it is true, a similar cultural impulse towards religious affirmation, and their contemporaneity within the Counter-Reformation produces a certain identity in themes and images. But in their aesthetic treatment of those themes all identity disappears. In the more popular tradition which both reflected and intensified the devotionalism that gripped Spain in the seventeenth century, artistic control is often relaxed in favour of a voluptuous surrender to sensuous experience, which at weaker moments can lead to a perilous reliance upon the stock responses of sentimentalism.

The cult of Mary Magdalene, so pervasive in this era, is a case in point. She was a New Testament figure ideally suited to the missionary aims of the Jesuit order in its attempt to inspire a resurgence of religious faith and a sense of inward rededication to Christ's teachings.[19] As a penitent renouncing the pleasures of fleshly love in favour of the divine, she served as the perfect examplar of contrition, conveying the heartening message that the repentant sinner, so far from being disqualified by past sins, would be welcomed with more joy into the arms of the church than the virtuous Christians who had self-righteously condemned her. It may be added that the self-abnegation implicit in her bathing Christ's feet with her tears and drying them with her hair had a touch of theatricality about it particularly appealing to an age inclined to the extremes of religious fervour, ecstasy, and self-abasement; and although the brief story in the New Testament is related there with simplicity and restraint, the seventeenth-century versions readily hyperbolized the tears into gushing fountains.

The cult's less obvious appeal, however, lay in the means whereby the lesson was disseminated, for the biblical allusion to Mary Magdalene's past sins lent an aura of eroticism to the new accounts which, perhaps unconsciously, placed within a Christian setting what was ecclesiastically condemned outside. In Ribera's portrait of *St. Agnes in Prison* (a variation on the Magdalene theme) a naked and very beautiful young girl kneels in prayer on the prison floor modestly clutching to her bosom a sackcloth which just fails to cover her breast, while above her a flying cherub, ostensibly holding the precariously poised cloth in place, looks for all the world as though he is about to twitch it completely away. And the same holds true of the crypto-sadism implicit in almost all melodrama. The pictorial representations of flagellations, of gruesome martyrdoms, and of ascetic self-torture which abound in this era are not to be divorced from the extravagances of the Jacobean stage. They were excused and, indeed, encouraged by the Church on the grounds that they fulfilled the Loyolan call for an imaginative identification with the sufferings of the saints. 'Delicious wounds', 'baths of blood', and 'crystal tears' of repentance became the stock-in-trade of religious poetry, while the diamond teardrops affixed to Luisa Roldan's polychrome statue *The Virgin of the Macerena* (which served as the bullfighters' icon) literally translated into the plastic arts the hackneyed images of such poetry.

It would be patently unfair to condemn this entire school of popular religious art on the grounds of cliché. The *Pietà* of Fernandez at Valladolid, the *St. Ignatius* of Montanez in Seville, and the delicate wooden figures of Pedro de Mena achieve an artistic purity and grace far removed from vulgarity; and Murillo himself can at times be a moving and sensitive religious painter, as his altarpiece *The Two Trinities* testifies. However, their aesthetic success is attained at those very moments when they refuse to employ the stock techniques which spoil so much devotional art. The difference, in fact, between Donne and Crashaw lies at this crucial point. Crashaw seems even in his most admired poems to be oblivious of the distasteful implications of his imagery, whilst Donne, in his most audaciously provocative moods, remains in firm artistic control, foreseeing the apparent absurdity or discrepancy and preparing to trap his reader by twisting it suddenly to his own advantage. Crashaw's scholarly advocates, Austin Warren and Ruth Wallerstein, for all their valuable analysis of his background and of his stylistic techniques, leave this major objection unanswered, and one closes their books with the disappointing feeling that they have proved everything *except* his stature as a poet. As his main argument, Warren maintains (incorrectly, I believe) that most antipathy to Crashaw is extra-literary, based on a feeling of the poet's insincerity; yet the defence he himself offers seems scarcely less extra-literary. 'On its sensuous surface', Warren informs us in summarizing the grounds for his admiration of the poet, 'his imagination sparkles with constant metamorphosis: tears turn into soft and fluid things like milk, cream, wine, dew; into hard things like stars, pearls, and diamonds. Beneath, the same experiences engage poet and poem. All things flow. Crashaw's imagery runs in streams; the streams run together; image turns into image.'[20] But metamorphosis in imagery is not in itself a poetic virtue; it must be justified by the way it is employed. Tears do turn into milk in one of his best-known stanzas from 'The Weeper':

> Upwards thou dost weepe,
> Heav'ns bosome drinkes the gentle streame,
> Where the milky Rivers creepe
> Thine floates above, and is the creame.

But what perturbs the sensitive reader even more than the metamorphosis of tears into milk and cream is the extraordinary image of a bosom drinking. Robert M. Adams cheerfully defends the dairy metaphors as being deliberately grotesque—associated with 'cud-chewing, angelic saliva, and a delicate series of cosmic belches' in order to express Crashaw's concept of man as a sort of joke in the eyes of his God. He compares such grotesquerie to a landscape by Salvador Dali and argues that, since the purpose of both is to shock, criteria of good and bad taste are irrelevant.[21] The argument would be more convincing if there were in Crashaw's poetry a hint of sardonic wit to justify the assumption of deliberate shock tactics, but on the contrary the predominant tone is one of quiet, unquestioning faith. If, however, we put entirely to one side any consideration of the appropriateness of dairy imagery as such, the question remains whether a drinking bosom can, in the context of this poem, be anything but a failure of the poetic imagination. It is a classic instance of the unrealized metaphor which, instead of exploiting the multiplicity of poetic response, relies upon a fuzzy, unfocused reading, and appeals to stock response in place of metaphorical precision. It suggests that milk, cream, and bosoms all imply richness and nutriment, and as long as the cream rises to the top we are not to ask why, for example, the river 'creeps' instead of flowing.[22] The parallel to this vagueness of imagery in the painting of this time is the moon on which Murillo's Virgins stand in the various versions of *The Immaculate Conception*, with one foot placed firmly and un-astronomically within the crescent itself. There is no hint here of a purposeful transgression of natural law as in an El Greco painting, nor the conscious suspension of disbelief suggested by Coleridge's moon, bearing a star within its nether tip. The assumption is more simple: the moon, conventionally associated with Marian benevolence, is imported as a tinsel stage-prop, unrelated to the lunar sphere itself. It is a visual cliché.

Where, then, within the definitions of mannerism and baroque offered here do Murillo and Crashaw belong? They obviously have no share in the introspective self-searching of mannerism, and in fact have always been recognized as belonging to the baroque; yet there is no trace in their work of that weighty, dogmatic assertion which serves as the main baroque thrust. But perhaps here lies the source of their aesthetic ineffectiveness—for Crashaw and Murillo depict, I would suggest, the effulgent, heavenly opulence painted on the ceiling of a baroque cathedral but without the massivity of the dark structure below which creates the powerful aesthetic tensions of the true baroque. Theirs is a surrender without a struggle, a celestial reward achieved so effortlessly that it savours of voluptuous self-indulgence. Hence the myriads of rosy-cheeked cherubs, the mystic rapture, and the images of maternal suckling which create the over-rich texture of their work. St. Teresa, in Crashaw's 'Hymn', rises to heaven, where 'the moon of maiden stars' awaits her, ready to shower her with blessings:

> O what delight when she shall stand,
> And teach thy Lips heaven, with her hand,
> On which thou now mayst to thy wishes,
> Heap up thy consecrated kisses.
> What joy shall seize thy soul when she
> Bending her blessed eyes on thee
> Those second smiles of heaven shall dart,
> Her mild rays through thy melting heart . . .

My intention here is not to elevate Donne by denigrating Crashaw, nor to dignify El Greco by disparaging Murillo; but rather to suggest the danger of grouping them with the less talented practitioners of this Spanish-centred revival, and of assuming from a certain identity of theme, a similar identity of artistic technique and achievement. A tranquil and trusting piety is in itself as legitimate a theme for poetry as troubled self-scrutiny, and it is not there that the distinction lies, but in the means of translating the religious experience into aesthetic form. At times Donne too employs the conventional, hyperbolic vocabulary of the Counter-

Reformation on which Crashaw draws so heavily, referring in one poem, for example, to the 'flood' of tears shed by the repentant sinner. But instead of leaning on it as a substitute for artistic creativity, he startles us by the inversion of the familiar, reinvigorating the cliché by placing it within a new setting. The biblical flood becomes a classical Lethe, in preparation for the climactic sequence of 'memorie' and 'forget' which constitute the central theme of the poem:

> . . . of thine onely worthy blood,
> And my teares, make a heavenly Lethean flood,
> And drowne in it my sinnes black memorie;
> That thou remember them, some claime as debt,
> I thinke it mercy, if thou wilt forget.[23]

It would, indeed, be hard to think of any poet less interested than Donne in appeal to popular sentiment, or more ruthless in his parody of platitude and stereotype.

The upward gaze of an El Greco saint is similarly to be distinguished from the conventional depictions by such artists as Dolci. El Greco's St. Francis (Plate 6) suggests no voluptuous surrender to a shower of blessings, but rather a sensitive striving away from the impediments of the flesh towards release from what Donne called in one sermon '. . . that miserable, perplexed, riddling condition of man', caught inextricably between the demands of body and soul, neither of which can achieve satisfaction in this earthly world:

I have not body enough for my body, and I have too much body for my soul; not body enough, not blood enough, not strength enough to sustain myself in *health*, and yet body enough to destroy my soul, and frustrate the grace of God in that miserable, perplexed, riddling condition of man; sin makes the body of man miserable, and the remedy of sin *mortification*, makes it miserable too; if we enjoy the good things of this world . . . we doe but carry an other wall about our prison, an other story of unwieldy flesh about our souls; and if wee give our selves as much *mortification* as our body needs, we live a life of *Fridays*, and see no *Sabbath* . . .[24]

The powerful inner dialectic of this passage follows, as we shall see, a typically mannerist movement in its development from an initially solipsistic concern to conclusions with universal implications for all mankind.

While it is always dangerous to speak categorically of cause and effect, it is now generally recognized that a firm interrelationship exists between the devotional literature emanating from Ignatius Loyola's *Spiritual Exercises* and the remarkable degree of self-projection into the final agonies of the martyr visible in the works of Donne and El Greco. Professor Martz has explored in considerable detail the filaments connecting the 'meditative' tradition in poetry and this introspective concern among the Jesuits. He has shown how Loyola adapted to the needs of his time a contemplative tradition long established within the Church, whereby the Christian worshipper had been encouraged to direct his thoughts to the suffering of Jesus or Mary and by a process of empathic re-enactment, or imaginative *imitatio Dei*, to attain an emotional identification amounting almost to visionary self-immolation. The stigmata, or marks of crucifixion, appearing on the hands and feet of St. Francis and others formed external, psychosomatic testimony to the intensity of the spiritual experience. In this tradition Loyola found a perfect instrument for diverting the probing intellectualism of his followers away from empirical inquiry into the realm of a highly individualized inward exploration. His book advocated a strict regimen of meditative exercises in which the Jesuit was to direct his thoughts at fixed times of the day to specific moments of agony or revelation in Christian history and by this exercise to stimulate artificially a sharp emotional realism. By contemplating the physical details of the Crucifixion or of a saint's martyrdom, they learned imaginatively to immerse themselves in the experience and to return from this act of devotion with a sharpened awareness of their own spiritual deficiencies and with an increased determination to overcome those deficiencies by a process of self-purification. Luis de la Puente summarized the exercise:

Then I am to set before mine eyes Christ Jesus crucified, beholding his heade crowned with thornes; his face spit upon; his eyes obscured; his arms disioincted; his tongue distasted with gall, and viniger; his handes, and feete peerced with nailes; his backe, and shoulders torne with whippes; and his side opened with a launce: and then pondering

that hee suffereth all this for my sinnes, I will drawe sundrye
affections from the inwardest parte of my heart, sometimes trembling
at the rigour of God's justice . . . sometimes bewailing my sinnes
which were the cause of these dolours.[25]

Martz identifies this cult of emotional intensity with the baroque
rather than with mannerism, but the distinctions we have been
making between that broader movement and mannerism itself
apply here no less; for it is exclusively within religious mannerism
that this sharp focus upon *personal* salvation becomes paramount.
It is always concerned with the lonely self, whether in the form of
the *Sprecher* responding to the epiphanous scene or the preacher
meditating his own spiritual predicament as the paradigm for all
Christian suffering. In contrast, the baroque artist ultimately invokes the universal, theological framework—the power, the vastness, and the energy of that cosmic vision which can alone lend form
and purpose to the life of the individual. In Milton's epic, the
theodical intent is, as we have noted, the acknowledged *raison d'être*
of the work, his determination to find a justification for God's
actions which should convey its lesson to all mankind. Yet even in
his more personal drama, *Samson Agonistes*, he enlarges and expands
elements from his own experience into the mythic figures of Samson and Job in order to elevate them to heroic proportions.[26] The
personal must find its justification in the archetype. In Donne
the opposite process is at work. Universal truth must be checked
against the individual experience and its application reduced to the
isolated self before it can be accorded any validity; and a comparison
between two of their best-known sonnets affords an instructive
illustration of these contrary techniques at work.

Milton's sonnet on his blindness opens on a remarkably un-
Miltonic note—a touchingly personal lament for his own suffering
and the apparent pointlessness of his existence. He stands alone and
helpless in a wide, unfriendly world, longing to serve his Maker,
but rendered impotent by the deprivation of his sight:

> When I consider how my light is spent,
>   Ere half my days, in this dark world and wide,
>   And that one Talent which is death to hide,
>   Lodg'd with me useless, though my Soul more bent

> To serve therewith my Maker, and present
> My true account, lest he returning chide.

But the disconsolate note of the opening lines is slowly replaced by a renewed confidence as he raises his eyes from his immediate and depressing surroundings to the heavens. It is there in the vast cosmic system above, where thousands speed to perform their Master's bidding, that he finds his comfort. The resonant tone of the baroque rises in volume to inspire and encourage the poet, whose personal doubts are sublimated in the busy movements of the innumerable host of heaven:

> 'Doth God exact day-labour, light denied?'
> I fondly ask; But patience to prevent
> That murmur soon replies, 'God doth not need
> Either man's work or his own gifts; who best
> Bears his mild yoke, they serve him best; his State
> Is Kingly. Thousands at his bidding speed
> And post o'er Land and Ocean without rest:
> They also serve who only stand and wait.'

The dark, heavy opening represents, in a sense, the lonely worshipper overwhelmed as he enters the huge, dark cathedral, and the latter half symbolizes his growing reassurance as he raises his eyes to the bright infinity of the painted ceiling, where the myriad angels perform God's will.

Donne's sonnet is the very reverse. It begins with the magniloquence of the baroque—a Miltonic voice rare in his own poetry. The octave speaks with the reverberating authority of a prophet, commanding the angels to trumpet forth the advent of the Day of Judgement:

> At the round earth's imagin'd corners, blow
> Your trumpets, Angells, and arise, arise
> From death, you numberlesse infinities
> Of soules, and to your scattered bodies goe,
> All whom the flood did, and fire shall overthrow,
> All whom warre, dearth, age, agues, tyrannies,
> Despaire, law, chance, hath slaine, and you whose eyes,
> Shall behold God, and never tast deaths woe.

The baroque crescendo reaches its climax with the vision of the
countless infinities of souls gathering before the divine throne for
judgement. But at that moment the thunder of the Apocalypse is
silenced and the quiet voice of the speaker's own soul is heard as he
tremblingly recalls his own dire plight, his own need for personal
repentance and divine mercy:

> But let them sleepe, Lord, and mee mourne a space,
> For, if above all these, my sinnes abound,
> 'Tis late to ask abundance of thy grace,
> When we are there; here on this lowly ground,
> Teach me how to repent; for that's as good
> As if thou' hadst seal'd my pardon, with thy blood.

From his vision of the spacious heavens, the focus suddenly narrows
as he shrinks into himself in fear and doubt. The sole comfort upon
which his hope can finally rest is not the vision of an omnipotent,
kingly God dispatching thousands to perform his bidding, but
the intimate and personal relationship of *thy* blood and *my* pardon.
If Donne proved to be among the finest of English preachers, one
substantial reason was his refusal to preach down to his audience in
the name of an authoritative church, but rather to share with his
listeners the drama of his own spiritual agony as imaging forth the
struggle of each individual Christian. Walton was not alone among
his contemporaries in testifying to the introspective intensity of
the sermons, but he was perhaps the most eloquent. He portrays
Donne as

... preaching the Word so, as shewed his own heart was possest with
those very thoughts and joyes that he laboured to distill into others:
A Preacher in earnest; weeping sometimes for his Auditory, sometimes with them; always preaching to himself, like an Angel from a
cloud, but in none ... and, all this with a most particular grace and
an unexpressible addition of comeliness.

He was indeed preaching to himself, and the sermons repeatedly
acknowledge that his subject-matter was his own personal anguish,
in which he found the symbol for all Christian suffering:

I preach but the sense of Gods indignation upon mine own soul, in
a conscience of mine own sins, I impute nothing to another, that I

confesse not of my selfe, I call none of you to confession to me, I doe
but confesse my self to God and you, I rack no man's memory, what
he did last year, last week, last night, I onely gather into my memory,
and powr out in the presence of my God, and his Church, the sinfull
history of mine own youth.[27]

Even when he is not consciously resisting (as he is here) the distasteful picture of a complacent dean condescendingly chastising
the sinners in his flock, the language of the sermons itself disarms
any such suspicions. Stylistically, his is the inverted pyramid which,
in defiance of gravity, rests on the single soul and grows outwards
and upwards in its vitality and power. And when his vision does at
last open out into the infinity of heaven, it is not a universal and
impersonalized *they* who also serve, but *we* who are weighed, each
alone on the scale at that fateful moment which includes on its
scrupulous balance the soul's most secret, inward affliction:

. . . when I shall need peace, because there is none but thou, O Lord,
that should stand for me, and then shall finde, that all the wounds
that I have, come from thy hand, all the arrowes that stick in me,
from thy quiver; when I shall see, that because I have given my selfe
to my corrupt nature, thou hast changed thine; and because I am all
evill towards thee, therefore thou hast given over being good towards
me; When it comes to this height that the fever is not in the humors,
but in the spirits, that mine enemy is not an imaginary enemy,
fortune, nor a transitory enemy, malice in great persons, but a reall,
and an irresistible, and an inexorable, and an everlasting enemy, the
Lord of Hosts himselfe, the Almighty God himselfe, the Almighty God
himselfe onely knowes the waight of this affliction, and except hee
put in that *pondus gloriae*, that exceeding waight of eternall glory,
with his owne hand, into the other scale, we are waighed downe, we
are swallowed up, irreparably, irrevocably, irrecoverably, irremedi-
ably.[28]

The reiteration of the phrase '. . . the Almighty God himselfe, the
Almighty God himselfe onely knowes the waight' highlights a further
and no less significant aspect of this mannerist introspection—the
sense of intimacy it creates as though the reader or spectator were
at that moment eavesdropping on some private communion between
the speaker and his God or, in Donne's love poetry, between the

speaker and his mistress. This effect, however, is in itself illusory, for in the final analysis it is really not a dialogue to which we are listening but a communion between the *persona* and himself. Hence the technique of the dramatic monologue which lends a sense of immediacy to the urgent argument, an argument repeatedly doubling back upon itself to check, to modify, or to reverse the apparently convincing conclusion reached a line before. El Greco's *Agony in the Garden* communicates that emotional dialectic visually, even though the difficulty of conveying such complex mobility is far greater in an art form frozen to one moment of time; for the calm joy on Christ's face as he perceives the angelic vision is powerfully counterpointed by the convulsive agony of the twisted rock and the whirling hollow in which the disciples sleep. In the religious paintings of Zurburan and El Greco, the central figure is invariably sensitive, intelligent, and with a touch of the ascetic about him; there are no coarse beggars or peasants such as fill the canvases of Breughel. For in effect the artist is projecting part of himself into the picture—arguing, contradicting, exploring that inner being which can alone lead him towards some final, spiritual truth. So in Donne much of the wit as well as the soul-searching arises from this sophisticated dialogue, intended only for the perceptive, finely attuned reader—his other self. It is perhaps for that reason that he rarely externalizes his sinful impulses in the form of a Satan or Mephistopheles for it is the complexity of the inner soul that continually fascinates him, not the pressure of outward forces or universal evils. In Milton the inward conflict is no less poignant, and no responsive reader can miss the turbulent undercurrents swirling beneath the majestic surface of his verse. But the artistic form he adopts for his epic writing is that of the authoritarian poet who has already discovered the answers to the human predicament, and has received a divine call to transmit them to mankind in the name of God. Where the baroque artist stands back to gaze in admiration at the infinite and omnipotent heavens which lend dignity and splendour to his own existence, the mannerist transmutes his own perturbation into art in a dematerialized world where the only ultimate substantiality is the spiritual.

For many readers the brief definition of mannerism offered here will, I have no doubt, appear too restricted to be valid. This contrast between the massivity of the baroque and the spiritualizing dematerialization of mannerism ignores, for example, the element of caprice present in so many forms of mannerism—such *trompe l'œil* effects as the stairway in the Laurentian library whose sections appear to travel in contrary directions, and buildings which seem to sink into the ground or topple down on to the viewer. This aspect of mannerist art is without doubt of central importance for an understanding of the wit in Donne's poetry, and I must ask the reader to be patient as it will, in fact, occupy a major place in the more detailed study to follow. A more serious charge would be that this definition excludes from the mannerist school those very writers and artists whom modern critics such as Hauser are beginning to place centrally within it—Shakespeare in his Jacobean phase, Cervantes, Bologna, Vasari, Bronzino, and others. To this charge there is a twofold answer. First, it should be noted that I have deliberately introduced the term *religious mannerism* in order to isolate that specific area of mannerist art to which I believe a study of Donne can be most fruitfully related. The placing of Donne within his artistic milieu is in itself of merely historical interest unless it adds to our critical understanding of his poetry and prose, and it is his relationship to the Jesuit form of mannerism typified by Tintoretto and El Greco that I propose to explore. The attenuated or foreshortened figures in Parmigianino and Titian, the intellectual sensuality of the pearly nudes in Bronzino's *Venus, Cupid, Folly, and Time*, all these art styles have a distinct bearing on Donne's work. But within religious mannerism they are, it seems to me, subordinated to an ultimate purpose in a way that transfigures them almost beyond recognition, and it is in this setting that they can be most profitably explored.

Secondly, I remain doubtful how valid it is to place *Hamlet* or *Lear* centrally within the mannerist tradition, despite the many attractions of the theory. The mood of world-weariness, the striving for self-knowledge in a paradoxical and perplexing universe, the preoccupation, in short, with the inner anguish of man rather than his place in a harmonious universe, these are qualities which appear to divorce Shakespeare's Jacobean phase from the Elizabethan and to suggest a shift in sensibility from Renaissance to mannerist art. The connection, moreover, between the Yorick scene and those skulls conspicuous in the meditative paintings by Georges de la Tour, Zurburan, El Greco, and others is clearly neither fortuitous nor trivial, since the skull, in both its dramatic and its pictorial setting, functions as a symbol of the central theme—the implications of death and after-life in a transitory world. The introspection of a soul divided within itself is dominant in both *Hamlet* and *Lear*, and the protagonists must work their way painfully towards some meaningful resolution of the inner discord.

Yet with all these correspondences, there is so much of the vigorous Renaissance within both plays that I would place them at most within the transitional phase leading into mannerism, the phase represented most accurately by Michelangelo. The latter's *Dying Slave* points forward in its twisting, serpentine form to the mannerist concern with spiritual suffering while yet retaining the muscular realism of the Renaissance, and its classical delight in the beauty of the human body. In the same way, though Hamlet seems overwhelmed by the corruption of man in both the moral and the fleshly sense he is aware no less of man's potential nobility and of his actual achievement on this side of the grave. He himself is melancholic, and disillusioned by human frailty, but he is also the accomplished courtier, the eager student, theatre-goer, and skilful swordsman. His philosophical perspective, like that of Macbeth, Othello, and Lear, belongs to the Renaissance, relying upon a concrete, visible world. Hamlet will have proof of his father's murder before he acts, Othello demands tangible evidence of his cuckoldry in the form of a handkerchief, and Lear insists on the audible verbalization of Cordelia's love. And this reliance on physical actuality is not restricted to their failings but extended to their moments of perspicacity. Hamlet can tell a hawk from a handsaw even when the wind is not southerly. To befuddle Polonius he will pretend that yon cloud is very like a camel, but his own mind preserves a clear distinction between fact and fiction. He establishes no paradoxical identity between the two which traverses the visible divisions of the empirical world, and in this he remains no more than transitional in his mannerist tendency.

Moreover, there is in Shakespeare's Jacobean drama a superbly balanced structure whose artistic organization creates an over-all impression of naturalism—the interlocking themes of Lear and Gloucester, of Hamlet and Laertes which, obvious as they may be to the literary analyst, seem to arise naturally and effortlessly in the theatre itself. We might compare this naturalistic, harmoniously designed structure to Da Vinci's *Last Supper* where the initial impact upon the viewer is of dramatic excitement, conveying the shock of Christ's pronouncement that one of his disciples will betray him. There is a troubled movement, a startled regrouping of figures, and only closer inspection reveals the subtle counterpointing of the figures, the balance which preserves the dominant calmness of the scene while yet suggesting its disturbed movement. In Shakespeare as in Da Vinci there are no atectonic figures bursting spasmodically out of the framework like the giants in Giulio Romano's Palazzo del Té. There, in the dimly lit hall, the rebellious Titans lie sprawling beneath the ruins of their temple, clutching wildly at the fractured pillars which seem to be falling forward from the walls on to the head of the spectator himself. Instead, Shakespeare preserves the laws of perspective, and Lear's rage, enormously impressive in its power, is yet contained within the confines of the storm, subordinated to, and at no time outstripping the mightier forces of nature. Lear would never reduce the sun to a meddlesome Peeping Tom as Donne's speaker so casually does, nor make it run ludicrously behind the racing lovers as in Marvell's 'Coy Mistress'. It is only in the last of the great tragedies (which we shall examine more closely in a later chapter) that Shakespeare's heroes appear to outdistance sun and moon.

Lastly, the new complexity of character apparent in these later dramas is as much allied to the High Renaissance as it is to the mannerist aesthetic, and the theory that the inner tension of the tragic figures belongs to the latter school is again only partially valid. Hamlet jealously guards the mystery of his inner self as the central element in his being and treasures his own complexity in a way not discernible in earlier drama. Angrily he thrusts a pipe into the hands of the reluctant, unmusical Guildenstern, and peremptorily commands him to play:

Why, look you now, how unworthy a thing you make of me! You would play upon me; you would seem to know my stops; you would pluck out the heart of my mystery, you would sound me from my lowest note to the top of my compass; and there is much music, excellent voice in this little organ; yet cannot you make it speak. 'Sblood, do you think that I am easier to be played on than a pipe? Call me what instrument you will, though you can fret me, you cannot play upon me.

But is this a mannerist or a Renaissance phenomenon? It was at the height of the Renaissance itself that Da Vinci introduced into art the pictorial form of this human complexity. His remarkable technique of *sfumato*, the delicate shading at the corners of eye and mouth in his portraits, lent a new air of mystery and depth to his paintings, leaving us wondering whether the enigmatic Mona Lisa is smiling in pleasure, in sadness, or in mockery—or, indeed, whether she is smiling at all. To hold Ghirlandaio's sensitive but two-dimensional *Portrait of a Girl* beside Da Vinci's *Virgin with St. Anne* is to perceive the advance from Shakespeare's simple characterization of King John to the complex brilliance of his Lear. We should beware, therefore, of attaching too readily the term mannerist to Shakespeare's Jacobean phase. There deserves to be recognized in that period a leaning towards the mannerist art form rather than a full exemplification of its aesthetic assumptions.

For our present purpose, then, it is I think valid to concentrate upon that specific form of mannerism most relevant to a study of Donne, while neither denying nor ignoring the rich variety of mannerist art in either its embryonic or more developed form, which is less applicable to such a study. If it is true, as I have argued here, that the common denominator of religious mannerism is the dematerialization of the physical universe and the tormented striving towards a more satisfying spiritual reality beyond the empirically verifiable world, we may set aside the current evaluation of it as devoted merely to 'knowing poses' and 'abused ingenuity' in favour of a more sensitive and positive response. For it is a movement achieving in its finest form the fulfilment of a purpose different from, but in no sense intrinsically inferior to, that of the Renaissance, and we should cease judging it by standards drawn from the very style it was attempting to supplant. The more sympathetic interpretation which results can, I believe, prove valuable in offering yet another avenue of approach to Donne's vision and to the artistic techniques whereby he transformed it into poetry.

III

SHIMMERING LOGIC

ANY attempt to place Donne within the illusory insubstantiality of the mannerist world would appear at first sight to be invalidated by the pattern of firm, demonstrative argumentation which shapes the dialectic of his verse. The triumphant 'thens' and conclusive 'therefores' which consummate arguments carefully buttressed by evidence drawn from recondite alchemical or cosmographical sources suggest a very obvious solidity arising from a respect for the concrete and provable. It was, indeed, this demonstrative tone which particularly irritated his readers during those periods when his reputation was in eclipse. Tender protestations of love, traditionally expressed with the melancholy lyricism of the sonneteer, became in his hands subjected to an analytical scrutiny and a process of deductive reasoning more often associated with the proof of a geometrical theorem. We can at least understand, if not finally accept, Dryden's stricture that Donne perplexed the minds of the fair sex with nice speculations of philosophy when he ought to have been entertaining them with the softness of love. Fortunately for those of us who respond more positively to his verse, Donne's mistresses, real or supposed, seem to have been made of tougher intellectual fibre than Dryden's; and with the distance afforded by history we may suspect that the virile dialectic of his love poetry provided them with a welcome change from the self-pitying laments of the Petrarchan school.

While the ratiocinative texture of his poetry is sufficiently evident both to his admirers and his detractors, the difficulty of pin-pointing its precise nature has been amply illustrated by the polarized response it has evoked from critics. Miss Rosemond Tuve, for example, unequivocally identified Donne some years ago as '. . . the strictest poet-logician of his times', even tracing his system of reasoning to a specific philosopher, the French anti-Aristotelian

Ramus, whose work was being so widely discussed at the universities during the period when Donne was a student. She regarded as particularly Ramist the tendency in his verse towards intellectual probing as a substitute for rhetorical persuasion—a tendency which in her view led him to investigate the true nature of a subject rather than to adopt established conventions. Her attribution of metaphysical modes of thought to Ramist sources has since been challenged, notably by William Empson, and it is now generally acknowledged that this metaphysical preference for exploratory analysis owes more to the growth of Renaissance empiricism at large than to the writings of any particular philosopher. Ramus should thus be regarded as symptomatic of the new humanist inquiry rather than as its philosophical instigator. What does emerge from her theory, however, is her conviction of the tough rationalism of Donne's mental processes which in her view resembled Ramist philosophy by regarding all thought as part of '. . . a vast orderly arrangement in which argument was hooked into argument, lesser attached to greater, word to concept, concept to larger concept, in an unbroken reasonable pattern. The inevitability of a conception of imagery as logically functional, given this understanding of the nature of thought and hence of all discourse, is obvious.'[1] Miss Tuve is not alone in her judgement, and Donne criticism abounds with affirmations of the firm logical pattern of his poetry, constructed, as one critic put it, '. . . on a basis of the hardest mathematics'.

Interestingly enough, Miss Tuve herself refrains from any detailed analysis of Donne's verse on the grounds that any unprejudiced reader can find the obvious examples of such logic for himself, and she turns instead to Henry King as the main illustrator of her theory. But if we do look for those 'obvious' examples within Donne's poetry, the very reverse becomes apparent—that Donne will not stand up to any close scrutiny as a logical practitioner. It is not merely that exceptions can be found—she admits, for example, that 'The Will' is based on 'tenuous' logical connections—but that the poems most typical of Donne's individualistic style employ, in fact, a pseudo-logical progression whose speciousness, it can be shown, is unquestionably deliberate. Miss Tuve is too perceptive a critic to be unaware of the outrageousness of Donne's more extravagant statements or images, but these she explains away as examples of catachresis (perverse hyperbole or meiosis) in which the reader is expected to 'sheer off irrelevant suggestions' leaving the sharp logical relevancy on which the image is based. It is difficult to see how her theory can possibly be applied to so characteristic an opening as:

> My name engrav'd herein,
> Doth contribute my firmnesse to this glasse,
> Which, ever since that charme, hath beene
> As hard, as that which grav'd it, was;

To imagine that the glass is less fragile now that the lover's name appears upon it cannot be termed a mere exaggeration. It is a patent absurdity, achieved by treating the metaphorical 'firmness' of love as if it were the physical firmness of unbreakable glass, and hence solemnly converting a whimsical fancy into a supposedly verifiable fact. Moreover, the absurdity forms an integral part of the poetic argumentation, by no means to be discarded as irrelevant. The initial dislocation of logic on which the witty superstructure is built is allowed to engage and mildly disturb the reader at a subdued level throughout the poem, until the final stanza at last acknowledges the 'idle' nonsensicality of such reasoning, amusingly twisting it into a further proof of love:

> But glasse, and lines must bee,
> No meanes our firme substantiall love to keepe;
> Neere death inflicts this lethargie,
> And this I murmure in my sleepe;
> Impute this idle talk to that I goe,
> For dying men talke often so.[2]

The reader who has failed to respond to the spuriousness of the initial reasoning, with its smooth equation of the literal and figurative meanings of 'firm', will be lost when he reaches the concluding volteface. Any 'sheering off' of logical irrelevancies would serve merely to deaden both the wit and its subsequent exploitation. And this is no isolated instance. A close reading of almost any poem by Donne will confirm the centrality of such lightly camouflaged illogicality which the perceptive reader (at whom Donne invariably aims his verse) is intended to grasp, whether at the conscious or subconscious level. The deception is not always based on a blurring of the line between metaphor and fact, frequently consisting of a series of intellectual acrobatics which subtly contradict the accepted laws of reasoning while yet achieving a new and revitalized rationale of their own. The carefully structured opening of 'A Feaver' reaches a conclusion which slily subverts the original assertion of undying love on which the poem is based:

> Oh doe not die, for I shall hate
> All women so, when thou art gone,
> That thee I shall not celebrate,
> When I remember, thou wast one.

Such circular argumentation which ends by pulling the rug from under its own feet suggests that to categorize Donne the strict poet-logician he has so often been called is to miss one of the main delights of his verse—his sparkling irreverence towards that new idol of the Renaissance, logic or right Reason.

In the opposite camp are ranged those critics for whom Donne is simply the fashionable logic-chopper, the university wit engaging like the Mercutios and Hamlets of the Elizabethan stage in swift punning repartee with their student friends for the sheer pleasure of displaying a fecundity of extravagant invention. According to J. E. V. Crofts, Donne, while carefully preserving the steps in his logic, is '. . . nearly always careless of its direction', using it to defend a manifest sophistry as readily as to serve what may be truth.[3] It is a picture of Donne which attractively fits into the conventions of the age. The cult of paradox in the Renaissance formed part of the general revival of classical literature, having occupied an honoured place there. Ovid's and Lucian's exercises in rhetorical frivolity, such as the extravagant encomium on a nut, found numerous imitators among the new humanists, eager to prove their mastery of the form. It constituted a sophisticated game, with the rules set out by a learned coterie of players skilled in its subtleties. In Castiglione's *Courtier*, Lady Emilia can demand an amusing account of the lover's escapades on the grounds that as '. . . there have bene men so wittie and eloquent that thei have not wanted matter to make a book in the praise of a flie, other in praise of a quartaine fever, an other in the praise of bauldnes, doth not your hert serve you to finde out somewhat to saie for one nyght of courting'.[4] There is no doubt that Donne's 'Feaver' derives from this same source, but the description of him as the frivolous logic-chopper and punster, careless of the direction his logic leads him, while it may be applied to the most trifling of his verse, has little bearing on the poetry for which Donne is famed, where the witty or paradoxical inversion of normal assumptions leads towards some revelatory experience, a feeling at the conclusion of the poem that the reader has been privileged to glimpse an intimate and rare mystery, whether of human or divine origin. Nor can this final revelation be divorced from the outward logical pattern of the stanzas preceding it; for it can, I believe, be shown that the complex movement of the poems, so far from carrying Donne along haphazardly, is constructed with extraordinary subtlety specifically in order to create a spring-board for the leap into the mysterious or transcendental. To call this play with logic a whimsical trick of style or the gesture of fashionable dandyism is to miss its deeper resonance as an expression of the spiritual and cultural concerns of the age.

Some years ago, S. L. Bethell, a lone voice among critics, published an article in the *Northern Miscellany* in which he expressed reservations concerning Miss Tuve's book and hesitatingly suggested that Donne is often less logical than has been generally assumed. Observing that seventeenth-century England, although so rich in poetic creativity—notably in the poetry of wit—had produced virtually no treatises defining the nature of that wit, he decided to turn to the Continent for critical sources which might throw light upon the theory behind metaphysical poetry. This decision was more justifiable than might appear as Donne was well read in the Spanish schools of theology and literature, once commenting in a letter to Buckingham that '. . . in my poor library . . . I can turne mine eye towards no shelf, in any profession from the mistress of my youth, Poetry, to the wife of mine age, Divinity, but that I meet more authors of that nation than of any other'.[5]

The first of these critical works to which Bethell refers the reader is Baltasar Gracian's *Agudeza y Arte Ingenio* ('Conceit and the Art of Wit') published in 1642, the work of a Spanish Jesuit. Its central theme is to distinguish between wit and judgement, on the grounds that judgement is contented with truth alone, while wit aspires after beauty. There is already a hint, therefore, that wit reaches beyond demonstrable truth, and in fact Gracian maintains, in a manner closely reflecting the shifting use of 'firm' in Donne's poem on the window-inscription, that there exists a form of wit which '. . . consists more in the words, in such a way that if one departs from them, the meaning disappears also, nor can they be translated into another language; of this type are equivoques . . .'. Gracian's definition of wit merges with that of Bethell's second theorist, the Italian Emanuele Tesauro, whose *Il cannocchiale aristotelico* ('The Aristotelian Perspective-Glass') of 1654 unambiguously asserted that perfect conceits take the form of 'arguments urbanely fallacious'. Combining the two critics, Bethell deduces that there exist for them three clearly distinguishable modes—dialectic, rhetoric, and wit. The purpose of dialectic is to establish truth, while rhetoric aims exclusively at persuasion, at times employing false reasoning to attain its ends. Wit, on the other hand—and this is the main point towards which the article has been leading—has a different intent: to reveal supernatural truths or that divine order of the universe which unites the apparently disparate. There is in this final phrase a very obvious parallel to the various definitions of metaphysical wit from Johnson to Eliot, seeing it as yoking the most heterogeneous ideas together and creating thereby a new unity. But it adds a new dimension, the search for a supernatural truth which unifies the disparate in a manner more profound than that of a passing mood or whimsy.

The originality of Bethell's article is its perception that Donne's poetry employed the extravagant or fallacious conceit not merely as an entertainment device, but as a means for gesturing towards a transcendent verity. Unfortunately, in what he himself termed only a preliminary article, never developed into the full book he promised, Bethell proves disappointingly unpersuasive in applying this insight to the poetry itself. In the brief final section of the article, which could alone have justified his lengthy and detailed analysis of such obscure terms as 'enthymeme' and 'cavillation' in Gracian and Tesauro, he does little more than glance at the relevance to Donne. He quotes, for example, from 'The Sunne Rising':

> Thine age askes ease, and since thy duties bee
> To warme the world, that's done in warming us.

pointing out that the word 'age' in this passage deliberately shifts ground from the astronomical antiquity of the sun to the decrepitude of human old age (though he might have noted that the opening phrase of the poem 'Busie old foole . . .' had done that already). He offers, however, no indication of the method whereby such false reasoning leads on to that truth which the Gracian–Tesauro theory had demanded as the ultimate purpose of the logical fallacy. In an examination of this poem in an earlier chapter, I have already suggested how in fact it does lead towards an impressive reassertion of the traditional man-centred world in the face of Copernican heliocentricity. The ludicrous depiction of the sun as a weary, aging factotum functions metaphorically to shrink and reduce to subservience the awe-inspiring vastness and eternity of the newly discovered solar system, an achievement which goes beyond surface wit and amusing word-play.

Moreover, valuable as his central idea may be, Bethell's relating of Donne's wit to such continental theorists is misleading. Neither Gracian's book nor Tesauro's could have found their way on to Donne's shelves for all his interest in Spanish and other writings, for both were first published long after his death in 1631. At the very most, they are late critical formulations of ideas generated much earlier during the Counter-Reformation itself, and it is there that Donne's sources must be sought. Gracian, for example, defined true wit as an *equivoque*, a term which had in fact attained currency some forty years earlier at the turn of the century in connection with Jesuit casuistry. The trial of Father Garnet for complicity in the Gunpowder Plot had riveted public attention on the strange explanation offered by the priest to justify his original denial of the charge. What seemed in Protestant eyes to be no less than a barefaced lie by a man in holy orders (from whom some degree of veracity might be expected even if he belonged to an opposition sect) was, he argued, theologically defensible as an 'equivocation'. John Chamberlaine recorded the contemporary distaste for such quibbling:

> With which being charged he stifly denied it . . . till at last being confronted with Hall he was driven to confess; And being now asked in this Audience how he could salve this lewd Perjury, he answered that *so long as he thought they had no Proof he was not bound to accuse himself*; *but when he saw they had Proof, he stood not long in it.* And then fell into a large Discourse of defending *Equivocations* with many weak and frivolous Distinctions.[6]

Shakespeare could play on the word in the Porter scene on the safe assumption that his audience would at once identify the obvious allusion to the Jesuits:

> Knock, knock. Who's there, i' th' other devil's name?—Faith, here's an equivocator, that could swear in both the scales against either scale; who committed treason enough for God's sake, yet could not equivocate to heaven: O! come in equivocator.
>
> (Macbeth, II. iii. 7.)

It might appear that such equivocation was simply the result of political expediency. In those troubled times, it has been argued, a disguised priest whose identity was challenged by his persecutors, needed some means of deflecting the charge in order to preserve his life, while yet avoiding actual falsehood. He found his solution in the reply, 'I am no priest', to which he would add the unspoken mental reservation '. . . of Apollo'. I suspect, however, that these 'frivolous distinctions' for which the Jesuits became notorious had deeper roots than contemporary political conditions. This was not the first time in Christian history that priests and missionaries had been subjected to persecution and martyrdom, yet until this period Augustine's flat condemnation of such prevarication had remained virtually unchallenged. In the spirit of 'Let thy yea be yea, and thy nay, nay', he had argued that no true Christian was entitled to corrupt his own soul by such sly falsehood, even to save his own or another's life. It was only in the sixteenth century, when the Jesuits of Valladolid approached Martin Aspicuelta for his ruling on the point that the Doctor of Navarre's lengthy justification of 'mental reservation' gave theological sanction to the previously tentative discussion. The Jesuits resorted to his ruling frequently during the following century, until Pope Innocent XI eventually condemned the practice in 1679 on the grounds that it had never been in accordance with true Christian principles.

In other words, the popular association of equivocation with the Jesuits had a basis in fact. Not only did its theological sanctioning coincide historically with the rise of the movement, allowing them to be its main utilizers, but it arose at their instigation because it accorded so closely with their own philosophical outlook. It formed one facet of what their detractors decried as Jesuit 'casuistry', but they themselves saw as the validation of inward, spiritual truth if necessary at the expense of outward consistency. It was a reflection in fact of the contrast between introspective withdrawal from the world advocated by the *Spiritual Exercises* and the militant practicality of the Jesuit movement as a whole. Ignatius himself, severely ascetic in his private life from the moment of his conversion, had in effect turned his back on earthly joys, reaffirming the old injunction of dying to this world in order to live for the divine. But he was faced with a practical dilemma, for at the same time he saw his immediate task as existing within the temporal world as a missionary winning back souls to virtue. The solution he found, and one adopted by his successors, was to erect a façade of deference to worldly wealth and human prestige while behind it he preserved his own abstemiousness and *contemptus mundi*. His disciple, Diego Laynez, the theoretician of the early Jesuits, took as his watchword *destrezza*, dexterity or 'accommodation' to the worldly, whereby the despised actuality of existence—the habits and customs of the secular world—were adopted almost cynically in order to allow the movement to penetrate with its religious message into the very citadels of the profane. That 'accommodation' in later years was to bring lasting discredit on the Jesuits when Pascal, quoting chapter and verse, accused them of indulging in moral juggling to attain political ends. But in its earlier phase, before the order had become a political power, their renewed medieval contempt for the temporal world led them in all sincerity to attach less importance to the actual deeds committed by Christians than to the moral intention or spiritual condition which had prompted them. Within the over-all Christian framework, it constituted a shift in emphasis from outer to inner reality and, in contrast to Augustine's ruling, it meant that they dismissed as comparatively negligible the external, spoken word of the equivocator, provided that his inner integrity and purity of motive were preserved. Hence it was, for example, that Gracian (himself a Jesuit) could select the term *equivoque* with no hint of its pejorative connotation and in fundamentally the same sense, to describe the highest form of wit—the transcending of literal paradox or falsehood to convey an eternal truth.

The sources of Gracian's theory are thus to be found within the earlier Counter-Reformation itself, and there is, I would argue, an unmistakable parallel between the Jesuit concept of prevarication and the witty, quibbling, and shifting word-play of Donne's verse, which sought out beyond the deceptive plausibility of existence some ultimate authenticity. This is the link between the apparently frivolous wit of the poems and the haunting sense of mystery to which it seems so inexplicably to lead. The recent suggestion, incidentally, that Donne may not after all have received a speci-fically Jesuit training in his youth is irrelevant.[7] 'I had my first breeding and conversation', he tells us, 'with men of a suppressed and afflicted religion': and the Catholic upbringing would certainly have exposed him to the new winds blowing from the Continent even if his education was not formally in Jesuit hands.

This disruption of logic although intended to express his own misgivings over the final authority of the empirical process, was certainly no indication of a fundamental antipathy to Reason on Donne's part. On the contrary, it betrayed a delighted fascination with Reason, which so nearly fulfils its delicious promises, but coquettishly turns from him at the last moment leaving him sad-dened but not embittered. One feels his own excitement in following its teasing course, leaping upon logical pointers which send him doubling back to revise a seemingly unassailable conclusion. The nuances of his argumentation give his verse its sharp brilliance of organization and imagery, while the false analogues are intended to convey to the reader, often jocosely, Donne's own final conviction that, for all its manifold attractions, logic is an unreliable and even treacherous friend. The purposes to which he applies this false reasoning range too wide for neat definition at this stage, and the problems involved in dating his poetry make it even more difficult to speak of any chronological development in its usage; but we can at least distinguish between the light-hearted dalliance with the fickleness of logic in his poems of wit and the almost despairing rejection of Reason in his religious verse, where he finally and reluctantly disqualifies it as a means of approaching divine truth. Even in this latter context, his dismissal of rationalism involves no angry recrimination or contempt, but rather a note of sadness that so promising an ally, the supposed representative of God on earth, should fail him at the moment of his greatest need:

> Reason your viceroy in mee, mee should defend,
> But is captiv'd, and proves weake or untrue.

The image he offered in his *Essays in Divinity* conveys vividly his own realization that empirical 'demonstration' cannot attain to ultimate truths. Those men, he argues, who seek God by reason and natural strength

. . . are like Mariners, which voyaged before the invention of the Compass, which were but Costars [coasters] and unwillingly left the sight of the land. Such are they which would arrive at God by this world, and contemplate him onely in his Creatures and seeming Demonstration. Certainly, every Creature shewes God, as a glass, but glimmeringly and transitorily, by the frailty both of the receiver, and beholder.

The warning is clear—the demonstrable is mere seeming, and human knowledge is deception. But such dogmatism is unusual in Donne, and elsewhere, in a passage from a Christmas sermon delivered in 1621 remarkable not only in the sensitivity of its imagery but also in its emotional resonance, he recognizes that human knowledge must be pursued and exploited to its utmost limits before being deserted at the end of the trail in favour of a superior and intuitive knowledge.

Knowledge cannot save us, but we cannot be saved without Knowledge; Faith is not on this side Knowledge, but beyond it; we must necessarily come to *Knowledge* first, though we must not stay at it, when we are come thither. For, a regenerate Christian, being now *a new Creature*, hath also *a new facultie of Reason*: and so believeth the Mysteries of Religion, out of another Reason, then as a meere naturall Man, he believed naturall and morall things. He believeth them for their own sake, by *Faith*, though he take *Knowledge* of them before, by that common Reason, and by those humane Arguments, which worke upon other men, in naturall or morall things. Divers men may walke by the Sea side, and the same beames of the Sunne giving light to them all, one gathereth by the benefit of that light pebles, or speckled shells, for curious vanitie, and another gathers precious Pearle, or medicinall Ambar, by the same light. So the common light of reason illumins us all; but one imployes this light upon the searching of impertinent vanities, another by a better use of the same light, finds out the Mysteries of Religion; and when he hath found them, loves them, not for the lights sake, but for the naturall and true worth of the thing it self.[8]

The light of reason which shines equally upon all men can, therefore, be used or abused in accordance with the purpose to which it is applied. But in the continuation of the above sermon, Donne manipulates the image to suggest that in fact there are two lights and hence two forms of knowledge. The natural reason of man seems at first sight to glow brilliantly, but it is in fact 'a Torch in a misty night', which merely appears brighter because it has illumined the thick and gross air around it; while the inner light burns purely and shall 'grow up from a *faire hope*, to a modest assurance and *infallibility*, that that light shall never go out, nor the *works* of darknesse, nor the *Prince of darknesse* ever prevaile upon thee . . .'. Clearly, such impassioned and resolute conviction of the limitation to human reason cannot be applied retrospectively to Donne's early writings, which are exploratory, playful, and as yet uncommitted; but it does suggest the burgeoning of Donne's suspicion of logic as he moves from the trivial games of wit which dominate his *Juvenilia*, through the increasing sense of mystery which so often transmutes and enriches the maturer poems without dislodging completely the casual and flippant, and on to the magnificent devotional poems and sermons where paradox—disturbing, daring, but finally triumphant —symbolizes the culmination of that reaching out beyond logic which he terms in this passage the inner vision of 'infallibility'.

The pattern of Donne's spiritual development may be examined in isolation as the lonely journey of a sensitive, troubled individual, distracted by personal doubts in the midst of his apparent gaiety, and expressing with a rare sense of the bizarre and the droll his gradual progression from a secular to a holy discontent. The stylistic techniques he employed to translate his thoughts and to project his experiences into literary form have an unmistakably individualistic and even idiosyncratic tone which would seem to point to his uniqueness rather than to membership in any larger mode. Yet as we respond to Donne's amused undercutting of rationalistic authority and to his increasing suspicion of contemporary scientific pronouncements, it becomes apparent that he is, like all true artists, crystallizing within the aesthetic expression of his personal odyssey a complex change in the cultural configuration of his era. Shakespeare had defined as the task of the ideal poet-dramatist to show the very age and body of the time its form and pressure, and in the same way Donne's apparently perverse use of sophistry and his supposedly wilful or frivolous inversion of accepted norms, once they are seen as expressions of the era's profoundest concerns, not only take on a fresh significance, transcending the merely quixotic, but also introduce a new dimension into a reading of his poetry. The wit, in fact, is seen to arise even in its apparently most trivial form from more serious causes than simply the desire to entertain. However, to argue for such broader significance in his work might well prove abortive were the attempt based exclusively on a conjectural interpretation of the motives behind his stylistic caprice. For that reason, I have turned to those modes within the plastic and visual arts which were immediately contemporary with Donne, in search of some verification. One finds there a dissatisfaction with Renaissance norms remarkably similar in character to that suggested for Donne, together with a range of new artistic techniques for expressing that disturbance which more than confirm the suspicion that he was not alone in his search for a set of values based upon inner rather than outer truth.

The connection between Donne's pseudo-logic and the mannerist movement we have been following is that in both art forms the firmness and rationality of Renaissance perspective, and the solidity of its three-dimensional effect has been discarded in favour of the hallucinatory, the fluid, and the unstable—not through a nihilistic scepticism as has so often been assumed, nor even through an unresolved 'tension' between the worlds of the spirit and the flesh, but through the feeling that syllogistic proofs or naturalistic realism had become prosaic and nugatory beside the energizing power of the spiritual and the paradoxical. All forms of religious belief which deny the final validity of the temporal tend towards such paradoxical inversions of accepted truths, not only to provide a catch-phrase for awakening the potential convert from his torpor but also because such paradox is implicit in the reversal of values which forms the basis of the faith. There arises a new logic, dependent on the heart rather than the mind, bearing with it a reassessment of the data and the very criteria for truth. Christianity had been no exception in enunciating its tenets in phrases which sounded absurd as they struck the hearer's ear—'The first shall be last, and the last shall be first', or 'Whoever loses his life shall preserve it'. It has not, however, employed such inversions with equal cogency in all eras. Arising as it did in a land long familiar with prophets and visionaries proclaiming that the dry bones will put on flesh, and the mountains and hills be laid low, Christianity in its earliest form had little that it needed to invert. Certainly, it placed a greater emphasis than did Judaism on ascetic withdrawal from the ephemeral world, and its more urgent demand that man prepare for the apocalyptic Day of Judgement produced a more obviously eschatological concern; but for all that, Christianity constituted a change of direction rather than a complete reversal, Jesus himself declaring that he had come '. . . not to deny but to fulfil' the law and the prophets. Paradox continued to occupy a prominent place in Christian writing during later eras, as it was bound to in a religion affirming the Incarnation and stressing the transitoriness of earthly life. But in the Middle Ages, for example, when the power of the Church over men's minds was almost unchallenged, its usage was less aggressive and the pronouncement 'In the midst of life we are in death' was a grim reminder of acknowledged truth rather than a provocative overturning of prevalent belief. In the Counter-Renaissance, however, religious paradox takes on a new significance and with it a new vitality in the struggle to subvert the intimidating authority of Reason. Rationalism, as part of the classical revival of the sixteenth century and, indeed, as part of the rediscovery of this-worldliness which lies at the heart of the Renaissance, had permeated every corner of the art, philosophy, and literature of the day, even the sceptics resorting to rational arguments to support their scepticism. Among those attempting to undermine its influence, whether they were consciously attacking an identifiable opposition or in fact arguing against their inner selves, paradox became a finely honed weapon for combating the assumptions of contemporary scientific thought. Tintoretto and El Greco depict the liquescence of actuality with a more obviously devotional intent, while Donne, in contrast, particularly in his earlier period, rejoices in the *reductio ad absurdum*, revealing at times facetiously and at times with a fervour far from humorous, his distrust of that demonstrative logic on which the new science prided itself. Donne's blend of piquant wit and religious commitment is uniquely his own, and it would be pointless to search among practitioners of the visual arts for any single artist who combines in exact parallel the subtle and complex artistry that results; but while the religious painters of the mannerist school provide no counterpart to the coruscating wit of Donne's secular writings, within the wider ramifications of mannerism a delight in visual trickery reflects his own verbal legerdemain, and there too the prankishness of the technique is often modified by an underlying seriousness.

The 'wetting-stools' of Buontalenti which sprayed jets of water on the unwary have already been quoted as an instance of mannerist vagary; but they should perhaps be regarded less as the quirk of an architectural joker than as the surface symptom of a more profound movement of ideas. Since a building, if it is not to collapse, must by its very nature conform to the laws ensuring stability and solidity, it might appear far-fetched to search in architecture for examples of the fluid, the inverted, and the illusory; yet in fact these are among the most characteristic features of mannerist structures. This same Buontalenti, for example, designed an altar—originally for the Church of S. Trinita in 1574 but removed later to S. Stefano in Florence—which consists of a raised balustraded area with two short flights of stairs leading up to it from the centre towards right and left (Plate 7). As one draws closer, the steps seem to melt away, revealing themselves not as stairs at all but as shell-shaped ornamentation impossible to climb, with the real stairs concealed behind the balustrade on either side. In the setting of a holy church, before the altar itself, the deception is (unlike the wetting-stools) intended neither to provoke laughter nor even mild amusement but to create a sense of shifting perspective and architectural instability.

There is a similar *trompe l'œil* effect in the anteroom to the Laurentian Library designed by Michelangelo. Nikolaus Pevsner has provided a detailed analysis of the mannerist features of this room, from the scroll brackets supporting nothing, to the pillars which taper downwards in defiance of the normal rules for physical and even visual stability.[9] Most prominent of all is the strange staircase whose central section seems to spill downwards in widening circles, suggesting that any attempt to ascend would be like wading against the current of a cascading river. This is visual fluidity carried almost to its fullest extent; but in the Villa Farnesina, Baldassare Peruzzi constructed an even more remarkable instance in 1513. An impressive salon opens at one side on to a large, airy loggia flanked by alcoved statues, and offering a fine view over the rooftops of Rome. Yet as one approaches, it becomes apparent that the entire section—loggia, marble columns, statues, alcoves, and even the view of Rome—is an illusion painted on what is, in fact, a continuous flat wall.

Baroque architecture, we should remember, is equally deceptive in its techniques, but the nature of the deception illustrates once again the distinction suggested in an earlier chapter which divorces mannerism from the baroque. In a baroque cathedral marble columns are visually stretched into the distant heavens by extensions deceptively painted on the flat ceiling to look as though they belong to the columns themselves. Similarly, a brick wall will be faced with stone, or otherwise concealed in order to produce an effect of grandeur and to contribute to the over-all monumentality of the edifice. Such devices, however, are intended to deceive, and only the architectural engineer or repair worker removing the stone façade will uncover the brickwork behind. In contrast, mannerist illusion is, like Donne's logic, constructed with the specific intention of being detected, and its purpose is opposite to that of the baroque—to create a feeling of insubstantiality and a mistrust of the apparently tangible at the moment when the illusion is discovered. Such instances as the non-existent loggia, or the façade of Giulio Romano's own house in Mantua, whose basement windows, just peeping above ground level, appear to be sinking into the earth, are indeed 'wilful' as they have so often been called; but like the metaphysical conceit, they are wilful for a purpose, expressing with a kind of shock tactics (which pop art and the modern psychedelic groups have again made fashionable) a rejection of the serenity and security traditionally associated with masterpieces of art.

The shimmering logic of Donne's poetry was not created in a vacuum but had, like all such movements, absorbed, adapted, and reapplied techniques inherited from the preceding era. An intellectual diversion popular in Donne's student day, with its roots in the rhetorical training of the scholastic tradition and in that rediscovery of Lucian and Ovid discussed above, was the mock disputation in which the participants were required to offer a perverse defence of ludicrously untenable propositions. Like debaters in the Oxford or Cambridge Unions today (with the difference that then it actually formed part of the curriculum, formal dialectic occupying a prominent place in study towards a bachelor's degree), students would solemnly argue for or against extravagant assumptions for the sole purpose of exercising their wit and displaying their forensic virtuosity. In the *Juvenilia: or certain Paradoxes, and Problemes* Donne has left us a typical collection of such exercises. He inquires into the inordinate length of Puritan sermons, and gravely concludes that it arises '. . . out of a zealous imagination that, It is their duty to Preach on till their Auditory wake'. He patiently investigates 'why doth the poxe so much affect to undermine the nose', and offers a number of learned and, for the most part indecent suggestions, such as the similarity in shape to the member which originally contracted the disease. And in defending the nonsensical hypothesis that a wise man may be recognized by his tendency to laughter, he concludes with the dubious proof that '. . . I think all wise men, if any wise man do read this Paradox, will laugh both at it and me'. Donne made no

claims for the value of these trivia, describing them as 'but swagger-
ers' written 'rather to deceave tyme than her daughther truth', and
he begged the friend to whom he sent them on no account to make
copies as they are 'nothings' of which he was almost ashamed.[10] His
partiality for the absurd spilled over into his early verse, which
sparkles with the same mischievous delight in defending the patently
indefensible. Elegie ii insists with tongue firmly in cheek that the
ugly Flavia deserves to be admired for her beauty. She possesses, he
argues, all the charms of an attractive woman, and the fact that
these features are misplaced is, on the analogy of an anagram, quite
unimportant. Her cheeks may be yellow, but her hair is red; though
her eyes are dim, she herself is light enough:

> These things are beauties elements, where these
> Meet in one, that one must, as perfect, please.
> If red and white, and each good quality
> Be in thy wench, ne'r aske where it doth lye.
> In buying things perfum'd, we aske; if there
> Be muske and amber in it, but not where.

In another poem, 'Loves Warre', he refuses a call to martial glory
in favour of the more urgent tasks awaiting him in his mistress's
bed. There, he argues, he is assisting the war effort far more effectively in his own way:

> . . . Thousands we see which travaile not
> To warres, but stay, swords, armes and shot
> To make at home: And shall not I do then
> More glorious service, staying to make men?

In connection with such trivia, E. R. Curtius has broadened the
term 'mannerism' to describe a phenomenon not confined to the
sixteenth or seventeenth centuries, but forming part of a cyclical
pattern of history. It occurs, he believes, in every era reacting to
formal classicism. His use of the art term is, as he himself acknowledges, no more than a peg on which to hang the literary version of
such anti-classical tendencies, and is not intended to imply any
profound parallels with the more specific application of the term
in the Renaissance. However, he interestingly traces the ingenuity
of such 'mannerist' writing to the early Greeks. It appears, for

example, that Pindar's teacher, the sixth-century poet Lasus, wrote 'lipogrammatic' verse in which the letter *sigma* was carefully avoided (no mean feat, incidentally, as, like the letter *s* in English, it is one of the most common in the Greek language); and the technique was imitated later by Nestor of Laranda who wrote an *Iliad*, each book of which was distinguished by the omission of a different letter of the alphabet. In the late Roman period, such devices were extended beyond art and literature to the banqueting table, where feasts were planned, the various courses of which were selected not for their gastronomical compatibility but for the more prosaic reason that their names bore the same initial letter. The familiar 'figure poetry' of Herbert's 'Altar' or 'Easter Wings', which are set out on the page in such a way that their outward shapes suggest the content or theme, are shown to have ancient antecedents among the Greek bucolic poets.[11] All this is undoubtedly true, and provided we use the term 'mannerism' in Curtius's specific sense as a preference for the abnormal, the artificial, and the affected, we are justified in regarding it as a recurrent phase in all European literature. The writings of the metaphysical poets are in this context merely a seventeenth-century version of an intermittent literary phenomenon, prizing virtuosity for its own sake. Yet in the final analysis, this cyclical view of mannerism is, I believe, as relevant to Donne's greatest poetry as a study of Kyd's *Spanish Tragedy* for an understanding of *Hamlet*. It focuses attention on the soil out of which the work grew rather than on the artistic process which has filtered the life-giving elements from that soil and transformed them into a living plant. The contrived sophistry of the anti-classical mode explains the type of Donne's verse we have just examined, or such of his flippant epigrams as 'The Lame Begger':

> I am unable, yonder begger cries,
> To stand or move; if he says true, hee *lies*.

But it has little bearing on 'A Valediction: forbidding Mourning' which, as we shall see, is a mannerist poem in the fullest sense of the term.

In fact, the danger in passing from such amusing persiflage to the more famous poetry is that the unwary reader may assume such sophistry continues to be entirely frivolous in purpose, offering no more than a pyrotechnic display of intellectual prowess. The capricious reasoning in the anagram elegy was certainly a harbinger of the metaphysical conceit as it was to be fully developed in his subsequent verse, but it is as remote from the resonant paradoxes of the mature poetry as are Buontalenti's wetting-stools from the luminous mysticism of Tintoretto. The disconcerting element in Donne's writing is his unique capacity for embracing both mannerist extremes—the teasing and the solemn—often within the same poem. In the early verse, his proclivity for the absurd expresses itself for the most part in light-hearted exhibitions of virtuosity which reflect the caprice of Arcimboldo, noted earlier, who grotesquely composed the faces in his portraits out of gnarled roots, dead fish, or a disarranged pile of books. Elegie xviii employs a very similar technique when the mistress's features are fantastically transformed into promontories, anchorages, and creeks in the interest of bawdy innuendo. On his voyage of exploration, the lover reaches the Fortunate Islands of her lips, and there:

> . . . in a creeke where chosen pearles doe swell
> The Remora, her cleavinge tongue doth dwell.
> These, and the glorious promontorye, her chinne,
> O'rpast; and the straight Hellespont between
> The Sestos and Abydos of her brests,
> Not of two Lovers, but two Loves, the nests,
> Succeeds a boundless sea . . .
> Though thence the currant be thy pilot made,
> Yet ere thou bee where thou wouldst bee embay'd,
> Thou shalt upon another forrest set
> Where some doe shipwracke, and no farther gett.

In contrast to the overt playfulness of these *juvenilia*, the meditations, sermons, and religious poems of his last phase are charged with an intensity of feeling and a solemnity of purpose which might appear to divorce them completely from such facetiousness. Yet though he may have exchanged the fashionable cloak of the dandy for a dean's surplice, and with it the theme of lovemaking for the theme of grace, the patterns of thought which had animated his early verse, including his love of the riddlingly perverse and his provocative inversion of convention continue to characterize his ecclesiastical writings, though of course with different intent. The movement from mischievousness to solemnity in his treatment of paradox is exemplified in one of the recurring motifs of his early years. As part of his revelling in the perverse, on more than one occasion he argued that the only constant element in women was their inconstancy, quizzically defending it as their most outstanding virtue. 'Every simple fellow can bespeak the change of the *Moon* a great while beforehand: but I would fain have the learnedst man so skilfull, as to tell when the simplest Woman meaneth to vary . . . And what reason is there to clog any woman with one man, be he never so singular?'[12] In a poetic treatment of the same theme, he poses as the angry lover knowing beyond doubt that tomorrow his mistress will deny all today's protestations of love:

Wilt thou then Antedate some new made vow?
Or say that now
We are not just those persons, which we were?
Or, that oathes made in reverentiall feare
Of Love, and his wrath, any may forsweare?

Ironically, he entitles the poem 'Womans Constancy' playing on the same paradox of her consistent inconsistency and, concluding it with a light-hearted admission of her right to variety in love, he turns the tables by glibly demanding the same right for himself. The same paradox has its place in the divine poems too, but there with totally different effect in a mood of grave and anguished devotion:

Oh, to vex me, contraryes meete in one:
Inconstancy unnaturally hath begott
A constant habit; that when I would not
I change in vowes, and in devotione.

The wit is muted. He is no longer amused at the paradox, nor delighted at displaying his mastery of labyrinthine reasoning. Instead, the paradox expresses a weary admission of the complexity of human fickleness and the deviousness of Satanic temptation- The virtuous habit of prayer dulls the sharpness of contrition, and the very sincerity of renewed faith may nullify the penitent oaths sworn yesterday:

As humorous is my contritione
As my prophane love, and as soone forgott:
As ridlingly distemperd, cold and hott,
As praying, as mute; as infinite, as none.
I durst not view heaven yesterday; and to day
In prayers, and flattering speaches I court God:
To morrow I quake with true feare of his rod.
So my devout fitts come and go away
Like a fantastique Ague: save that here
Those are my best dayes, when I shake with feare.

The concluding line returns to paradox in a quietly moving admission of the discrepancy between spiritual and rationalistic values. The contrast posed between the trembling of the physical ague which threatens death, and the trembling of divine fear which promises life epitomizes the theme which animates Donne's later verse, where the devotee, gazing into the concave mirror of inner experience, discovers that the truly meaningful is in fact an inversion of the worldly.

As one moves from the casual exercises in student wit to the more resonant poems, so the gap between surface bravura and the underlying vein of seriousness grows wider, creating that subtle interplay of intellect and passion which has been recognized as a hallmark of Donne's art. The conceit in this more mature, but as yet not fully committed, form leaves more room for the flash of exuberance or audacious juxtaposition of the incongruous. But there is a subtle change. Now in almost all instances the bravura is either immediately modified by the authenticity of the emotional response, or alternatively leads on to a resolution which retrospectively endows the initial incongruity with a validity it had not originally possessed. It had required, after all, no high degree of poetic insight or inventiveness to compare a mistress's lips to two islands as a prelude to a bawdy joke about her protective 'forest' below; but the metaphysical conceit at its best pulsates in its apparent absurdity with a genuineness of feeling which envelops and absorbs the surface ebullience. 'The Expiration' is a case in point.

So, so, breake off this last lamenting kisse,
Which sucks two soules and vapors both away,

Turn thou ghost that way, and let mee turne this,
　And let our selves benight our happiest day,
We ask'd none leave to love; nor will we owe
　Any, so cheape a death, as saying, Goe;

Goe; and if that word have not quite kil'd thee,
　Ease mee with death, by bidding mee goe too.
Oh, if it have, let my word worke on mee,
　And a just office on a murderer doe.
Except it bee too late, to kill me so,
Being double dead, going, and bidding, goe.

The scene is the last desperate moment of parting, in which the speaker surprisingly insists on breaking off the final kiss rather than prolonging it. There is a touch of perversity in the proceedings, as we witness a lover, deeply involved in the pathos of their separation, yet juggling with such outlandish notions as ghosts, vapours, or the pretence that words can slay. This is the emotional dichotomy which has so often exasperated readers who prefer a more conventional and unified depiction of human response. Yet the poem does succeed in catching with remarkable vividness the parting of two grief-stricken lovers and it achieves its effect by two primary means.

The first derives from the extravagance of the imagery itself—the succession of deliberately flimsy arguments which are in fact snatched at as straws to shore up a hopeless case rather than to convince. Intellectually the lover recognizes the inevitability of their parting and that, for the lady's sake as well as his own, one clean break would be preferable to a protracted tearing apart of souls. But his heart tempts him to stay, spinning out a series of fantastic images to stretch out their last few moments together. The thinness of argument is thus not a literary failing exposed by the rigorously demanding reader, but an intrinsic part of the dramatic accuracy of the scene, conveying the despair of the speaker himself as his instincts battle against his resolution.

Secondly, although the apparently far-fetched images—such as the kiss which sucks away the lovers' souls—strike the superficially bizarre note necessary for conveying the psychological conflict of the scene, they are at the same time delicately modulated by the setting. The ceremonious grief of the parting presented in the form of a stately dance of death, with one partner turning this way and the other that before the pronouncement of the fatal word, takes us one remove away from the actual to symbolize the inner attempt at restraint and the refusal to collapse into grief. Yet at a more profound level the extravagance of the image is muted also by its ultimate appropriateness, relying as it does upon an established archetypal idea. A concept common to many ancient cultures had long identified the breath with the soul or spirit of man, animating him both literally and metaphorically. God, for example, creates Adam from the dust by breathing life into his nostrils. Of course Donne's lovers will not literally die of breathlessness from the final kiss that 'sucks' their souls away, but emotionally the breathing out of the fatal word 'Go!' marks for them the end of all that makes life worthy of the name. The last sighing kiss in which they surrender all hope of earthly joy is thus a spiritual *expiration* only slightly removed from death itself, and whether Donne or a later editor assigned that title to the poem, its aptness in catching the latent theme is evident. The two have met as lovers, but will part as soulless ghosts, and the speaker who bravely must first utter the parting word is in that sense doubly dead '. . . going, and bidding, goe'. There is in this poem less an ironic tension between the worlds of intellect and passion as has usually been described than an initial illusion of witty extravagance which is subsequently authenticated emotionally.

The same technique is apparent in Donne's use of word-play, for there is perhaps no English poet who exploits so startlingly the deeper implications of the pun. Since Empson's day we have learned to acknowledge the omnipresence in poetry of meaningful ambiguity whereby the concealed associations or connotations of a word are unconsciously imbibed by the reader to create a new level of meaning, to manipulate a response, or to reinforce a submerged theme. The uniqueness in Donne's practice is that instead of concealing the *double-entendre*, he thrusts the ambivalence at us almost derisively, as though it were no more than a piece of flamboyant word-play in the tradition of the University Wits. He seems at first to be merely utilizing the fortuitous overlapping of two meanings within one word for a display of intellectual agility—like Hamlet's jest with the grave-digger over the meaning of *lie*: 'Thou dost lie in't, to be in't, and say it is thine', or the latter's reply "'Tis a *quick* lie, sir; 'twill away again from me to you.' There is no hint of any deeper significance here in the two meanings of 'quick'. What gradually permeates the consciousness in Donne's usage, however, is the realization that the surface word-play is in fact rooted in a cultural rather than a surface or semantic ambivalence. Frequently the ambiguity exploits the almost forgotten literal meaning out of which a metaphorical term grew, before it broke away to gain its independent meaning. In the course of a famous meditation, Donne offers the grotesque picture of a newly baptized child which is thereby '. . . connected to that Head which is my Head too, and engraffed into that body whereof I am a member'. The hint of anatomical monstrosity which creates the initial shock appears to arise arbitrarily from the ambiguous meaning of 'head', as a part of the human body and as the supreme ruler of the Church—an incongruity emphasized by the phrase '. . . which is my Head too'. But the harshness is wonderfully resolved by the concluding word 'member', which in this context suddenly shines forth in its literal and original meaning of 'limb'. It is as though Donne were gently chastising us for our sense of the grotesque, recalling that, as the term itself shows, the Church had from the very first demanded of its 'members' the intimate relationship of limb to head, and of limb to fellow limb. If his readers have forgotten the vitality of the original metaphor and allowed the terms to be dulled by usage, the fault, he suggests, is theirs, not his. Even in his word-play, therefore, the deeper reverberations of meaning eventually rise to authenticate the apparent *panache*, and this same technique operates in the lighter verse too, although there, of course, the reverberations are often treble rather than bass.

In 'A Jet Ring Sent', for example, the lover inquires whose qualities the ring is supposed to represent, his own or those of his faithless mistress:

> Thou art not so black, as my heart,
> Nor half so brittle, as her heart, thou art;
> What wouldst thou say? shall both our properties by thee bee spoke,
> Nothing more endlesse, nothing sooner broke?

Here 'endlesse' appears at first sight to be a casual pun, comparing the physical shape of the ring, which has no beginning and no end, with the metaphorical infinity of his own love. We might be inclined to dismiss it as no more than the ingenuity of a sonneteer working out an elaborate bagatelle based on chance points of contact between the object and its owner, were it not that the next stanza retrospectively illumines in its opening line the deeper justification for the jest:

> Marriage rings are not of this stuffe;

We are suddenly reminded that the pun is by no means arbitrary. Since ancient times, the choice of a ring to symbolize the contract of marriage had been based upon precisely this feature—that the simple, circular band of gold should represent the unending and ever-valued devotion of the donor. The humour which Donne has introduced is the realization that these particular lovers' rings made of jet (which had become popular in Donne's day)[13] contained in addition to their circular form the more dubious qualities of being cheap, black, and fragile, and hence introduced a rather less comforting symbolism when offered as gifts. Moreover, did the name 'jet', he wondered, mean also that in contrast to the wedding ring, it was to be (in its French meaning) 'jettisoned' or flung away when the brief affair was over:

> Marriage rings are not of this stuffe;
> Oh, why should ought lesse precious, or lesse tough
> Figure our loves? Except in thy name thou have bid it say,
> I am cheap, and nought but fashion, fling me away.

He is, in effect, satirizing the contemporary fashion of false love by suggesting that the nature of the ring is more appropriate than the donors had realized. The ambiguity he perceives in its symbolism reaches its culmination in the final stanza where, in his usual style, he swings the argument round, deciding to keep the ring not because his reading of the qualities it represents is wrong, but because the reading has unfortunately proved so right. At least, he muses, the ring still matches the endlessness of his own abiding love, and for that alone it deserves to be protected from her spite.

> Yet stay with mee since thou art come
> Circle this fingers top, which did'st her thombe.

Be justly proud, and gladly safe, that thou dost dwell with me,
She that, Oh, broke her faith, would soon break thee.

At the end he is clearly projecting on to the ring his own emotions, proud to have been the mistress's lover for however brief a period, and relieved, now that the affair is over, to be spared the cruelty and recriminations which marked the conclusion of their relationship. Through the supposedly far-fetched comparisons with which the poem opens there emerges a humorous but perfectly valid identity between the ring's symbolism and the lover's own case, and it draws upon deeper, more ancient sources than the surface bravura suggests.

In emotional resonance the two instances here adduced are obviously worlds apart. The meditation on the newly baptized 'member' touches upon the central mystery of ecclesiastical communion and the spiritual brotherhood such communion implies for all Christian worshippers. The amatory poem, though more subtle in its allusions than might at first appear, remains a casual piece intended to amuse. Despite this polarity, however, they share a quality which is central in Donne's writings—a penchant for erecting a façade of superficial wit or fortuitous word-play through which some more lasting truth is gradually perceived. It is a dangerous technique, attracting critical charges of literary or even moral irresponsibility, particularly from those who either fail to discern the authenticity or who object to the outward bravura. Historical causes can never justify literary blemishes, nor excuse stylistic and imaginative faults. It is not for that purpose that I have stressed the cultural background of Donne's age and his concern with impalpability. But a knowledge of the historical setting can make us more responsive to the topical immediacy such writing held for the author's contemporaries—like stripping off centuries-old varnish from a canvas to reveal the bright colours it displayed to contemporary viewers. Such immediacy is of especial importance for Donne, as it formed a significant part of the literary integrity of his work as well as of its motivation.

In his own day, Donne was a renowned poet and in his Anglican period drew thousands to Paul's Cross as one of the most powerful and moving preachers England had produced. The ebb in his literary reputation began at the time of Dryden, when the deeper purpose of his wit and paradox in seeking out and asserting new values for a troubled era had ceased to be relevant. The mechanistic universe ratified by Galileo, together with the empiricism of the New Philosophy, no longer posed a threat to spiritual tradition but had now been welcomed as the basis for an optimistic advocacy of rationalism, propriety, and perspicuity in the literary and visual arts no less than in the Royal Society. Accordingly, Donne's bizarre juxtaposition of the dissimilar, now divorced from its ultimate purpose and regarded as an end rather than a means, seemed to the new generation merely flamboyant and idiosyncratic; and the neo-classical age, of which Dr. Johnson was a spokesman, inherited fundamentally similar views. Donne's reputation never recovered until the early part of the present century when it revived, to some extent under false colours, to supply a modern psychological need. He was then, as has been noted, welcomed and admired for his brilliant fusion of alchemy and poetry, of cosmography and love, in an age which seemed to have lost the ability to associate its own sensibilities. T. S. Eliot's own response to Donne, however, was inevitably more intimate; he was himself drawn closer to him by those religious propensities which separated Eliot from the main directional current of his own generation when writers and artists were for the most part finding their comfort in the new materialist religion of communism. Accordingly, his indebtedness to Donne goes beyond the technique of amalgamating disparate experience in order to create a poetic unity and included the primary impetus for that amalgamation, the latter's validation of paradoxical, spiritual truths. That they should both think of death in terms of rebirth is not in itself surprising—it forms, after all, a central belief of the Church, with its view of this world as a temporal and shadowy anteroom to the after-life of eternity. The specific quality they share, however, is the urgent need to argue with their own *alter ego*, their intellectual selves trained by the scientific eras into which they were born to accord final authority to the observable facts of the mechanistic universe. That instinctive respect for the material needed to be crushed or transcended if they were finally to assert in their eras the contradictory religious truth. Hence their insistence on thrusting the paradox at the reader, acknowledging the conflict between the factual and the spiritual, and then reducing the stubborn concrete reality to nothingness before the richness of the symbolic sense. Donne's symbolic West is his East whatever the cosmographers may say; and similarly that womb which all anatomists had identified as the bodily organ for generating new life is for him no more than a grave:

> . . . this deliverance from that death, the death of the wombe, is an entrance, a delivering over to another death, the manifold deathes of this world. We have a winding sheete in our Mothers wombe, which growes with us from our conception, and wee come into the world, wound up in that winding sheet, for wee come to seeke a grave.[14]

Birth becomes death, and death a form of birth; and the audible cries of the new-born infant or the visible putrefaction of the corpse's flesh serve merely to corroborate their reverse implications. So in the 'Journey of the Magi' Eliot creates a hallucinatory super-imposition of birth upon death, and death upon birth which achieves a new authenticity of its own:

> . . . but set down
> This set down
> This, were we led all that way for
> Birth or Death? There was a Birth, certainly,
> We had evidence and no doubt. I had seen birth and death,
> But had thought they were different; this Birth was
> Hard and bitter agony for us, like Death, our death.
> We returned to our places, these Kingdoms,
> But no longer at ease here, in the old dispensation,
> With an alien people, clutching their gods.
> I should be glad of another death.

There is 'Birth' and there is 'birth', 'death', and 'Death'; and with gentle mockery he assures us that even a scientist would have to admit that a birth had really taken place:

> There was a Birth, certainly,
> We had *evidence* and no doubt.

This is no chance aside, but integral to a poem whose purpose is to present the traditionally tinselled story of the Nativity in harshly contemporary terms. After the agony of his own conversion Eliot projects into his Magi the conflict between religious belief and those doubts which an analytically trained mind will constantly be struggling to supplant. He records earlier in the poem how they travelled towards the Nativity with '. . . voices singing in our ears, saying . . .' but instead of the expected *Gloria in excelsis* comes the sobering: 'That this was all folly'. His is not the Salvation Army conversion accompanied by hosannas; we witness instead the struggle of a man who has attained belief, but only by a hair's breadth. The Nativity represents for him as well as for the Magi the birth of a new era and the death of the past; but the past does not die so easily, and the lack of verifiable 'information' which thrusts itself so anachronistically into the New Testament setting would, he knew, continue to trouble his peace throughout his temporal life:

> Then we came to a tavern with vine-leaves over the lintel . . .
> But there was no information, and so we continued
> And arrived at evening, not a moment too soon,
> Finding the place; it was (you may say) satisfactory.

Eliot, while leaning in the same direction as Donne, is more hesitant, and Donne consequently achieves at times a richer effect. He not only accords precedence to the spiritual paradox but by charging the physical world with its vitality and finding in man's daily experience a similar pattern of illogical truth, suggests that the actual world in a strange way supports the paradoxical authenticity and hence undermines the assumptions of the pragmatists. As he once lay gravely ill after a succession of almost fatal sicknesses, he wryly compared himself to '. . . a porter in a great house, ever nearest the door but seldomest abroad'; and in a sermon on the uses of adversity, where he notes the strange fact that man discerns God's truth most clearly when he himself is in darkest fortune, Donne turned to the world of optics to corroborate the paradox: 'I can better know a man upon the top of a steeple, than if he were halfe that depth in a well; but yet for higher objects, I can better see the stars of heaven, in the bottome of a well, than if I stood upon the highest steeple upon earth.'[15] Moreover, he is more confident than Eliot in spurning those objections of the scientific world whose conclusions appear to contradict religious belief. He does not challenge the mechanistic universe of Copernicus, Galileo, and Kepler but transcends it as irrelevant to man's spiritual concerns. The opening lines of a sonnet we examined earlier illustrate this technique in its most impressive form. Intellectually Donne now knows beyond question that the earth is round, and acknowledges unhesitatingly that the traditional four-cornered world of biblical cosmology exists only as an *imagined* entity. Yet it is that imagined world which he requires as the setting for his awesome vision of Judgement Day. Hence, after a brief nod to the empirically proved fact of the earth's roundness, the imaginative power of the poem takes command, reducing it to a trivial technicality before the excited rhythms inspired by the apocalyptic vision:

> At the round earths imagin'd corners, blow
> Your trumpets, Angells, and arise, arise
> From death, you numberlessse infinities
> Of soules . . .

The command 'blow' reverberating into infinity as it sweeps across the run-on line serves to drown the pettiness of any empirical objection to the visionary call of Judgement. It was, I suspect, in this reaching out towards some ultimate imaginative reality beyond the restrictions of a cold scientism that Donne appealed to the lost generation of the twenties, and in particular to T. S. Eliot himself.

These positive assertions in his writing clearly militate against the traditional identification of Donne with the Pyrrhonic or libertine scepticism of the era, unless a powerful reservation is made which in effect cancels his membership of the school. For where the sceptics moved initially towards a negation of all belief and from there (ironical as it may seem) frequently towards a validation of empirical inquiry, Donne was being led by his doubts in an almost reverse direction. It has been rightly argued that the common denominator of the variegated Counter-Renaissance was its rejection of intellectual theorizing in favour of a stern insistence upon facts, and this tendency has been traced as far back as the thirteenth-century Franciscan, William of Ockham, the founder of 'nominalism'.[16] Ockham, in defiance of Plato's universalized 'ideals', had argued that all such philosophical concepts were mere names or empty words. In the course of time the epistemological approach joined forces with scepticism to create either a suspicion or an outright denial of all established scholarship, producing the famed Vanity of Learning. Montaigne, for example, with a wealth of lively instances drawn from the ancient philosophers, argued that reason itself was a fickle and untrustworthy mistress. Diogenes washing his vegetables for dinner, he pointed out, had caustically reproved Aristippus, when the latter was walking past on his way to a royal dinner, that had he only known how to wash cabbages, he would not be wasting his time by paying court to a tyrant; Aristippus replied aptly enough that if Diogenes had only known how to live among men, he would have no need to wash his own cabbages. 'See', cries Montaigne, 'how reason provides plausibility to different actions. It is a two-handled pot that can be grasped by the left or the right.'[17]

Much of this scepticism, in its most negative as well as in its later and more positive form can be traced to the new relativism implicit in Copernican cosmology, which rippled outward to embrace all areas of philosophy, ethics, and art. The geocentrically conceived universe, whether in the biblical or the Ptolemaic version (or in the peculiarly medieval conflation of the two) had accorded to man a sense of hierarchically ordered values in which his own importance, however limited, was secure and clearly defined. Although embedded in the mire, branded by original sin, and threatened with eternal damnation, he knew beyond doubt that the world existed for his sake. On the authority of the Bible itself, whether read in the Vulgate version or transmitted to him through the words of the preacher, he had learned that, moulded in the likeness of God, he formed the consummating act of Creation, that he possessed dominion over the earth and its creatures, which had been placed there by a provident Creator in order to supply his needs. By identifying the sun as the pivot of our planetary system instead of the earth, Copernicus had made the most familiar and cherished scenes of religious history almost impossible for man to conceive. The Ascension of Jesus into the heavens above was bewilderingly difficult for the sixteenth-century Christian to visualize when that tomb was seen as situated on the surface of a spinning globe, which itself orbited elliptically about the sun in the midst of similarly whirling planets. Where were the traditional horizontal and vertical planes, in what direction did the soul 'rise', and where in fact was God's heavenly throne in the newly gyrating universe?

The imaginative effort demanded for man's readjustment to the newly conceived universe included the realization that no single viewpoint could now be regarded as exclusively valid, either on a literal or figurative level. The Petrarchan sonneteer had often visualized the moon as gazing mournfully down upon earth in sympathy with the sonneteer's sad lot. It was less easy to reverse the roles and to think in terms of a sympathetic Earth gazing down on a lovesick moon-dweller. Yet such was the natural corollary of the Copernican theory, particularly as it was developed by Giordano Bruno, who argued for the plurality of inhabited planets (and paid for his views at the stake). In 1621 Robert Burton asserted: '. . . if the earth move, it is a planet and shines to them in the moon, and to other planetary inhabitants as the moon, and they to us upon the earth; but shine she doth, as Galileo, Kepler, and others prove, and then *per consequens*, the rest of the planets are inhabited as well as the moon.'[18] This cosmic relativity of viewpoint, which accorded equal validity to such vantage points as Jupiter, Venus, or even the sun itself, applied no less to the more intimate world of man, prompting Montaigne to gaze at himself experimentally through feline eyes: 'When I play with my cat, who knows if I am not a pastime to her more than she is to me?'[19] It was not an idle question posed for amusement, but in its context served to substantiate his view that man's claim to superiority over the animal kingdom is no more than empty, unjustified arrogance. The Great Chain of Being, with man joining and at the same time separating the beasts and the angels, was being sharply rattled, and found less firmly linked than had been imagined.

Bacon took the relativist argument even farther, raising a much more disturbing problem than the choice between a Ptolemaic and a Copernican system. For him '. . . the first question concerning the Celestial Bodies is *whether there be a system*, that is, whether the world or universe compose altogether one globe, with a centre; or whether the particular globes of earth and stars be scattered dispersedly, each on its own roots, without any system or common centre'.[20] Here too it required no mental leap to pass from such speculation about a universe devoid of an over-all, integrating order at the astronomical level to a similar querying of order within a social and ethical context. Machiavelli, dismissing as entirely irrelevant the traditional morality imposed by Sinaitic revelation and later bolstered by ecclesiastical prerogative, viewed the state with cool pragmatism as an isolated unit justifying its political decisions, its social structure, and its economic policies solely on the grounds of expediency. Stripped of his godlike attributes man was a grasping creature of appetite viewing the world solipsistically, and sceptical of all but his personal advantage. And what moral imperative in the new world of relativism was to deny him the right to pursue such selfish gain?

On the other hand, not only in connection with Donne, but in any analysis of the Renaissance as a whole, such scepticism which questioned the reliability of all criteria should be seen less as finally controverting confidence in right reason than as a transitional phase leading to a new and more positive application of rational thought. Where Richard Hooker had led the traditionalists in pointing to reason as the illuminator of a divinely ordered creation and the confirmer of established universal law, within the New Philosophy reason was eventually to fulfil a very different function, serving as a lodestar whose constancy lent the inquirers confidence to venture beyond familiar regions and, by taking their bearings from it, to charter the course of further exploration. It was the gateway to empiricism through which a number of the sceptics themselves began hesitantly to pass. Montaigne had indeed quoted with approval the Empedoclean doctrine that '. . . we sense nothing, we see nothing; all things are hidden from us; we cannot establish what any one of them is'; this was scepticism unadulterated. Yet one hears a more positive note entering his argument when he complains that '. . . we never test our common impressions. We do not probe the base, where the fault and weakness lies; we dispute about the branches. We do not ask whether this is true, but whether it has been understood this way or that.'[21] The new desire to test and probe, with its feeling that something valid and reliable would emerge from such unprejudiced inquiry, was to prove the basis of the embryonic empirical movement. Bacon gave most effective expression to the merger of these two tendencies, the pragmatic and the rational, in his *Novum Organum* which was to serve as the foundation on which the Royal Society was established some years later. Until his day, he argued, the two schools had remained completely divided. There were the materialists who relied solely on verifiable facts, and the dogmatists who relied solely upon their philosophical or intellectual theories. The ideal system, he maintained, was a combination of the two whereby men should apply their logical faculty to the material facts, and hence deduce from them by rational process the general and universal laws of nature. The materialists, he wrote picturesquely,

. . . like ants, only collect and put to use; dogmatic reasoners, like spiders, spin webs from within themselves. The bee's is the middle way: it extracts matter from the flowers of garden and field, but, using its own faculties, converts and digests it. The true operation of philosophy is not unlike this. It neither relies exclusively on the powers of the mind, nor simply deposits untouched in the memory the material provided by natural history and physical experiment. Rather it transforms and works on this material intellectually. Therefore we may have hopes of great results from an alliance, so far unconcluded, between the experimental and the rational methods.[22]

The sceptic, then, had denied all knowledge except for the chilling fact that he knew nothing; and on that assumption, he had irreverently slashed his way through the tangle of imposing philosophical and theological dogmas inherited from the past. In so doing, however, he had cleared a path for such early empiricists as Montaigne and Bacon who came to realize that by combining objective observation of facts with logical reasoning, they could create a new type of knowledge free from superstition or obscurantism. Donne clearly belongs to neither group, tempting as it may be to place him in so convenient a slot.[23] His 'Anatomy of the World', it is true, had given such eloquent expression to the sense of universal chaos engendered by the 'breaking of the circle' that it is probably the work most widely quoted by historians attempting to pin-point that despair:[24]

> And new Philosophy calls all in doubt,
> The Element of fire is quite put out;
> The Sun is lost, and th' earth, and no mans wit
> Can well direct him where to looke for it.
> And freely men confesse that this world's spent,
> When in the Planets and the Firmament
> They seeke so many new; then see that this
> Is crumbled out againe to his Atomies.
> 'Tis all in peeces, all cohaerence gone;
> All just supply, and all Relation.

This certainly sounds like the despairing cry of a sceptic who has lost faith in all but doubt itself. If the universe held together as the planets whirled and spun about each other, it now did so by a precarious fortuity rather than the solid laws of ordered and harmonious perfection which had previously integrated all aspects of an earth-centred and man-centred cosmos. Yet the assumption that Donne experienced a collapse of faith is denied by the poem itself, which refuses to accept the full implications of the new science, and is already reaching out beyond its discoveries to the mystery which can alone restore for him the lost harmony of the world. The 'Anniversaries', of which this is the first, are both elegies for the dead, and must therefore preserve a general feeling of mourning and gloom; but each statement of despair in the two poems is countered by the positive injunction to rise above the implications of Copernicanism and the theory that man is no more than an insect crawling on the surface of an indifferent globe:

> Shee, shee is dead; shee's dead: when thou knowest this
> Thou knowest how poore a trifling thing man is.
> And learn'st thus much by our Anatomie,
> The heart being perish'd, no part can be free.
> And that except thou feed (not banquet) on
> The supernaturall food, Religion,
> Thy better Growth growes withered, and scant;
> Be more than man, or thou'rt lesse than an Ant.

This is the positive assertion of the 'Anniversaries' which must not be ignored in assessing Donne's philosophical standpoint and which isolates him from the general group of sceptics—his conviction in the face of all contrary evidence that there is still room for faith:

> Up, up my drowsie Soule, where thy new eare
> Shall in the Angls songs no discord heare;
> Where thou shalt see the blessed Mother-maid . . .

Like the sceptics, he distrusts the authority of supposedly indisputable facts, regarding them in the final analysis as fluid and unreliable. However, his scepticism led him not only away from empiricism but also away from nihilism, towards a deepening awareness of a religious truth existing above and beyond the physical world.

Donne's poetic wit, with its grotesque juxtapositions and deceptive reasoning, offered a perfect medium for expressing that mistrust of the objective. Within the plastic arts of the Counter-Renaissance such illusionism is more sharply polarized. There are, for example, the amusing Zuccaro doorways (Plate 8) sculpted in the form of gaping mouths about to swallow up any visitor rash enough to knock. They constitute, rather like Donne's ring image, a light-hearted play upon a serious theme, in which the monstrous mouth of hell gaping wide in medieval paintings to consume for eternity the wretched souls of the damned is incongruously applied to the courtier and his lady coming to pay their respects to the master of the house. On the one hand, from within the security of the Renaissance they ridicule the terrors of an earlier and past age, while on the other they obliquely question the security of that new confidence; for in the process of the joke, the noble edifice, transformed into the caricature of a human face, has lost its imposing solemnity and solidity. At the other end of the scale, the religious paintings of Tintoretto and El Greco are devoid of humour as they employ for serious, though ultimately similar purposes an unstable perspective and a translucent insubstantiality. That same range, less clearly compartmentalized into the humorous and the devotional, can be discerned within the corpus of Donne's writings, serving there as a main unifying force, and lending to much of his apparently casual verse the deeper resonance of truly metaphysical wit. It is that we shall now examine more closely.

IV

THE WIT OF ILLUSION

THE essence of wit is intellectual surprise. It assumes on the part of the listener a sophisticated immediacy of response, and a swift perception of the humour or incongruity implied. Comedy, in contrast, can be sustained, and if the situation in which the characters find themselves is intrinsically amusing—when Goldsmith's Marlow, for example, mistakes a private house for an inn and his proposed bride for a serving girl—we are more than content to watch the scene work itself out in its own good time and in all its varied ramifications. The quick-silver quality of wit, then, demands by its very nature a continual renewal, or the element of surprise will evaporate; and one of the main delights in Donne's specific form of wit is the agile elusiveness with which he tacks and veers in order to trap us intellectually just as we are congratulating ourselves on having grasped his previous point. He loves to coax us into a novel, unconventional viewpoint by means of a speaker whose adroit inversion of cliché and intellectual vitality it is hard to resist; but once coaxed into that viewpoint, we discover to our amused chagrin that we have been duped, and the speaker has already swung off in a new direction, leaving us beached on a dialectical sandbank. In the intricate series of tergiversations the apparently solid structure of argument disintegrates into absurdity, as we are led almost unaware into a final pattern of assumptions which belong outside the realm of logical proof.

'The Flea', for example, pulsates for all its surface raillery with an intellectual and emotional energy that belies its apparently casual tone. The modern reader has often assumed incorrectly that the humour depends primarily on the theme itself, the ludicrous incongruity of building upon so insignificant a creature as a flea a case for the passionate consummation of love. In fact, Donne's readers at the time of the poem's circulation in manuscript had read dozens of variations on this erotic 'flea' theme, of which the medieval *Carmen de Pulice*, ascribed to Ovid, was the model. They were so numerous that in 1582 Étienne Pasquier compiled in France an anthology of over fifty such poems written in various European and classical tongues, in order to celebrate the occasion of his having observed a flea on the fair skin of a certain Mademoiselle Catherine.[1] In these poems, the lover envies the parasite's freedom to nestle in his lady's bosom, to 'taste' the joys of her flesh, and even to 'die' at her hand. The humour of Donne's poem, therefore, owed little to the lover's claim that he deserved equal rights with a flea. It derived rather from the discrepancy between the firm, logical argumentation of its structural progression and the obvious untenability of the conclusions at which the argumentation arrives. To assert in the second stanza that destroying the flea is tantamount to suicide, murder, and sacrilege is so patently absurd that we know beyond doubt the reasoning has fallen apart somewhere *en route*. It is less easy, however, to discern during the course of reading the poem the exact points in the argument where the flea has become cunningly transformed into a theological sanction, or to discover what rational camouflage has led us to be at least momentarily deceived, particularly as the swift movement of the poem in its arrestingly dramatic form is calculated to discourage critical deliberation. Here, at our leisure, we can afford to dissect the poem into its component parts, and to scrutinize more closely the nature of its subtle dissimulation.

The implicit parodying of the empirical process is evident from the very opening lines of the poem. There the lover, adopting the stance of the confident, scientific experimenter, points to the observable items on his laboratory table, upon which his 'proof' will be based:

> Marke but this flea, and marke in this,
> How little that which thou deny'st me is;
> Mee it suck'd first, and now sucks thee,
> And in this flea, our two bloods mingled bee;

Nothing but the simplest monosyllabic terms within the balanced structure of a geometrical theorem. To deduce from such cold scientism any vibrant moral validation for love seems so wildly improbable that one wonders how, within the context of the poem itself, we are led even momentarily to accept the argument. And it is here that the technique of subtle misdirection is at work—that artful camouflaging which, as in Buontalenti's stairs, creates an illusory substantiality dissolving on closer inspection.

It is obvious enough that the main logical elision in the opening stanza derives from the ambivalence of '. . . our two bloods mingled bee'. In those days it was believed, on the basis of Aristotelian physiology, that sexual intercourse produced the fusion of two drops of blood within the female,[2] and the lover here blandly assumes that it is immaterial whether the mingling occurs within the mistress's body or within the flea's. In fact, however, the dialectical deception is more subtle. It is cunningly concealed within the trivial pronoun 'this', which in the four times it appears in the opening stanza slides back and forth in reference so that the word changes its inner meaning while yet preserving its outer form. On its first appearance

> Marke but this flea, and marke in *this*

it refers unequivocally to the evidence to be supplied by the flea (as the humorous side-glance of 'little' confirms), and the factual reference is at once reinforced by the description of its busy foraging in search of nourishment. The lover can afford to ridicule any moral strictures applied to such harmless, natural activity:

> . . . *this* cannot be said
> A sinne, or shame, or losse of maidenhead,
>   Yet *this* enjoyes before it wooe,
> And pamper'd swells with one blood made of two,
> And *this*, alas, is more then wee would doe.

The final line has slily transferred the demonstrable innocence of the flea to the proposed surrender of chastity. It is the well-tried conjuror's trick of diverting the audience's attention to a brightly coloured kerchief held in his left hand while his right hand manipulates the articles in the hat. So here, the pronoun preserves the appearance of logicality, but as we are busy watching it, the argument itself has unobtrusively switched tracks.

Donne is, as usual, a step or two ahead of his reader, and before we can pin-point precisely where we have been tricked, he moves swiftly off in a new direction, again preserving an outward consistency. For the next deception is made to appear smoothly continuous by the connection it shares with the theme of blood. On biblical authority he accepts the principle that the blood is the soul; and absurdly extrapolating the dictum to apply to every drop of blood whether inside or outside the human body, he gravely endows the spilling of the drops within the flea with all the moral weightiness of the metaphorical term 'bloodshed'. Killing the flea is therefore both murder and suicide, with the flea's life added for good measure as a further dastardly crime. Like the elongated figures in an El Greco painting, logic is being stretched out of all proportion. And once more we are whirled away into the next section on theological sanctions before the illogicality has been fully grasped, so that we return to this bloodshed theme at the end of the stanza with the vague feeling that it had been proved earlier:

> Oh stay, three lives in one flea spare,
> Where wee almost, nay more then maryed are:
> This flea is you and I, and this
> Our mariage bed and mariage temple is;
> Though parents grudge, and you, w'are met,
> And cloysterd in these living walls of Jet.
> Though use make thee apt to kill mee,
> Let not to this, selfe murder added bee,
> And sacrilege, three sinnes in killing three.

We now approach the climax of the poem, and that deeper theme which so often lies beneath the surface *panache*. For the lady at this point calls his bluff, coolly taking the common-sense line of reasoning, and adopting that very empirical viewpoint from which the poem had begun. The speaker had extravagantly claimed that killing the flea was tantamount to murder and suicide. What better proof of his error than to crush the flea and point triumphantly to their own continued survival? With one finger, therefore, she demolishes his vain attempt to confuse verifiable facts with abstract metaphorical notions of 'bloodshed', and wins her point with glorious simplicity:

> Cruell and sodaine, hast thou since
> Purpled thy naile, in blood of innocence?

> In what could this flea guilty bee,
> Except in that drop which it suckt from thee?
> Yet thou triumph'st, and saist that thou
> Find'st not thy selfe, nor mee the weaker now;

Empiricism has won the day! Her victory, however, is short-lived; for she has in fact fallen into a neatly prepared trap—the trap towards which the entire poem has been moving. By employing his favourite device of *reductio ad absurdum*, Donne has forced his fair opponent (and through her, the reader) into the admission that in a world relying on the exclusive validity of observable facts, there is no longer room for such traditional moral concepts as 'honour' and chastity:

> 'Tis true, then learne how false feares bee;
> Just so much honour, when thou yeeld'st to mee,
> Will wast, as this flea's death tooke life from thee.

As in Huxley's day, such ethical notions had, by the objective criteria of physiology and scientific analysis, become meaningless metaphors, unrelated to the act of sexual union. Which side of the dispute Donne himself takes is as yet undecided. Ostensibly arguing against the young lady, his speaker would appear to side with the amoralists, happy to be released from the fetters of social or moral imperatives and welcoming the ethical self-determination of his pragmatist. Yet the deliberate speciousness of the reasoning allows him to play a double role and to preserve an ambiguity in his final position. What intrigues him at this stage is the conflict itself, the need to choose between the world of the spirit with all its illogicality and unverifiable elusiveness, and the empirical world which, for all its welcome clarity, reduces us ultimately to the level of an insect or flea. One thing at least is apparent—that the scintillating thrust and parry of his dialectic, for all its realism, is carefully staged to expose by subtle ridicule the weakness of ratiocination itself.

One aspect of Donne's specious reasoning which has long been recognized as characteristic of his verse is the device of volte-face. Donald Guss has pointed out that the problem for most Petrarchists is to find a witty conceit, and once that basic conceit has been found, presented, and elaborated, the poem holds few subsequent surprises; the few it does hold are generally the unannounced appearance of some further Petrarchan cliché.[3] Donne, however, even in his most conventional moods, continually catches us off guard after having misled us into assuming he is merely developing a cliché. The teasing impudence with which he overturns his carefully structured argument, while it functions in the amatory poems as the casual flick of the glove to create the note of libertine scepticism, serves in addition to throw the reader off balance and to implant within him a suspicion of the very rhetorical patterns on which the preceding dialectic had been based. Donne's reversal strategy is most often seen in the concluding phrase or couplet which subverts the moral or normative framework of the poem. After railing at the inconstancy of his mistress who tomorrow will no doubt invent a series of trumped-up excuses to conceal her base perfidy, he puckishly concludes in one poem:

> Vaine lunatique, against these scapes I could
>   Dispute, and conquer, if I would,
>   Which I abstaine to doe,
> For by to morrow, I may thinke so too.[4]

This device is familiar enough at the end of a poem. It may be, however, that insufficient attention has been paid to the less obvious tessellation of intricate rebuffs and paralogical twists which runs through the body of the poems themselves, alternately arousing and frustrating expectations in preparation for the crowning reversal, and contributing in no small part to the liveliness and wit of the verse. At times Donne seems determined not merely to amuse, but to baffle by the repeated misdirections, destroying the reader's sense of spatial security in order to fabricate in its place a new and preternatural perspective of his own. In 'Loves Growth', the twisting and backtracking of the opening lines can be intended only to bewilder; and the more sensitive the reader's response, the more sure he is to be trapped in the deliberately labyrinthine convolutions of the poem. If the reader will bear with me for a moment, I should like to focus almost microscopically on the opening section in order to distinguish the subtle shifts and veering in logic which create this illusory effect. But first let us see it as a whole.

LOVES GROWTH

I scarce beleeve my love to be so pure
  As I had thought it was,
  Because it doth endure
Vicissitude, and season, as the grasse;
Me thinkes I lyed all winter, when I swore,
My love was infinite, if spring make it more.
But if this medicine, love, which cures all sorrow
  With more, not onely bee no quintessence,
  But mixt of all stuffes, paining soule, or sense,
And of the Sunne his working vigour borrow,
Love's not so pure, and abstract, as they use
To say, which have no Mistresse but their Muse,
But as all else, being elemented too,
Love sometimes would contemplate, sometimes do.

And yet not greater, but more eminent,
  Love by the spring is growne;
  As, in the firmament,
Starres by the Sunne are not inlarg'd, but showne.
Gentle love deeds, as blossomes on a bough,
From loves awaken'd root do bud out now.
If, as in water stir'd more circles bee
  Produc'd by one, love such additions take,
  Those like to many spheares, but one heaven make,
For, they are all concentrique unto thee;
And though each spring doe adde to love new heate,
As princes doe in times of action get
New taxes, and remit them not in peace,
No winter shall abate the springs encrease.

For the purpose of this analysis, we must imagine that we are reading the poem for the first time—which is, after all, the only fair way of analysing any poem. It becomes apparent that the initial six lines are teasingly ambiguous throughout. Like one of those puzzle drawings for children which can be held up either way to show a different human face, so there are here two contradictory ways of understanding the text, and we are deliberately nudged into the incorrect reading, until the final word reveals that we have been

fooled. The first false pointer is the word 'scarce', with its disturbing hint of a double negative.

> I scarce beleeve my love to be so pure
> As I had thought it was . . .

The most gifted logician would, I suspect, be hard pressed to determine at this stage whether the speaker does or does not believe his
love to be pure; and we must wait for the following line to offer the
needed explanation:

> I scarce beleeve my love to be so pure
> As I had thought it was
> Because it doth endure

Ah, we cry, here at last is a clear statement of fact—his love *has*
endured. But the end of the line is not the end of the sentence, and
the next word reverses the meaning completely. 'Endure' is seen to
have been used not in its normal sense of 'to last', but the very
opposite—to 'suffer' change:

> Because it doth endure
> Vicissitude and season, as the grasse;

After the momentary dislocation of argument, a new, securer
pattern of meaning emerges. For the seventeenth-century reader
nurtured on the Bible, the immediate association of grass in such a
setting would inevitably have been with ephemerality and decay—
'The grass withereth, the flower fadeth'.[5] Accordingly, the biblical
allusion directs us to read 'vicissitude' negatively, as a falling-off in
love's strength, and the meaning of the opening lines at last appears
clear. It would read in paraphrase: 'My love, it seems, is less pure
than I had imagined, because it suffers change and withers as the
grass.' The impression of disillusionment with love is at once
reinforced by the admission:

> Me thinkes I lyed all winter, when I swore
> My love was infinite . . .

But the next and final phrase of this section overturns the entire
sequence, revealing how thoroughly we have been duped.

> Me thinkes I lyed all winter, when I swore
> My love was infinite, if spring make it *more*.

We must, as it were, retrospectively re-read the entire section in the light of this conclusion, but now in terms of a paean to the limitless splendour of true love, instead of as a lament for its passing.

Unlike the previous quotation from 'Womans Constancy' where the pose of the devoted lover was uniformly preserved throughout the poem until the casual libertine shrug of the concluding line unexpectedly contradicted the established mood, here a series of subtle misdirections sends us scurrying back and forth along the wrong trails almost from the opening word. Even when the poem is read at normal speed, at the revelatory 'more' we instantly recognize in retrospect that the preceding passage has been perfectly consistent with the newly disclosed meaning. The 'fault', as it were, was ours for having misread the implications of 'endure', 'vicissitude', or 'grasse' by relying on the false pointers cunningly planted within the text. The over-all effect is precisely what Donne needed in order to produce a shifting, unreliable perspective. Words change their meaning as we gaze at them, logic doubles back on itself to contradict its own conclusions, and familiar objects lose their firm outline in the shimmering haze. What had first appeared to be a conventional complaint at love's ephemerality emerges as a tribute to its awesome defiance of limitation, as it paradoxically perfects its own perfection and impossibly outgrows its own infinity. The mercurial quality of the opening lines is therefore far more than an intellectual game. It creates by its disintegration of logic the conditions for the mannerist transcendence of natural law and the validation of para-dox—'... this medicine, love, which cures all sorrow / With more'. And the process continues. The 'buts' and 'yets' take over, shifting the angle of vision as soon as it appears to be established, and hence questioning the authenticity of any single controlling viewpoint other than a metaphysical faith in the ultimate complexity of all human experience.

From within the natural world Donne selects those instances which themselves contravene, or at least appear to contravene, the prosaic rules of a mechanistic universe. In violation of the evidence of one's eyes, stars do not *emerge* at night but are merely made visible by an absent sun; the miracle of spring creates blossom on boughs that yesterday were naked; and stirred water, despite the economy of nature, produces an infinite and ever-widening series of circles. From these contradictory truths in nature, he glides across with increased confidence to the ideal verities of Neoplatonism, the harmony of the heavenly spheres, and the heaven of harmonious love:

> If, as in water stir'd more circles bee
> Produc'd by one, love such additions take,
> Those like so many spheares, but one heaven make,
> For, they are all concentrique unto thee;

Unpredictable as ever, just as he has established the perfection and harmony of love he introduces to this music of the spheres a jarringly cacophonous note, drawn from the mundane world of fiscal policy—the non-remittance of taxes. It is as though he were whimsically reminding us that paradox is not the exclusive prerogative of the celestial, but is to be found no less in the supposedly ordered world of commerce and statehood—although there the effect on the unfortunate taxpayer may prove less pleasing. And after that modernistic disruption of a harmony so carefully achieved —the kind of disruption that endeared him to his twentieth-century rediscoverers—he rounds off the poem on a note of peace, the concluding line once again confirming with quiet confidence love's outstripping of the common laws of nature:

> No winter shall abate the springs encrease.

Our concern here with the quasi-logical progression of argument in 'Loves Growth', necessary as it was for analysing Donne's hallucinatory manipulation of perspective, should not be allowed to obscure the delicate humour, readily intelligible even to one who has not grasped the full subtleties of the illusionist technique. For the opening of the poem is one of those teasing compliments to a mistress which any lover might use today: 'I don't love you as much as I thought I did', he might sadly remark, adding as her face falls, 'I love you much *more*!' In its extravagant employment of such misdirection, however, the poem certainly casts doubt on the widely accepted assessment of Donne as the poet-logician *par excellence*.

Most poetry, it might be argued, tends towards the imaginative or the ambivalent, fabricating in place of the actual an illusory world of heightened sensibility and multi-levelled response. But there is in Donne's reaching out beyond logic and nature a poetic quality which distinguishes him from his contemporaries, as it does even from his imitators. While he comprehends the real world of philandering, of alchemy or of exploration with an astonishing sharpness of vision and a lively, even passionate interest, he is intrigued primarily by the inconsistencies, absurdities, and incongruities he finds within the phenomenal world, which together suggest to him that any ultimately satisfying patterns must be sought elsewhere. His implicit disqualification of the actual as a final norm is both disturbing and reassuring; for while he discredits conventional criteria by exposing their inherent contradictions, he discovers within those contradictions support for a fideistic conclusion, reposing his final trust in the ultra-rational. The uniqueness this imparts to his poetry can perhaps best be seen by placing beside 'Loves Growth' the closest contemporary treatment of the same theme. In subject matter, the following Shakespeare sonnet is almost identical; a lover describes how an unanticipated increase in affection has belied an earlier asseveration that his love could grow no more. It will be seen, however, that unlike Donne's poem, the sonnet remains for all its colourful imagery, securely bounded by the conventional, tactile world, drawing its illustrations exclusively from within the rational framework of human experience.

SONNET CXV

Those lines that I before have writ, do lie;
Even those that said I could not love you dearer;
Yet then my judgment knew no reason why
My most full flame should afterwards burn clearer.
But reckoning time, whose million'd accidents
Creep in 'twixt vows, and change decrees of kings,
Tan sacred beauty, blunt the sharp'st intents,
Divert strong minds to the course of altering things;
Alas! why, fearing of Time's tyranny,
Might I not then say, 'Now I love you best,'
When I was certain o'er uncertainty,
Crowning the present, doubting of the rest?
　　Love is a babe; then might I not say so,
　　To give full growth to that which still doth grow?

This is a poem of wit no less than Donne's, but it chooses to remain within a firmly logical pattern. The speaker justifies his previous assertion that his love was perfect on the grounds that it was then complete for that stage of its growth—just as an infant can be a perfect and complete infant even though it will eventually grow into manhood. Time's tyranny here remains secure and unchallenged, the universal hierarchy being tacitly assumed and upheld, and the resolution of the poem has no desire to transcend normal chronological development nor the limitations of nature. There is no hallucinatory denial of factuality, nor any disruption of logical patterns to assert the rich paradox of love, but rather a quiet acceptance of the place assigned to man in the settled chain of being. In 'Loves Growth', however, despite the momentary pretence of seasonal change, love—as so often in Donne's poetry—stands outside the four-dimensional restrictions of the universe, and the difference can be felt in the cosmic range of the imagery as well as in the very texture of the verse itself. The swivelling, contradictory argumentation, the elusive Protean words, and the sliding metaphors which have so long been described even by his most admiring critics as the amusing extravagances of wit, can be seen in this larger context as affording legitimate expression, in their humour as well as their seriousness, for Donne's celebration of the boundless, the paradoxical, and the irrational.

'Sweetest Love', that most gentle and melodious of lyrics, may appear far removed from such devious reasoning and from the purposeful misdirections of 'Loves Growth'; yet the extraordinary vividness of its sentiment is in fact achieved by a similar illusionist technique. From the time of Walton onwards, the delicate precision with which the song conveys the tenderness of parting has made it hard to resist the assumption that it was written to record a specific occasion in his life, perhaps as a leave-taking from his young wife. But whether such an assumption is historically valid or whether the poem once again illustrates Donne's flair for psychologically projecting himself into an imaginary situation is irrelevant in explaining how, from the literary viewpoint, the lyric succeeds in creating so vividly the impression of an actual, intimately shared experience. The source of this emotional realism can, I think, be traced to the subtle discrepancy between the speaker's outward, spoken words and the inner feelings he attempts unsuccessfully to conceal but which eventually become visible through the apparently firm exterior. Ostensibly he is offering masculine comfort and reassurance to his grieving mistress, lending his strength to help sustain her during his absence. Initially posing as the gallant, he pretends to misunderstand her tears as being prompted by suspicions of his infidelity, and jestingly explains in a neatly turned compliment that his real reason for leaving is to inure himself to the pain of death. But the confident stance is belied even in this opening stanza by the strong metrical undertow, whose contrary pull betrays how badly he himself is in need of such comfort. Although in this passage, the wording itself is casual and self-assured, the enjambment throbs across the line-endings as though the stanzaic form were incapable of containing his grief, and the short, broken, monosyllabic phrases which conclude the stanza reflect the frustration with which he reluctantly submits to fate:

> Sweetest love, I do not goe
> For wearinesse of thee,
> Nor in hope the world can show
> A fitter Love for mee;
> But since that I
> Must dye at last, 'tis best,
> To use my selfe in jest
> Thus by fain'd deaths to dye.

As yet we can only rely on the powerful rhythmic clues to suspect what lies behind the façade as, with apparently unassailable logic, the speaker continues by demonstrating how certain he is to return safely from his journey. But the logic here is as specious as ever, intended to deceive only the distraught lady. The sun, he assures her, has less reason for returning each day, yet does so without mishap. Why, then, should she fear for his welfare who has so much stronger a desire to return? The sun, however, as both he and we know only too well, returns each day precisely *because* it has no desire or sense—because it is an enormous inanimate object; while he, unlike the sun, is susceptible to those accidents of mortality which fill her with such foreboding:

> Yesternight the Sunne went hence,
>   And yet is here to day,
> He hath no desire or sense,
>   Nor halfe so short a way:
>   Then feare not mee,
> But beleeve that I shall make
> Speedier journeyes, since I take
>   More wings and spurres then hee.

On the falsely triumphant note of wings and spurs, the façade suddenly collapses as he recognizes that the pretence has failed to convince even her. The illusion, as in all mannerist art, was fabricated in order to be exposed, and in an emotional volte-face, the concealed sorrow floods out at the word 'feeble' to reveal how completely he has all the time shared her sorrow and premonitions. The only plea he can now make for her to restrain her tears is to consider the suffering they cause him, kind as their motivation may be:

> O how feeble is mans power,
>   That if good fortune fall,
> Cannot adde another houre,
>   Nor a lost houre recall!
>   But come bad chance,
> And wee joyne to it our strength,
> And wee teach it art and length,
>   It selfe o'r us to advance.

> When thou sigh'st, thou sigh'st not winde,
>   But sigh'st my soule away,
> When thou weep'st, unkindly kinde,
>   My life's blood doth decay.
>   It cannot bee
> That thou lov'st mee, as thou say'st,
> If in thine my life thou waste,
>   Thou art the best of mee.

The pose of the gallant has been discarded, the pretended confidence exposed, and the concluding stanza, now openly acknowledging the forebodings they share at the dangers facing him on his journey, offers as their sole comfort and recourse the transcendent strength of their love. By a brilliant metrical device, the indivisible phrase 'keep alive' welds the final couplet together despite the disruptive rhyme sequence, as though to convey both visually and aurally the lovers' spiritual victory over their spatial separation:

> Let not thy divining heart
> Forethinke me any ill,
> Destiny may take thy part,
> And may thy feares fulfill;
> But thinke that wee
> Are but turn'd aside to sleepe;
> They who one another keepe
> Alive, ne'r parted bee.

Among the loveliest of Donne's lyrics, it is marked by an outward simplicity which, as we have noted, might seem to set it apart from the insolent, amusing, or riddling tone characterizing at least the surface texture of so much of his verse. But the mannerist elements are at work here none the less, creating a *chiaroscuro* effect—the gloom of earthly parting illumined by the ray of extra-terrestrial hope. Beneath the melodic flow of words, the disjunction of argument is muted; yet it is largely through the effect of double vision it produces that the blend of solicitous assurance and mournful apprehension is so convincingly attained.

This illusionist technique is employed in many of his poems. His famous 'Valediction: forbidding Mourning', for example, while it has been widely admired, has also been criticized adversely on the grounds that the initial image of death is never developed in the poem, and remains extraneous to the central theme. Such critics have been particularly disturbed by Donne's failure to develop his conceits or to preserve an underlying coherence in his movement from stanza to stanza. But within the context of this oblique treatment of theme the apparent inconsequence can be seen as a merely outward inconsistency which creates an extraordinary inner realism. We are led to believe in the first stanza of this poem that the sole function of the death image is to illustrate that quiet imperceptibility of parting or silent melting away which the speaker advocates for the lovers' own valediction:

> As virtuous men passe mildly away,
> And whisper to their soules, to goe,

    Whilst some of their sad friends doe say,
      The breath goes now, and some say, no:

So let us melt, and make no noise,
    No tear-floods, nor sigh-tempests move,
'Twere prophanation of our joyes
    To tell the layetie our love.

Moving of the earth brings harmes and feares,
    Men reckon what it did and meant,
But trepidation of the spheares,
    Though greater farre, is innocent.

The breathless silence of the opening line conveys with rare sensitivity the quiet melting away which should serve as the model for saintly lovers. There is, however, an intimate link between this initial image and the submerged, almost unacknowledged theme of the poem—the dread of a fatal ending to his journey abroad. As in 'Sweetest Love', the conscious purpose is to allay the lady's fears with the assurance that, if she be firm, he will return from his distant travels. Yet at the moment of the speaker's surest confidence in the inviolability of their spiritual union in this world, the threat of that final, mortal separation, which can alone disrupt it, remains ominously present.

The imagery and diction of the poem ensure that the equipoise is maintained throughout. The title (which may well have been Donne's own) forbids 'mourning', with its unambiguously funereal associations, and the implications are in any case at once confirmed by the hushed death-bed scene of the opening stanza. What seems to have been missed by those critics disturbed at the apparent lack of structural unity is the series of unobtrusive pointers to the storms and other natural hazards awaiting the defenceless traveller on the journey which lies ahead of him—the concealed hints in 'tear-floods', 'sigh-tempests', and 'moving' of the earth, culminating in the final ambivalence of 'trepidation'. The surface confidence now soars to new heights as, with the contemptuous pun on 'sense' and 'absence', the refinement of their affection is contrasted with the merely bodily needs of others. Boundless and transcendent, their love, composed of mind and soul and metaphorically situated in the highest heavens, spurns, it would seem, such trivialities as physical parting, and we wait for the firm assurance that they care *not* for bodily touch. The unexpected admission that they 'Care *lesse*, eyes, lips, and hands to misse' ruefully acknowledges that they are grieving mortals for all their spirituality, and their pain is momentarily glimpsed through the attempt at self-delusion.

> Dull sublunary lovers love
>   (Whose soul is sense) cannot admit
> Absence, because it doth remove
>   Those things which elemented it.
>
> But we by a love, so much refin'd,
>   That our selves know not what it is,
> Inter-assured of the mind,
>   Care lesse, eyes, lips, and hands to misse.

With all due reverence for the spiritual quality of their love, the bodily contact remains a very necessary and indeed vital part of their relationship.

In the next stanza, too, within the graceful image of the beaten gold, reflecting the rarity and pricelessness of their love, there lurks a dark reminder of those underlying, unstated fears of parting. The grim word *yet* points tremblingly towards that ultimate mortal separation which will one day transform the 'expansion' of their united soul into a dreaded and eternal breach:

> Our two soules, therefore, which are one,
>   Though I must goe, endure not yet
> A breach but an expansion,
>   Like gold to ayery thinnesse beate.

At this point, the shimmering, illusory logic of Donne takes control once again. The oneness of their united souls has been demonstrated with a forceful *therefore* as the culmination of the carefully developed argument; yet as he shifts to a different image, he discards the proof with a casual 'If they be two . . .', as though admitting with an unconcerned shrug that rational consistency is nugatory beside the emotional reality. In the splendid compass image, which Donne may have borrowed from Guarini,[6] the circular harmony of love and the spiritual interdependence of the two parted lovers is combined to perfection. In this context, however, the image impinges even more powerfully on our emotions because it is projected against a silently brooding background—those unuttered qualms for his safety which suggest that the image is, after all, less a conclusive proof as it is meant to sound, than an attempt to soothe and comfort. Animate and inanimate cannot be so easily equated. The predictable movements of a scientific instrument which will, under given circumstances, return precisely to its point of departure offer no real parallel for a vulnerable human embarking on the perilous sea voyage of Donne's day; and at a subdued level we are aware that the lady's firmness, be it ever so perfect, will prove but poor protection against drowning should the ship founder in mid ocean:

> If they be two, they are two so
> As stiffe twin compasses are two,
> Thy soule the fixt foot, makes no show
> To move, but doth, if the other doe.
>
> And though it in the center sit,
> Yet when the other far doth rome,
> It leanes, and hearkens after it,
> And growes erect, as it comes home.

The words we hear spoken lose their firmness as the feelings they are attempting to conceal become visible through the gossamer screen of speech; and the interplay between word and feeling creates a realism of such intensity that we are made to feel like eavesdroppers overhearing the exchanges of two lovers engaged in the most intimate discourse. This discrepancy between feeling and speech, or rather between heart and mind, wins our final sympathy for the validity of the heart, suggesting that if the image of a unified golden soul beaten to an airy thinness will not in the final account allow the lovers to triumph over the accidents of fate, it lends them none the less a splendour and nobility which fate itself can never hope to touch.

Any reader familiar with mannerist painting will recognize here a further technique characteristic of the school—the irrational or unpredictable use of space whereby the main figure or incident is relegated to a background position of apparent insignificance, while the emotional force of the scene is conveyed indirectly through the phosphorescent colouring or violent movement of the canvas as a whole, or through the structural device of purposeful misdirection. In Tintoretto's *Presentation of the Virgin* (Plate 9), for example, the complex structuring misleads us into imagining for a moment that the young girl placed prominently in the centre foreground at the foot of the imposing stairs is herself the Virgin about to ascend, particularly as the woman beside her appears to be coaxing her forward for a formal presentation. Only on closer inspection do we discover that the girl is really a spectator to whom the woman is merely pointing out the scene, while the true Virgin, identifiable by her halo, is standing alone before the patriarchal figure at the head of the stairs. By directing our sight first to the young girl and through her on and upwards to the Virgin herself, the artist has tricked us into visually ascending the intimidating stairway ourselves. What many critics have called Tintoretto's eccentric use of space in fact involves us dramatically here in the solemnity of the ascent, fulfilling in visual form the Loyolan call for an imaginative identification with the martyrs and heroes of the Church at the climactic moments of their lives.

Of all Donne's poetic innovations, the most distinctive is this duality of apprehension whereby the concrete and the conceptual, the spoken word and the unheard emotional response, manifest themselves in his verse with equal vividness, not as separate entities but as cognate, intimately related aspects of experience, merging into each other while yet retaining their individuality. It is a quality which differentiates him not only from his predecessors, but also from that school of poets with which he has so long been associated. In contrast to Crashaw, for example, who as a devotional poet sees the natural world almost exclusively in terms of its religious symbolism, Donne imparts to his dramatic scenes the sharply tactile quality of direct, unfiltered experience. He discards the sweet-scented lyricism and stylized imagery of the sonneteers in favour of an almost brutal colloquialism, addressing his own heart in one of his love poems with the brusque, everyday familiarity one would use towards a drinking companion:

Meet mee at London, then,
Twenty dayes hence, and thou shalt see
Mee fresher, and more fat, by being with men,
Then if I had staid still with her and thee.[7]

The added quality which transforms this otherwise mundane realism into a deeply felt experience has been described by a number of critics as his 'complexity of attitudes' which, in the Bruno tradition, allows him to swerve from one vantage point to another, and thereby hold in ironic counterpoint such antithetical philosophies as those of religionist and libertine, Platonist and empiricist, without according final preference to any one view. According to this theory, these contrasting viewpoints are drawn from a wide variety of sources, being introduced and elaborated in order to convey with greater dramatic realism the intricacies of the human character. In the classic formulation of this critical standpoint, Leonard Unger identifies this complexity as 'the distinguishing and characteristic feature of Donne's *Songs and Sonets*', and he attributes to it the primary value and appeal of the poetry:

This complexity may itself be regarded as a value. It might be so held on the basis that recognition of complexity of attitudes is *realistic*, since life is extremely complex: there are various standards of interpretation that are opposed to each other; individuals seldom share identical attitudes; there are conflicts between the individual and society, and conflicts among the various interests of the same individual. Complexity of attitudes reflects, thus, the actual differences among persons and the psychological nature of the individual. There appears, then, to be a further basis for the value of complexity. It brings into prominence the *psychology of the individual*, which is itself interesting. And the emphasis on human individuality, especially when the individual maintains or is involved in an opposition of attitudes, makes for dramatic quality, which is, like psychology, self-evident in its value.[8]

In his view, therefore, the poetic achievement of Donne rests principally on the psychological realism with which the individuals are presented. What a deflatingly limited achievement, if Mr. Unger is right! According to this view, the key to the vibrant metaphysical quality of 'The Canonization' or 'The Funerall' is their presentation of the lovers as psychologically interesting, and we are to see a passage such as the following (which is as characteristic of Donne's verse as anything he wrote) distinguished primarily by the accuracy of its characterization:

> Who ever comes to shroud me, do not harme
>   Nor question much
> That subtile wreath of haire, which crowns mine arme;
> The mystery, the signe you must not touch,
>   For 'tis my outward Soule,
> Viceroy to that, which then to heaven being gone,
>   Will leave this to controule,
> And keepe these limbes, her Provinces, from dissolution.

The hush of sanctity in these lines, investing the bleakness of the grave and shroud with a lambent mystery and blending the worlds of flesh and spirit has surely more significance in identifying its specifically metaphysical timbre than mere realism, psychological or otherwise. On the contrary, we are deliberately drawn away from the actual and the mundane into a hauntingly unfamiliar world where the real has been transmuted by the touch of eternity, and the tired conventions of Petrarchist poetry are seen suddenly anew, as touching affirmations of faith by virtue of the reverence with which the love token is treated. Within his book, Unger carefully confines his discussion to the *Songs and Sonets*, leaving the devotional poems untouched. Since, however, the acknowledged purpose of his study is to define the essence of metaphysical poetry as such, his theory must be equally applicable to the divine writings if it is to be valid. Yet there it would be patently untenable to argue that the poetic vigour of Donne's 'Hymne to God my God, in my Sicknesse' arises from the 'lively realism' with which he contrasts the psychological viewpoints of physicians and preachers. Certainly that contrast is present in the poem, but only as a symptom of a profounder theme, the two polarized concepts of death medically as the grievous cessation of human life, and Christianly as the joyful threshold of eternal rebirth.

The theory that the mainspring of Donne's poetry is its complexity of attitudes explains too small a part of his creative genius to serve as more than a starting-point in analysing the originality of his contribution to poetry. Browning, for example, was in later years to imitate in the dramatic characters of his own verse the psychological complexity of Donne's speakers, borrowing with it the technique of a lively and colloquial monologue. The bishop ordering his tomb at St. Praxed's is a superlatively credible figure, precisely because he believes unquestioningly in the holiness and peace of the Church, in the existence of the heavenly angels, and in the efficacy of prayer, while at the same time unhesitatingly indulging his worldly jealousies, greed, and lust; and Browning identifies himself neither with the asceticism demanded by the Church, nor with the excesses of his very human ecclesiast. Yet for all its brilliant realism and the persuasive complexity of attitudes, it contains no hint of that transcendent, *metaphysical* quality inherent in Donne's poetry as the latter joins, divorces, contrasts, and blends the terrestrial and ethereal levels of human experience.

There is, I would suggest, a very real complexity of attitudes at the heart of Donne's verse but it is a far more profound and at the same time more cohesive complexity than the casual juxtaposition of libertine and lover, alchemist and scholiast, physician and preacher, contrasted for the purpose of realistic portrayal and variety of vignette. For these antithetical viewpoints should be seen as symptoms rather than ends in themselves, expressing in polarized form Donne's experimentation with the pragmatic and fideistic interpretations of reality, each stimulating and attractive to him in itself, yet not easily to be reconciled with its counterpart. Moreover, the subtle, ironic interplay between these polarized views, at times suggesting a commitment to the one, at times to the other, is reflected in what might be called his 'double vision' of the world. He invests the tactile and the concrete, in all its sharp brilliance of depiction, with an added diaphanous quality which allows us by a sudden shift in lighting to see through it into the world of the spirit. Whether or not we return to reality after that glimpse, we are left with a heightened awareness that the visible and the tangible form only part of the totality of human experience and gain their validity only when that further truth is perceived. Just as the logical pattern of his verse dissolves into paradox while the fascination with reasoning remains fresh and unimpaired, so the joys of sensory response become attenuated and etherealized not at the expense of the sensory but as an enriching extension of it. The libertine in Donne's poetry embodies the initial aspect of this duality —he delights in the flesh, his roving hands excitedly exploring the splendid curves and crevices of the female body '. . . behind, before, above, between, below'; while in contrast the devoted lover shares with his mistress a refined spirituality of love by perceiving the celestial through and beyond the flesh. The two types of lovers do not remain at opposite poles, but are held in complementary unison, often within the same individual as Donne shifts the focus of the emotional response from the tactile to the ethereal. The eager explorer of the flesh '. . . behind, before, above, between . . .' avows a moment later that all women '. . . are mystique bookes, which only wee / Whom their imputed grace will dignify / Must see reveal'd . . .' and we have glimpsed the celestial through the corporeal. Hence that characteristic refusal in Donne to divorce his amatory from his devotional verse. The intermingling of secular imagery with sacred reflects this impinging of inner upon outer reality as the plane of perception is adjusted.

If the theory suggested here is correct—that the sliding metaphors, reversals of logic, and illusory wit of Donne's verse derive ultimately from his 'transpicuous' vision of the universe with its refusal to accord any final validity to the actual—to what extent can Donne's viewpoint be identified with Neoplatonism which in its Renaissance form swept through Europe in the fifteenth and sixteenth centuries, reviving in men's minds the Socratic distinction between the real and 'ideal' levels of existence? The actual world, according to this philosophy, consists only of shadows, each object and even each behavioural pattern being merely specific instances, localized in time and place, of the ideal form it adumbrates. A triangle is by definition a flat, three-sided figure, but man is only capable of visualizing specific forms of it—isosceles, acute-angled, equilateral. Socrates deduced from this human limitation the existence in a superior world of a single 'ideal' triangle which embraces all possible variations. Similarly, a single act of courage on a specific battlefield is only a faint worldly reflection of the universal and all-inclusive idea of courage of which it is a shadow. Within this philosophical system, man strives to ascend from the particularized phenomenal world towards the universal, moving ever nearer in his spiritual ascent to that divine pinnacle which, comprising all subordinate ideals, epitomizes in totality the eternal, the beautiful, the perfect, the true, and the good. Alternatively, in the mythic pattern more popular during the Renaissance, the human spirit swings in circular motion from the mundane, up through the sacred, and back into the temporal, now bearing with it the knowledge newly attained through having perceived the divine. Here are the two worlds of body and soul, of terrestrial and ethereal, to which at first sight Donne's own twofold vision might appear to conform.

Of his familiarity with such tenets of Neoplatonism and his indebtedness to the Renaissance form of it, there can be no doubt. He employs its images of perfect spheres and circles (even after Kepler's discovery of the elliptical orbiting of the stars) with an ease as well as a confidence of being understood which testify to the thoroughness of its absorption into the era; and his conception of the refinement and divinity of pure love owes much in its specifics as well as its more general features to the theories developed by the Alexandrian school of the third century in which Neoplatonism was born. Plotinus, the leading figure of that school, had even introduced as a central element in that philosophical system (and advocated by his personal example) the cult of ecstasy, whereby the soul temporarily leaves the body to bask in the splendour of divine light. By the time of Donne, Platonism had been sufficiently assimilated by Christianity for him to have no need to turn directly to Plotinus, and the similarities discernible in his own outlook show how much he had in common with the philosophical school as a whole, as well as with its contemporary revival.

However, the identification of Donne with that tradition is liable to obscure as much as it illumines. It is true that he found there a valuable vocabulary of images for his own exploration of the relationship between spirit and flesh, their interdependence in this world, and their separation at the moment of death; but he was far from being a Neoplatonist himself. For Platonism, in its original form as well as in its subsequent Christian varieties, presupposed as the corner-stone of its philosophy the essential harmony and stability of the relationship between real and ideal. The beauty and (as Plato himself admitted in his later work *The Laws*, whose influence never superseded that of his earlier writings) the impracticability of the utopian Republic he envisaged, is that the tangible and specific in this world are connected by straight, undeviating filaments to their superior and logically identifiable *ideas*; and once the *idea* has been recognized and defined, the means of working towards it must itself be simple and direct. The perfect soldier, Socrates argues, is the man who can best ensure the military defence of the city-state; he needs therefore to be nurtured and trained from childhood towards the fulfilment of that designated function, and all other criteria, including personal ambition and pleasure, must be subordinated to that purpose, or discarded as irrelevant if they do not contribute towards its achievement. The masses, Socrates reluctantly admits, will never grasp this beautiful simplicity and will continue to crave other satisfactions from life.[9] The true philosopher, however, knows that there is only one ultimate good under which all the lesser ideals such as soldiership are subsumed. At the apex of the system stands absolute perfection, for which Plato employed the compound name *calocagathia*, the 'Beautiful-and-Good' which presides majestically over all. The philosopher who has once perceived this perfect cosmic structure will never doubt its truth again, even though he will be reproached and maligned by those who have remained in the cave and have never learnt to distinguish the shadows from the originals. Out of this basic tenet arises the conviction pervading all Platonic thought, that no man commits wrong knowingly; it is only through ignorance of the splendid master-plan that he confuses minor, immediate pleasure with the ultimate pleasure of contributing to the absolute good.

The golden optimism which glows throughout Plato's writings, reflecting the ordered harmony shining above the particular and the mundane, derived its energy from the Pythagorean theories of geometrical and musical patterns which Plato, after coming into contact with the Pythagorean communities of the West, absorbed into the central cluster of dialogues on which his reputation rests— the *Meno, Phaedo, Symposium, Phaedrus,* and *Republic.* Pythagoras had been among the first to perceive that the musical scale, like the laws of geometry and mathematics, followed complex but consistent rules of behaviour which suggested an over-all system of nature integrated in perfect mystical accord. Not only were the numerical divisions of the harmonic scale an indivisible part of mathematical notation, but the circular orbiting of the spheres themselves produced as they whirled through the skies a harmonious music inaudible to human ears. Interestingly enough, Pythagoras is believed to have been the first to apply to the universe the term *cosmos*, which in Greek means both 'beauty' and 'order', and it was a small if profoundly important step for Plato to extend this theory of universal consonance to moral behaviour. The perfecting of the soul in the human microcosm restores it to full participation in the cosmic harmony, ensuring recognition of the beautiful and good as the guiding principles of the ideal world:

On these accounts, therefore, Glauco, said I, is not education in music of the greatest importance, because the measure and harmony enter in the strongest manner into the inward part of the soul, and most powerfully affect it, introducing decency along with it into the mind, and making every one decent if he is properly educated, and the reverse if he is not. And, moreover, because the man who hath here been educated as he ought, perceives in the quickest manner whatever workmanship is defective, and whatever execution is unhandsome, or whatever productions are of that kind; and being disgusted in a proper manner, he will praise what is beautiful, rejoicing in it, and receiving it into his soul, be nourished by it, and become a worthy and good man; but whatever is ugly, he will in a proper manner despise and hate, whilst yet he is young, and before he is able to understand reason; and when reason comes, such an one as hath been thus educated will embrace it, recognising it perfectly well from its intimate familiarity with him.[10]

Reason, beauty, music, and moral decency all constitute facets here of the same supreme perfection towards which the entire universe aspires. In Plotinus, the identification of harmony with rational thought was even more marked, and the apex of his philosophical system is no longer the 'Beautiful-and-Good', but the *Nous* which, as far as it can be translated into English, may be rendered as the 'intellectual principle' or 'Spirit of Intuitive Reason'. It stood above the soul in importance, and when Christianity assimilated its concepts more fully, *Logos* or Reason began to be identified with the divine. Thus, however far-fetched it may appear today, the opening verse of St. John's Gospel 'In the beginning was the Word (*Logos*)' meant in this context 'In the beginning was Reason, and Reason was with God, and Reason was God.' Subordinate to this *Nous* was the soul, identified with non-intuitive rational thought and functioning by the process of logical development from premiss to conclusion. These two supreme principles, the divine Intellect and the rational Soul, consummated the order of cosmic being in the universe as conceived by Plotinus. Among such Renaissance thinkers as Ficino, Castiglione, and Pico, the primary attraction of Neoplatonism was its splendidly harmonious and hierarchical order. Within the broader stream of Neoplatonism as it emerged in the Renaissance, there existed numerous eddies and cross-currents, as the more Thomistically inclined accepted Aristotle's affirmation of the interdependence of body and soul in contrast to Plato's identification of the body with the tomb. But whatever the internal differences, their adherents were united in accepting as the central philosophical concept the symbol of a graduated ascent in the stages of love, beginning with an admiration of beauty in its physical form (whether or not this included physical union), moving upward to a perception of the lady's inner and truer loveliness, and culminating in the splendid vision of Eternal Beauty which marked the apex of the ascent. The music of the spheres, even if inaudible to human ears, provided by its very existence an assurance that the imperfect of this world could rise smoothly and rationally towards divine perfection. Spenser, in his 'Hymn of Heavenly Beauty', catches melodiously the nature of such hierarchical ascent:

> And as these heavens still by degrees arise
> Until they come to their first mover's bound,
> That in his mighty compass doth comprise
> And carry all the rest with him around;
> So those likewise do by degrees redound
> And rise more fair, till they at last arrive
> To the most fair, whereto they all do strive.

The golden glow of concordant perfection has been preserved here almost untouched from the earliest sources of Platonism.

Where in such a world of euphonious, reasoned order are we to place the dislocated logic, the deliberate cacophonies, and the taut inner restlessness of Donne, as he reaches out in near despair for those paradoxes which could alone create some semblance of meaning out of the chaos he saw around him? For the Counter-Renaissance, the harmony of the spheres had played itself out, and the sun now stole with 'couzening line', failing even to perfect its circle; reason which had promised so much had proved weak or untrue; and the world's beauty and proportion were decayed, all coherence gone. This grim mood of disillusionment was not permanent with Donne; it was modified even at its more extreme moments by a disposition to find consolation in the world of the spirit. But his was an anguished faith in its earlier as well as its later phase, a 'holy discontent' which repudiated serene trust as dangerous complacency, choosing instead the path of rigorous, ever-dissatisfied introspection. Within his view of the world, the spiritual ideal was to be attained not by a calm rung-by-rung ascent of the ladder of love, nor by a gently circular movement from mundane to divine, but rather by the tortuous path which about must and about must go, a path beset by traps and twisting contradictions. Even so apparently simple an ideal as fear of God becomes in his labyrinthine soul both a virtue and a sin. His best days are those in which he shakes with a divine fear testifying to the power of his faith; and yet at the same time he knows that that very fear can be a pit of damnation—the 'sinne of feare' betraying a failure of trust in divine mercy. Either way is treacherous, and there is no middle path for man to walk. In the same way, longing to understand and through understanding to enlarge his trust, he recognizes the danger that knowledge can bring and prays with a moving contrariness for a limit to his own reason—that recurring mannerist metaphor of man's need at a certain point to close his eyes to the visible in order to see the truth:

> Let not my minde be blinder by more light
> Nor Faith, by Reason added, lose her sight.[11]

Such are the riddling paradoxes of love, both secular and divine, which divorce Donne's vision from the Neoplatonic. The discrepancy is unmistakable in the devotional poetry; but even in the amatory verse, where the similarities have been most often discerned, a gulf exists between them none the less. The poem most obviously related to the Neoplatonic tradition in its theme, terminology, and images is, of course, 'The Extasie' with its disembodied souls ascending to the rarefied atmosphere of heaven to engage in the dialogue of pure love. Probably more critical ink has been expended on this one poem than on any of Donne's writings, particularly since Pierre Legouis created a fluttering in the scholarly dovecots by suggesting it was a poem of seduction. His contention was energetically rebutted, and critical opinion has settled down since then to the view that it is, after all, genuine in its Platonic idealization of love. In fact, I find it difficult to read the poem as anything but a parody, almost a burlesque, of Neoplatonic conventions, particularly in its opening section.[12] There, with mock solemnity he depicts the Platonic lovers lying motionless side by side throughout *all* the long day, as cold and unfeeling as if their bodies were made of stone, while their souls 'negotiate' above:

> Wee like sepulchrall statues lay;
> All day, the same our postures were,
> And wee said nothing, all the day.

It is the *reductio ad absurdum* of the tradition. And Donne continues the gentle ridicule by describing how the refined lover—should there be any worthy of the name—would be even further purified by overhearing their celestial and unisex dialogue, provided (Donne adds circumspectly) that he happens to stand within 'convenient' distance:

> If any, so by love refin'd,
> That he soules language understood,
> And by good love were grown all minde,
> Within convenient distance stood,
>
> He (though he knew not which soule spake,
> Because both meant, both spake the same)
> Might thence a new concoction take,
> And part farre purer then he came.

Only when the idealistic exaggerations of Neoplatonism have been put aside as faintly absurd, does he advocate a healthy recognition of the need to mingle the ethereal elements of love with the bodily.

Behind this merging of celestial and mundane love lies a complex tradition whose origins go back beyond the fifteenth-century revival of Platonism to the ancient conflict between Eros and Agape which had almost split early Christianity, and had continued in a suppressed but scarcely less dangerous form long after the apparent victory of the Church. The pioneer studies of C. S. Lewis, De Rougemont, and D'Arcy have revealed within the courtly-love tradition an extraordinary fusion of paganism and Christianity in which the Gnostic and Manicheist heresies had reasserted themselves.[13] Prominent among the pagan elements assimilated by these heresies from ancient primitive cults was the worship of Eros—a worship very different from the popular conception of it today. So far from being an orgiastic gratification of sexual desire for its own sake, it was almost the reverse—a craving for abstract, deified love as a refuge from the wearisome constrictions of the finite world. The primal impulse was a death wish in which symbolically the dark lady of love conducted the devotee of Eros from the world of the flesh into mystic union with the spirit of the infinite. When the sixteenth-century poet punned on the dual meaning of 'die' as the terminal moment both of love and of mortal life, he was touching a chord whose echoes reverberated into the primitive past.

The contempt for carnal love among the worshippers of a deified Eros meant that marriage had no attraction for them, and they rejected it as a symbol of enslavement to the flesh. Their own physical outlets they sought outside wedlock in a frenzied urge to exorcise their bodily lusts and purge themselves in preparation for their ultimate escape from the corporeal. As a result, the act of love on earth was not the culmination of a noble meeting of souls, the physical expression of a mutual tenderness and regard, but arose instead from an essentially egoistical impulse, a narcissistic desire for self-purgation in which the participation of the female was a distasteful but unavoidable necessity. Although it was never to become a dominant mode of the Renaissance, this disgust with the sexual act flowed as a powerful undercurrent whose turbulent eddies are visible at such moments as Lear's tirade against the bestiality of copulation or the famous Shakespearean sonnet on lust in action as an expense of spirit in a waste of shame. It is a mood which emerges at times in Donne's own love poetry, incompatible as it may seem with that idealization of love which became the keynote of his verse. When the pagan Eros surfaces momentarily from the dark recesses of Donne's mind, woman represents neither virtue nor beauty, but shrinks to a genital orifice constructed to supply man's lustful needs:

> Rich Nature hath in woman wisely made
> Two purses, and their mouthes aversely laid;
> They then which to the lower tribute owe
> That way which that exchequer lookes must goe.
> Hee which doth not, his error is as greate
> As who by Clyster gave the stomach meate.[14]

His own disgust is patent in the nauseating image with which the passage concludes—an image which retains its emetic effect despite the worldly pose of unshockable bravado. It was a mood of disgust most clearly visible in the early elegies from which the above quotation is taken, but it appears occasionally in the midst of the love poems themselves, creating a disquieting, jarring note in the predominantly passionate tenor of these amatory pieces. For there, even in his most libertine and philandering moods, woman is for Donne's lovers the delightfully attractive object of pursuit, and it is only at rare moments that one catches the echo of this pagan revulsion at the corrupting fleshliness of human lust, and a despairing feeling that all attempts to imbue the sexual act with spiritual content are mere self-delusion:

> That loving wretch that sweares,
> 'Tis not the bodies marry, but the mindes,
> Which he in her Angelique finds,
> Would sweare as justly, that he heares,
> In that dayes rude hoarse minstralsey, the spheares.
> Hope not for minde in women; at their best
> Sweetnesse and wit, they are but *Mummy*, possest.[15]

In contrast to this need for orgiastic purgation of contemptible lust, Christian Agape saw in the Incarnation of Jesus a partial sanctification of mortal flesh. The other-worldliness of Christian belief attached, of course, no less importance than did the cult of Eros to escape from the corporeal through death—in Christianity the sole theological justification for temporal existence. Nevertheless, within the earthly setting, it recognized that love between man and his lawful wife could in its noblest form offer some terrestrial adumbration, an inkling however minuscule, of God's love and understanding for his creatures. Wedded love, therefore, was condoned and even blessed by the Church as a sacramental union. It requires, however, no great knowledge of ecclesiastical history to recall that, for all its official approval of marriage, there was from its inception, particularly in its Pauline sources, an idealization of the celibate life which reduced marriage to the level of a refuge for the weak, tolerated with the greatest reluctance by the Church. The celibacy of Christ's own life, as well as the centrality in Christian theology of the Virgin Birth, left little room for the positive encouragement of sexual activity, and the Old Testament's firm injunction for mankind to be fruitful and multiply was quietly ignored until the Reformation, on the unwarranted assumption that it had been superseded by the Gospels. Even within the Reformed church, with its ostentatious rejection of celibacy even for the priesthood, it was to take many years before the Protestant could rid himself of a sense of guilt when lawfully procreating within the bonds of marriage, and the stern maxim 'omnis ardentior amator propriae uxoris adulter est' ('any man too passionately in love with his own wife is an adulterer') continued to cast its shadow over the Protestant home too. In certain ways, therefore, Eros and Agape were not as antagonistic as they might first appear. Both strove for union with the divine and the infinite, both despised the physical gratification of love, and both tended to regard the body itself as a vile encumbrance to the soul.

Within the Renaissance, however, Christian Agape moved further away from Eros in response to a revival of what Dean Inge once called the only philosophy with which Christianity can work without friction. In its purest form, the Florentine renascence of Neoplatonism endowed human amatory experience with new dignity and, if it showed little concern whether such love found its expression inside or outside the marital framework, it viewed it none the less as both valid in itself and as a legitimate foothold for ascending towards the divine. Yet within Neoplatonism there remained a broad range of opinions from which to choose. Behind the rarefied intellectual arguments and the fine distinctions can frequently be felt—as so often in the lofty realms of philosophy—that instead of embarking in accordance with Socrates' ideal on an uncommitted search for truth wherever it may lead, the Neoplatonists were merely clothing their personal predilections in dialectical garb. Leon Ebreo, whose *Dialoghi d'Amore* exerted wide influence in this period, was really the Jewish philosopher Abarbanel writing under a pseudonym and attempting to reconcile Neoplatonism with Judaism. Accordingly, in the rabbinical tradition (which saw marriage as a divine injunction incumbent upon mankind) he validated the act of bodily union, maintaining that thereby '. . . spiritual love is augmented and made more perfect'. But there were extremer views on either side of his more liberal attitude. Ficino, while following Plato's Diotima in admitting that procreation arose from a laudable desire for immortality or self-perpetuation, could nevertheless discern no connection between divine love and mere procreation, regarding coitus as bestial and, what was more, as a dangerous temptation to desert the pursuit of higher love in favour of the vulgar and more ephemeral variety which had already been tasted and enjoyed. On the other hand, the influential Sperone Speroni, recognizing in man a centaur-like creature composed indivisibly of reason and desire, argued with a lively bluntness, that the celibate lover seeking an exclusively spiritual and refined love resembled one '. . . who, gulping his food without touching or masticating it, more harms than nourishes himself'.[16]

Such, then, were some of the more fundamental discrepancies within the larger body of Neoplatonism. But whatever the internal differences in their attitude to physical love, the Neoplatonists were united in accepting as their central concept the divinely harmonious relationship between the particular and the ideal, and the smoothness of the straight or perfectly circular ascent to the celestial. It is here that Donne's concern with glimpsing the conceptual through the concrete and finally invalidating the actual is divorced from the Neoplatonic tradition whatever similarities in terminology may appear to unite them. 'Twicknam Garden' is typical of Donne's reaching through the sharply visualized reality of the phenomenal world to the world of the spirit beyond, and might at first sight appear to participate in this merger of body and soul associated with Christian Neoplatonism. The setting here is a real garden (probably, if the title is authentic, one belonging to the Countess of Bedford) with its fresh flowing water, its stone fountains, and its trees laughing in the springtime. While the natural loveliness is seen and admired, the garden becomes at the same moment transfigured in the eyes of the sorrowing lover into the priestly administrant of extreme unction to his dying soul in a Christian setting redolent of the Eucharist:

> Blasted with sighs, and surrounded with teares,
>   Hither I come to seeke the spring,
>   And at mine eyes, and at mine eares,
> Receive such balmes, as else cure every thing;
>   But O, selfe traytor, I do bring
> The spider love, which transubstantiates all,
>   And can convert Manna to gall,
> And that this place may thoroughly be thought
> True Paradise, I have the serpent brought.

Here are indeed the two worlds of body and soul, of actual and spiritual; but the relationship between these two worlds, in contrast to the Platonic, is anguished, taut, and restless. The garden's loveliness fails to soothe, the extreme unction proves ineffective in its balm, and the act of transubstantiation has been usurped by an embittering spider love. That ordered harmony of creation lauded by Spenser has been blighted here; and in the concluding couplet of the stanza, the wit so characteristic of Donne illustrates once again that transparently counterfeit logic and responsiveness to paradox divorcing him from the Neoplatonic world with which he has so long been associated. The lover pretends ironically that he has brought the serpent envy with him into the innocent garden solely in order to convert the latter into 'true' Paradise—as if his desire for historical accuracy outweighed his longing for peace and contentment. Beneath the surface humour, however, is conveyed the tragic admission that man carries with him wherever he goes, even in the tranquil beauty and freshness of a garden, the seeds of his own despair. Such is the flawed universe in which Donne finds himself; a universe too perverse as well as too fascinating in its contradictions, delights, and sorrows to be neatly fitted into any idealized, harmonious scheme.

The uniqueness of Donne's 'transpicuous' vision, then, is that, while preserving the sensuous immediacy of the corporeal, he yet perceives through such actuality the iridescent realm of the spirit, allowing the perspective to be dictated by an inner rather than an outer reality; and he creates thereby a series of shifting angles of vision and a disturbing elongation or contraction of space. The originality it imparts to his verse lends it a Midas-like quality which can transform the most hackneyed theme into gold, as his poem 'The Dreame' illustrates. The sources of the poem within Renaissance convention and the specific analogues in continental as well as contemporary English poetry have been amply recorded by Mario Praz, who points out that few topics had been so harped on by sixteenth-century poets as this time-honoured theme of the 'love-dream'. In this tradition, the slumbering poet, envisaging that his cruel mistress has miraculously relented and has agreed to respond to his love, imagines her approaching his bedside in order to offer him a rich recompense for his suffering. Unfortunately, as he is just about to enjoy the long-awaited rapture, he awakens to the harsh reality of his solitude and, bemoaning his lot, reluctantly returns either for comfort or for revenge to the more satisfying visions of sleep. Thomas Watson, Sir Arthur Gorges, and numerous others had written commonplace treatments of the theme, and Praz, in acknowledging the success of Donne's version, attributes the superiority of his poem to '. . . its dramatic character, its metrical originality, its crabbed and poetic imagery'.[17] Certainly the dramatic character raises it above such other versions, for here the lady has actually entered the room and participates as a silent partner in the one-sided dialogue, her unheard responses in the intervals between stanzas dictating the speaker's next move.[18] However, important though these elements may be as contributory factors, the central feature which elevates Donne's poem so far above contemporary versions and from which both its poetic timbre and its delightful humour derive lies elsewhere. For while the other poets scrupulously preserve the normal distinctions between sleeping and waking, without which they lose the contrast between the delicious visions of slumber and the bleak loneliness of the lover's room, Donne daringly blends the two worlds, creating a hallucinatory merger of inner and outer experience which projects dream into reality, and extends reality back into dream. Although the literary effect is more playful here than in such solemn poems as 'Sweetest Love', it shares with them the conviction that the two planes of being are not to be finally divorced.

For the sake of contrast, it may be worth glancing at the central section of Sir Arthur Gorges's poem, the moment when the sleeper awakens from his dream and realizes that the lady is present only in his mind:

> Oh sweet Elusion straunge
> o marvell of delighte
> But oh how sone did chaunge
> the pleasure off this nighte
> For loe this soddayne Joye
> so strake me to the harte
> As that to myn annoye
> out of this sleepe I starte
> And yett dyd doubtfull stande
> tyll lyftinge upp my heade
> To kisse her comelye hande
> the shape awaye was fledd.

There is no overlapping of worlds here. The dream is a mere figment of the imagination; and if it takes a moment for the speaker to shake off the happy delusions of sleep, once his eyes are opened, the vision vanishes without a trace. In Donne's poem, however, the beautiful vision of sleep merges into a real lady standing before him in flesh and blood, and continuing his dream uninterrupted into the waking world. And the reverse also holds true; for by her timely entry, she is seen as having a moment earlier penetrated into his dream from the waking world in order to know precisely when to rouse him.

The imaginary and the actual interweave with each other, blurring the distinctions between fantasy and fact:

THE DREAME

Deare love, for nothing lesse then thee
Would I have broke this happy dreame,
    It was a theame
For reason, much too strong for phantasie,
    Therefore thou wakd'st me wisely; yet
My Dreame thou brok'st not, but continued'st it,
Thou art so true, that thoughts of thee suffice,
To make dreames truth; and fables histories;
Enter these armes, for since thou thoughtst it best,
Not to dreame all my dreame, let's do the rest.

The lover's aim is again to assuage the lady's qualms. The purpose on this occasion, however, is not to soothe her grief but quite simply to tempt her into bed. We watch him playfully fabricate a web of false reasoning in the hope of catching this lovely fly in its mesh, and the entertainment the scene affords us lies to no small degree in his admiring recognition that she is in fact far too clever to be caught. His attempt is a roguish game-gesture rather than a serious seduction, and the elaborate traps he prepares are intended primarily to amuse. Running parallel to the spoken word and creating a humorous effect of double vision is the reader's understanding of what has actually occurred. The lady, one may guess, had woken him out of a dreamless slumber by the noise of her entry; but he, with the resourcefulness of an experienced lover, is instantly awake, glibly exploiting his unexpected opportunity to the full by delicately turned compliments, by protestations of love, and above all by subtly implicating her in his own amatory designs.

The gracious tribute with which the poem opens—the assurance that nothing but she herself could have persuaded him to break off his delicious dream—reaches its apogee in 'wisely' to form the pivot upon which the comedy turns. In one word, he transforms her fortuitous entry into the calculated act of an omniscient being who had perceived the content of his dream and entered at the precise moment she did in order to take over in the flesh the role she had

seen herself acting within his sleep. In this way, he not only establishes with her the bond of intimacy and shared insights reserved
for true lovers, but slyly places upon her the responsibility for fulfilling her supposed (and most welcome) intent. The wit would be
less effective, however, were it not reinforced by one of those graver
assertions which in Donne's verse so often authenticate the apparently trivial—his belief that in her, all dreams and fables are
realized. We scarcely notice, as we read, that 'dream' here has
silently glided across from the meaning of 'reverie in slumber' to
that of 'longed-for ideal'. In the latter sense, as the embodiment of
his dream of love, she literally makes dreams truth; and as we return
to the haunting description of their 'dreaming his dream' jointly,
the image comes alive with that deeper verity. Lovers do indeed
share dreams in the waking world, and by entering his arms she
will be acting out a continuation of their joint *waking* dream, if not
of the dream of sleep interrupted by her entry. On the one hand the
humour demands that we recognize the factual discrepancy between
the two meanings of 'dream', while on the other hand the throb of
genuine passion acknowledges the triviality of such distinctions.
Where dreams of love are concerned, the two views, actual and
transcendental, are held simultaneously in mind as mutually enriching rather than mutually exclusive.

The intermediate stanza elaborates and extends the mingling of
imagination and fact. He was awakened, he blandly assures her, not
by the sound of her footsteps but by the silent radiance of her eyes;
and extrapolating the dream-like fantasy of logic, he erects on his
earlier and, in fact, baseless assumption that she had seen into and
shared his dream, the 'proof' that such insight places her even above
the angels.

> As lightning, or a Tapers light,
>   Thine eyes, and not thy noise wak'd mee;
>   Yet I thought thee
> (For thou lov'st truth) an Angell, at first sight,
>   But when I saw thou saw'st my heart,
> And knew'st my thoughts, beyond an Angel's art,
> When thou knew'st what I dreamt, when thou knew'st when
> Excesse of joy would wake me, and cam'st then,

> I doe confesse, it could not chuse but bee
> Prophane, to thinke thee any thing but thee.

As so often in Donne's poetry, his speaker is condemned ruefully to acknowledge that his flimsy reasoning, elaborate as it is, has failed to persuade; for the lady, to be worthy of his regard, must possess that degree of intelligent perception which Donne always assumes in his reader. The result is a sharpened and more lively exchange of wit. This technique of assuming a silent and mildly sceptical partner as participant in the dialogue serves, however, an additional function of no mean importance; for through her are expressed our own more prosaic reservations as Donne argues for this commitment to a transcendent ideal. As in 'The Flea', the lady preserves in the face of the speaker's encouragement to soar beyond reality and convention a sober awareness of where dreams end and social or moral responsibility begins, and her refusal to be beguiled by specious arguments persuades us to leave our own potential objections in her able hands. At the conclusion, however, it is Donne's speaker who wins our final sympathy, even where the poem is humorous, weaning us gradually away from her cooler appraisal by suggesting that love in the fullness of its ardour is ultimately more splendid than the prosaic reservations which she (and perhaps we) initially entertained.

The lady now has discerned the light-hearted attempt at seduction concealed within his fine words, and prudently rises to leave. Surely, he argues with the oldest love ploy in history, their love outstrips the petty restrictions applicable to lesser mortals and she would not wish to surrender by her sudden departure the place he has assigned her above the angels. Is she the 'thou' of his dreams, or the 'thou' of a more mundane and pedestrian world?

> Comming and staying show'd thee, thee,
> But rising makes me doubt, that now,
> Thou art not thou.
> That love is weake, where feare's as strong as hee;
> 'Tis not all spirit, pure and brave
> If mixture it of *Feare, Shame, Honor*, have.

Sadly for him, this argument too she lightly brushes aside, and he must reluctantly fall back upon his last comfort, the faint hope that, perhaps like torches which one lights and then extinguishes in order to ensure their readiness in time of need, she has frustrated his desire on this occasion only in order to prepare him for her imminent and (he trusts) more rewarding return. The very extravagance of the torch image, with its touch of absurdity in this context, is intended to suggest that he is not even fooling himself. As he reluctantly sinks back into the prosaic dreams of slumber which must serve as a substitute for that vastly superior dream he so nearly realized in the waking world, and the poem seems about to end disappointingly with the hackneyed 'revenge' conclusion, it is suddenly enlivened by his sly Parthian shot—the sexual pun in the final word 'die'.

> Perchance as torches, which must ready bee,
> Men light and put out, so thou deal'st with mee,
> Thou cam'st to kindle, goest to come; Then I
> Will dreame that hope againe, but else would die.

The well-known ambivalence of the concluding word compresses brilliantly in this context a polarization of the two selves in the poem —the idealized devotion of the Petrarchan male wasting away to death through grief at his unrequited passion and, together with it, the more pragmatic concerns of a libertine lover eager to consummate his love in the flesh. It is as usual more than mere word-play, crystallizing as it does the ambiguity sustained throughout the poem whereby ideal and flesh, reality and dream overlap, blend, and usurp each other's realms. In a world where fair ladies excel in their beauty the idealized angels of their lovers' dreams, and men can continue in sleep those dreams frustrated in the waking world, the distinctions between fantasy and fact become mercifully blurred. The objective and concrete become bathed in an exotic aura of reverie, while the chimerical is charged with the vividness and clarity of truth. It is this rare duality that raises it so far above the nugatory poem of Gorges and Watson both in its humour and its delicate perceptiveness.

'The Dreame' is clearly a lighter piece, amusing and fanciful; but, like so many of the secular poems, it embodies within its casual form a view of the universe which pervades Donne's serious as well as his less committed writings. The danger of assuming any direct chronological progression from secular to sacred has been widely acknowledged by critics, particularly as it is likely that some of the devotional poems were written during what was once regarded as his secular period. A poet of Donne's mercurial disposition who, if we are to judge from his verse, could punctuate the gravest discourse with sudden flashes of wit, and deepen the resonance of a flippant comment by a grim reminder of the tomb, would be unlikely in real life to have compartmentalized his religious and secular concerns. In a study of almost any other poet it would be unjustifiable, perhaps even ludicrous, to search for themes unifying the serious verse with those occasional poems thrown off in a humorous mood. T. S. Eliot's 'Macavity, the Mystery Cat' is scarcely the source for deepening one's understanding of *The Waste Land*;[19] but there can be no such distinction in Donne's work. His intermingling of spirit and flesh, of imagination and fact, creates in the light-hearted and the profligate poems as well as in the devotional hymns a series of shifting or merging planes of reality which do more to invest his poetry with its strictly metaphysical quality than that extravagant linking of heterogeneous ideas to which the latter has so long been attributed. When Dryden applied the term 'metaphysical' to Donne's verse, he used it in the more technical sense, derived from the title which had been arbitrarily affixed to Aristotle's work by his editor Nicodemus because it happened to come 'After the *Physics*' in his collected works.[20] Dryden meant it to denote, like the content of that book, theoretical and philosophical speculation, his purpose being to chide Donne for troubling the minds of the fair sex with abstruse philosophical reasoning when the ladies wished to hear of the pleasant dalliance of love. The label, however, has in the course of time become firmly affixed, and I suspect that it has done so to no small extent because of the more popular meaning of the term; for readers recognized instinctively that Donne concerned himself quite literally with the *meta*physical, that which lay beyond the physical, in a manner distinctive even in the realm of poetry, which is by its very nature more sensitive to the world of imaginative experience. Whether it be in an apparently trivial poem such as 'The Flea' or a tender parting such as 'Sweetest Love', Donne comprehends simultaneously and with extraordinary vividness the factual and emotional strata of human experience not as a mere amalgamation of equally valid entities but with a gradual yielding of his own allegiance to the spiritual essence which informs the actual—energizing, distorting, and transforming it out of its natural shape into a new and haunting reality of its own.

V

THE PARADOX OF FAITH

As we turn from Donne's light-hearted or tender love poems to the sombre devotional verse, there is an unexpected effect of *déjà vu*— a strange mingling of the familiar and the unfamiliar. The insolent philandering in a lady's chamber, and the satirical mocking at court fashions have indeed been replaced by the grave self-communing of an ascetic, meditating within a cloister or chapel. Yet if the bravura pose has evaporated together with the sly humour, and the theme is now the damnation of the soul instead of the pleasures of the flesh or love's ecstasies, there is none the less an over-all impression of a deepening continuity rather than a sudden break with the past. The scene and mood have darkened, but Donne's silhouette remains distinct within the gloom. He had, in fact, not repudiated his earlier concerns but allowed those themes submerged in his secular verse to rise to the surface and gain a new prominence in their religious setting. For even in the most outrageous and apparently blasphemous gestures of his early poetry, when his lovers, clasped in erotic embrace, had invoked the sacraments of the Church to image forth their love, the effect had been, in Donne's delicate handling, a purification of the earthly rather than a sullying of the divine. Moreover, in such poems as 'The Expiration', from behind the façade of ingenious word-play and hyperbolic image could be heard the vibrations of a more solemn concern with death and the eternity of the soul. In a sense, Donne's development from the Melancholy Lover—the pose he adopted for his youthful Lothian portrait—to the impassioned, yet still melancholy preacher of the later years involved a smoother transition than might at first appear. The superscription he chose for that early portrait, *Illumina tenebras nostras, Domina*, like so much of his verse, both parodies and affirms his deepest needs. Whimsically addressed here to his mortal mistress, it is none the less the same prayer as permeated his religious writing, the plea for light to illumine the darkness of his soul.

This inner continuity which, belying the surface differences, unites the secular with the devotional poetry, is of more than biographical interest, pointing as it does to a central feature of his literary achievement both as preacher and religious poet. For although he had moved out of the glare of the world into the silence of the study, he had taken with him that restless imagination and sharp intellectual curiosity which had helped to create the dramatic liveliness of his amatory verse. The latter surprises us by the sacramental quality which gradually permeates a vividly conceived and often erotic realism. In the religious verse the roles are reversed, as the predominantly devotional theme draws much of its vigour from the secular world of maritime navigation, medicine, the playhouse, cosmography and, not least, the most explicitly physical aspects of human love. It is not merely, as has so often been stated, that this mingling of sacred and profane is intended to shock, but that, although the focus of his interest might shift, Donne preserved throughout his life a remarkable catholicity of vision which in its instinctive validation of paradox, was more acutely aware of the subtle interrelationship of these two elements than of any artificially imposed divisions. He was temperamentally incapable of cutting himself off from the mundane and devoting himself exclusively to the divine; and this trait was destined to trouble him sorely during his ecclesiastical years. Inevitably it conflicted with the more conventional views of an ascetically oriented Church, with its traditional advocacy of a dichotomy between the spirit and the flesh. However, what Donne wearily regarded as a failing in his religious sensibility—his irrepressible interest in the everyday actuality about him—formed, in fact, a major source of his literary vigour. In a passage of self-mortification in which he castigates himself for this weakness, the prose leaps into life precisely because of that accuracy of perception which he bemoans:

I throw my selfe downe in my Chamber, and I call in, and invite God, and his Angels thither, and when they are there, I neglect God and his Angels for the noise of a Flie, for the ratling of a Coach, for the whining of a doore; I talke on, in the same posture of praying; Eyes lifted up; knees bowed downe; as though I prayed to God: and, if God, or his Angels should aske me, when I thought last of God in that prayer, I cannot tell: Sometimes I finde that I had forgot what I was about, but when I began to forget it, I cannot tell. A memory of yesterdays pleasures, a feare of to morrows dangers, a straw under my knee, a noise in mine eare, a light in mine eye, an any thing, a nothing, a fancy, a Chimera in my braine, troubles me in my prayer. So certainely is there nothing, nothing in spirituall things, perfect in this world.[1]

This supposed 'imperfection' in Donne's character, besides ensuring that his religious writing would retain the vividness of imagery which distinguished his secular verses, performed a passive function too. It proved an invaluable prophylactic against the most common weakness of devotional writing. Religious poetry is intrinsically a more treacherous vehicle than secular verse. It can too easily collapse into self-righteous sentimentality or theological cliché for reasons inherent in the religious impulse itself. That desire for original ideas or lively images which animates the secular poet tends to be replaced in hymnal writing by a need on the poet's part to attest to the orthodoxy of his beliefs and to his unreserved acceptance of official church doctrine; and what may be commendable in the eyes of his bishop, frequently proves disastrous for the author's poetic sensibility. There is, of course, the occasional exception, the poem of untroubled faith which soars above dull pietism, catching with refreshing unselfconsciousness a moment of genuine religious communion:

> How fresh, O Lord, how sweet and clean
> Are thy returns! ev'n as the flowers in spring;
> To which, besides their own demean,
> The late-past frosts tributes of pleasure bring.
> Grief melts away
> Like snow in May,
> As if there were no such cold thing.
>
> Who would have thought my shrivell'd heart
> Could have recover'd greennesse? It was gone
> Quite under ground; as flowers depart
> To see their mother-root, when they have blown;

> Where they together,
> All the hard weather,
> Dead to the world, keep house unknown.

But such moments are uncommon enough in devotional poetry. Some years ago Lord David Cecil, in his introduction to *The Oxford Book of Christian Verse*, warned his readers not to expect too much, as so large a proportion of religious verse is of poor quality; and he attributed the comparative paucity of great Christian poetry to the fact that in general the poet writing on religious themes '. . . does not say what he really feels, but what he thinks he ought to feel'. He imagines he should offer only the most unexceptionable sentiments in terms and symbols sanctified by usage and, as a result, speaks not in his own voice but in the solemn tones that seem fitting to his solemn subject. C. S. Lewis, on the other hand, in reviewing the anthology, felt that the more positive aspects of religious verse were being underplayed, and with his customary wit reversed the dictum to define that area in which devotional poetry has achieved its greatest literary success—when the poet takes as his subject not what he ought to feel, but '. . . the fact that he did not feel as he ought'.[2] In other words, when the theme approaches Christian *humility*, and is concerned with the poet's sense of failure, his yearning for redemption, or his near despair, then the complacent conviction of personal salvation or the dutiful affirmation of orthodox principles which so often lead to mawkishness, evaporate. Even George Herbert's 'The Flower', from which the above quotation was taken, although it appears so ingenuous in its trust, in fact draws its poetic strength from the sense of unworthiness which underlies it, the wonder that such calm should have succeeded the previous turbulence of his soul:

> And now in age I bud again,
> After so many deaths I live and write;
> I once more smell the dew and rain,
> And relish versing: O my onely light,
>   It cannot be
>   That I am he
> On whom the tempests fell all night.

Donne's natural penchant for the perverse, the complex, and the contradictory afforded him a rare protection against that pietism which has spoilt so much religious verse. In so far as anything is predictable in human affairs, one might have foretold from the dialectical subtlety of his earlier writing that his progress towards faith would never end in a quiet acceptance of orthodox belief, nor indeed in any secure conviction of his own salvation. For that reason, the comparison offered by his most recent biographer, R. C. Bald, is misleading. Bald discerned in the religious melancholia of Donne's Mitcham period, with its brooding upon damnation and decay a classic instance of the 'sick soul' as defined in William James's *Varieties of Religious Experience*. Such a soul, congenitally morbid, is, James informs us, oppressed by a pervasive sense of personal guilt or sin, and a belief that it is irrevocably cut off from true repentance and divine forgiveness, until a blinding conversion suddenly trans-figures the world and suffuses the previously divided soul with a new sense of spiritual integrity and contentment. Bald equates this melancholy period of Donne's life with the gloomy disillusionment of Bunyan and Tolstoy before the moment of their spiritual revela-tion,[3] and like many earlier critics, he quotes to substantiate this picture of Donne's hopelessness and dread the lines:

> I dare not move my dimme eyes any way,
> Despaire behind, and death before doth cast
> Such terrour, and my feebled flesh doth waste
> By sinne in it, which it t'wards hell doth weigh.

It has long been recognized that Donne experienced no sudden conversion to faith—there is no hint of such an epiphany as Bunyan's or Tolstoy's throughout his writings. But Bald's identification of Donne as a Jamesian 'sick soul' does imply that the Mitcham phase was the dark prelude to a later spiritual calm, while in fact that tortured, dissatisfied, and self-searching mood was to be the per-manent motive force of both his poetry and prose, as well as one of its most distinguished features. Certainly on entering the Church Donne was relieved of his more immediate financial pressures, and in time found a deepening satisfaction in his vocation as a preacher; but he continued throughout his years to be by his very nature more acutely aware of the straitness of the gate leading to eternal life, and the weight of sins he had accumulated than of the promise awaiting fulfilment. It was that awareness which lent the note of urgency and personal involvement even to the latest of his sermons.

> . . . when we looke upon our own weaknesse and unworthinesse, we cry out *Wretched men that wee are, who shall deliver us from the body of death?* For though we have the Spirit of life in us, we have a body of death upon us. How loving soever my Soule be, it will not stay in a diseased body; How loving soever the Spirit of life be, it will not stay in a diseased soule . . .[4]

He was too well versed in the writings of the church fathers and the subtleties of medieval theology to imagine that, apart from death-bed repentance, any single declaration or act of faith during a man's lifetime could win the assurance of eternal redemption; and the anguished knowledge that there lay before him a daily and even hourly struggle with sin and despair, which only the release of soul from body would end, allowed him to transfer to his devotional works the tensions, dislocation of argument, and validation of paradox which had characterized his amatory verse.

In this light, the bond linking profane with divine love in his secular poetry can be seen retrospectively to have been no casual image; for the contradictions and complexities which he had discerned in the relationship between man and woman were now projected with greater fervour to his own exploration of the relationship between man and God. Indeed, that very poem from which Bald quoted to illustrate Donne's unmitigated despair in the Mitcham period can be seen rather as revealing the intricacy of Donne's spiritual condition and his ability to wrest directly out of his despair the sustaining if limited hope on which he was to place his trust. Read in isolation the lines quoted above do express the panic of a doomed soul caught inescapably between despair and death. But the poem does not end there. It moves at once from despondency to comfort:

> Onely thou art above, and when towards thee
> By thy leave I can looke, I rise again;

In the hands of almost any other religious poet, the sonnet might

have closed here on a note of quiet faith; but Donne will have none
of it. His restless mind resists the hint of complacency the lines
imply, and he thrusts it aside with the inevitable 'but', familiar
from his amatory verse, as he reminds himself and us that Satan is
not so easily to be vanquished. There are no sudden hosannas in
heaven to mark the salvation of a soul as it pronounces its declaration of faith, but rather a long and agonizing fight with weakness
and temptation which must continue until death closes the account.
Ultimately his hope can rest only in that paradox which was to loom
so large in the final period of his writing, the sole means of accom-
modating the conflicting assertions of intellect and faith. This hope
achieves its formulation in the image of the sonnet's closing line—
the strange possibility that the stubbornness of his *iron* heart, which
seems to disqualify him for redemption, may prove eventually to
be the very quality making it susceptible to the magnetic force of
divine love:

> But our old subtle foe so tempteth me,
> That not one houre I can my selfe sustaine;
> Thy grace may wing me to prevent his art
> And thou like Adamant draw mine iron heart.

That closing image may, in fact, serve as the key to Donne's
religious writing as a whole. His obstinate determination to wrestle
both with God and himself to the last second of his existence upon
earth might well appear to be a religious failing, as it so often did to
Donne himself. But it contains within it a much higher estimation
than any conventional view would offer, of the spiritual battle to be
fought and the rigorous demands to be made upon the human soul.
Unlike so many penitents, he never discards his past sins as having
been atoned for by his self-reformation and by his determination to
sin no more. On the contrary, Donne seems to reach back to them in
need, almost to treasure them so that he may drive himself to greater
remorse and learn from their burning lusts how to cauterize his soul:

> But oh it must be burnt! alas the fire
> Of lust and envie have burnt it heretofore,
> And made it fouler; Let their flames retire,
> And burne me o Lord, with a fiery zeale
> Of thee and thy house, which doth in eating heale.

Donne's need for subtlety and complexity even in matters of faith—or perhaps most of all in a matter so momentous to him as faith—afforded him, therefore, a natural resistance to some of the main dangers of religious poetry. He was by no means entirely immune and, as in his secular verse, his ingenuity could lead him at times to excesses which reduce a supposedly devotional poem to the level of a mere game. There are, I suspect, few readers who, even if they are familiar with the typological tradition of the church fathers, can respond with any real sympathy to his far-fetched discovery of symbolic crosses in almost everything around him:

> Swimme, and at every stroake, thou art thy Crosse,
> The Mast and yard make one, where seas do tosse.
> Looke downe, thou spiest out Crosses in small things;
> Looke up, thou seest birds rais'd on crossed wings;
> All the Globes frame, and spheares, is nothing else
> But the Meridians crossing Parallels.
> Materiall Crosses then, good physicke bee,
> And yet spirituall have chiefe dignity.[5]

There are more persuasive methods of indicating divine omnipresence; and the weakness of the theme is reflected here in the dullness of the poetic form, notably in the regularly end-stopped lines which show no trace of the metrical subtlety visible when Donne's thoughts and emotions are genuinely engaged. Similarly, he can occasionally fall into the pietism he normally shuns—almost as though he had decided that an exercise in formal devotionalism was a necessary step in the fulfilment of his religious duties. Both 'A Litanie' and 'La Corona' desert the anxious self in favour of more general theological themes, and as a result a declamatory and consciously laudatory tone replaces there the usual urgency and resilience of his verse. Even Donne, then, can nod. On the other hand, no poet in the English language with the possible exception of Hopkins has, at his best, produced devotional verse of such poetic intensity and structural tautness—passionate in its commitment, and yet in the midst of that commitment acutely aware of the contradictions and the dangers inherent in belief itself.

Donne's distrust of conventional, established belief as a mere papering over of spiritual chasms is reflected in his tendency to overthrow the entire spectrum of values adopted by his contemporaries in assessing the human condition. In his later phase, he rejects all four dimensions as invalid standards of measurement—time now has meaning for him only in terms of death and eternity, place is irrelevant if the imagination is engaged elsewhere, and the material becomes immaterial as its spiritual essence is perceived. But this was a process discernible in a modified form even in his earlier writings. Stylistically, this challenging of accepted norms had been exemplified by one of his most characteristic features, those arresting opening lines which compel immediate attention by their explosive passion, their patent absurdity, or their idiosyncratic pose. The degree of Donne's deepening suspicion of the conventional is, however, expressed in the new way this stylistic device is employed. In both the love poetry and the religious, its function is, of course, to jolt the reader out of familiar preconceptions; but in its specific effect it ranges, like his use of paradox, from the trivial to the profound. In a more casual mood, his purpose is no more than to offer a mild parody of Petrarchan tradition by exposing the foolish extravagance of its assumptions. With mock seriousness, its imagery is pushed to ridiculous extremes—'When I dyed last . . .', or 'For the first twenty yeares since yesterday . . .'; and with echoes of those student exercises in wit, Donne proceeds ingeniously to defend the extravagances in terms of the very convention he is mocking.

At times, however, the technique of surprise takes on a greater seriousness both in weakening an established mode and in preparing the way for a subsequent assertion of new values. 'For Godsake hold your tongue and let me love . . .' is intended to disrupt that gentle, melodious tradition of the lyric in which the wan lover querulously pines away in fashionable passivity. It presents with welcome freshness the image of a more aggressive, volatile, and altogether more virile male angrily protecting the privacy of his love against the meddlesome incursions of inquisitive outsiders. Yet, by its abrasiveness, it serves too the important literary function of eliciting from the reader a readiness to discard previous assumptions and, in a more receptive frame of mind, to await with some curiosity the unconventional ideas on love that are about to be developed in the poem. Our responses have been manipulated in advance to make us amen-

8. Zuccaro. Doorway of Casa Zuccaro, Rome

9. Tintoretto, *The Presentation of the Virgin*

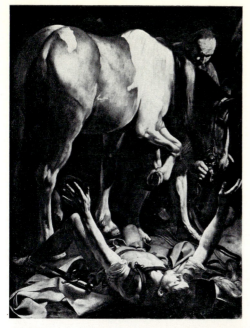

10. Caravaggio, *The Conversion of St. Paul*

11. Zurbaran, *The Vision of St. Peter Nolasco*

12. Bernini, *The Ecstasy of St. Teresa*

able to the originality of approach, whereby the almost sacrilegious particularity of ecclesiastical allusion within 'The Canonization' will transform the overworked love–saint equation of contemporary verse into a genuine sanctification of love. In this respect, the initial shock-device shows signs of approaching the solemnity of its usage within the body of the religious poetry, where an opening line such as 'What if this present were the worlds last night?' plucks us out of the leisurely world of courtly love and profane mistresses into a sudden confrontation with the immediacy of death and the need for spiritual repentance before the day of doom that is almost upon us.

Although Donne was almost alone among English poets of his period in the audacity with which he challenged or overthrew convention as a means of provoking a more fundamental reappraisal of outlook, or, to use Carew's description, of committing '. . . holy rapes upon our will', he is far from being an isolated figure within the broader patterns of European culture. One aspect of this Counter-Reformation context, his indebtedness to the meditative tradition, has been familiar to every student of Donne since Helen Gardner and Louis Martz reached their conclusions almost simultaneously.[6] In defining this indebtedness, Martz drew particular attention to the visual as well as the literary parallels of the time by choosing as the frontispiece for his book Georges de la Tour's *La Madeleine au Miroir*. It depicts the Magdalene as a Loyolan disciple gazing deep in thought at the reflection of a skull in the mirror before her, seeing as in a glass darkly the implications of mortality. In exploring the relationship between metaphysical poetry and the meditative mode, Martz concentrates primarily on establishing structural affinities such as the threefold sequence of memory, understanding, and will, which typified the Loyolan meditation and which, he argues, is discernible in much of the associated poetry. In analysing the first of these sections, memory, whereby the meditator attempts to conjure up the scene of a holy martyrdom before proceeding to apply the lessons to himself, Martz remarks on the greater vividness this practice lends to the opening passages of meditative poems, and he offers a particularly valuable comment in distinguishing between the initial brusqueness introducing most of Donne's holy sonnets, which corresponds to the more vigorous Jesuit train of meditation, and the 'silent tears' and gentler images of Herbert's poems reflecting the later form inaugurated by St. François de Sales. The latter had advocated '. . . a certain mildness and effortless ease' in the process of meditation. However, in general Martz has proved to be more valuable to the historian seeking the sources to which such poetry is indebted than to the critic attempting to discern the full literary implications of the poems themselves and the means whereby they achieve their effects.

In fact, there is far more to these turbulent openings of Donne's poems than has been recognized and they should be regarded less as an offshoot of the religious meditative tradition, than as expressing in literary form that central Counter-Reformation philosophy, of which the meditation formed one facet. The *Spiritual Exercises* had applied to devotional practices its desire to encourage a new spirit of self-dedication and personal purity within the Church; but in the literary and the plastic arts too that same impulse was at work, exploiting the means afforded by the different media to subvert the firmly established this-worldliness of the Renaissance and to replace the current faith in vigorous self-assertion by an introspective yearning for revelatory truth. It may, therefore, prove helpful to examine once again the effect this impulse produced in contemporary painting in order to apply the insights such a study may offer to a reading of the poems themselves; for the techniques they employ are, as we shall see, remarkably close to those developed in Donne's verse.

The religious paintings by Tintoretto, El Greco, and Rosso are patently devotional in their intent, the canvases quivering, as it were, with the mystical fervour of the artist. But it should be recalled that the same had not held true for the religious paintings of the High Renaissance. On the contrary, the aesthetic modes of the earlier period had demanded from even the most deeply committed Christian that, in his artistic depiction of biblical scenes, personal ardour should be subordinated to the newly adopted classical principles of harmony and restraint. His purpose was to create an impression of tranquil beauty, and the contemporary identification of beauty as a universal concept meant that it embraced all forms of art. Consequently, without a glance at the title, it is frequently impossible to distinguish religious from secular paintings. Had Da Vinci's *Mona Lisa*, the portrait of a Florentine lady, been originally named *The Madonna of the Folded Hands* I doubt whether anyone would ever have queried its religious character. In its gentle benevolence and serene countenance it stands clearly within the tradition of the numerous Madonna paintings being executed at that time by Perugino and others. And the reverse holds equally true. Where there is no distinguishing halo, a sacred figure from the Scriptures often becomes interchangeable with its pagan counterpart, and in general the trappings or setting offer little assistance. Titian's voluptuous *Magdalene*, coyly attempting to conceal her naked breasts in her long golden tresses, is a strange representative of the Christian faith to set beside his clothed, decorous, but technically pagan *Flora*; and it is obvious that the two were painted from the same model, as though the subject-matter of the painting were immaterial.

These are not chance anomalies but symptomatic of the overlapping of Christianity and heathenism implicit in the Renaissance itself. The rise in the status of the Virgin Mary in the later Middle Ages, with its introduction of a new matriarchal quality into Christianity, was almost certainly prompted by the need to provide a counter-force to the growing cult of Venus.[7] Those artists interested in identifying the mythological figures of classical antiquity with those of Christian history—whether as a mere excuse for their artistic depiction (as occurred during the transition from the Middle Ages), or in a genuine attempt to discern an underlying unity between the two traditions—had found in the Virgin the nearest equivalent to Venus, the classical goddess of Love; and the distinction between divine and human love was, of course, less clearly marked in a period impregnated with Christian Platonism. At all events, the Church, alarmed at this growing identification, retaliated by re-emphasizing the Virgin's chastity, to the extent even of suppressing the explicit references in the Gospel to Jesus' brothers and sisters (preferring to refer to them as 'cousins') in order that no hint of concupiscence be attached to so immaculate a personage. But the blurring of borders continued none the less, accounting, among numerous examples, for the otherwise incongruous presence in the centre of Botticelli's pagan *Primavera* of a typical Virgin Mary figure taken, as it were, straight out of a stained-glass chapel window. It accounts also for the phenomenon (which seems so far-fetched to a twentieth-century viewer) that so obviously heathen and erotic a theme as the rapes of Io, Danae, and Europa iconographically represented for the public of that day the snatching up of the Christian soul by the divine spirit. Only when we note the holy cherubs flitting with indulgent smiles above the scenes in Veronese's *Europa* or the self-conscious piety of the raped maiden in Guido Reni's version does it become apparent how deeply within the consciousness of this era was embedded this blending of the secular and the religious traditions.

This intertwining of the pagan and Christian worlds explains to some extent the rarity of any deep religious passion or emotional involvement within the devotional paintings of the time. Perhaps even without this overlapping, one may presume that the contemporary idealization of harmonious order would itself have produced a corresponding tendency among religious painters to emphasize the tranquil beauty of the holy scenes in order to evoke in the viewer a quiet confirmation of rationalist faith. Raphael's choice of the Madonna as a recurrent motif suggests in itself a proclivity for scenes of maternal, pastoral serenity, but even those biblical subjects which were by their nature dramatic, revelatory, disturbing, or miraculous were toned down by a delicate blending of colour, and careful balancing of the figures to produce a predominantly quiescent effect. Titian's *Noli Me Tangere*, painted in the full High Renaissance tradition, is exquisitely balanced, with the curving body of Jesus as he gently draws his shroud away from the Magdalene's touch delicately offset by a tree leaning slightly in the opposite direction and itself continuing the flowing line of the Magdalene's cloak. It requires a conscious effort to recall that in its original setting within the Gospels, this scene is one not of peaceful rusticity but of dramatic and awesome revelation—the first human confrontation with the risen Jesus. In Titian's version, the drama has been modified, filtered through the Renaissance imagination with its preference for an integrated serenity, and there is no hint in the painting of surprise or even of supernatural manifestation.

In contrast, the mannerist painter aims at a violent disruption of tranquillity. His purpose is to recapture the emotional shock of the original scene and thereby to compel the viewer to share vicariously in the spiritual upheaval of its participants. The painting is, in fact, a pictorial equivalent of the meditative exercise whereby Loyola exhorted his disciples to concentrate their thoughts upon a specific moment of torture, bliss, or epiphany experienced by a martyr or saint, to attempt imaginatively to relive that moment by visualizing the suffering or elation even in the smallest details, and hence to fulfil emotionally if not physically the ultimate Christian ideal of *imitatio Dei*. It was an exercise dangerously open to abuse, and was no doubt in large part responsible for such excesses as the notorious incident at Loudun where the nuns whipped themselves into orgiastic and murderous frenzies in the belief that they were fulfilling the dictates of their order. It produced too a morbid interest in dripping wounds, excruciating suffering, and blissful pieties; but in its original form as propounded by Ignatius, it was a sober exercise in contemplation, intended to heighten the religious dedication and ascetic commitment of the Christian by creating within him an imaginative empathy with the leading saints and martyrs of the Church at the climactic moments of their spiritual fulfilment. Moreover, it encouraged a revitalizing of the internalized world of the Jesuit and a consequent displacement of material reality, in that respect typifying the central theme of the Counter-Reformation in its resistance to the new materialism and 'this-worldliness' both of Protestantism and of the Renaissance at large.

The mannerist painter, therefore, in reflecting this meditative tradition had a dual purpose—to recreate the vivid emotional impact of the original scene and at the same time to draw the viewer into the event itself by establishing a sense of personal identification with its central figures. This assault on the viewer was not a casual side-product, but part of the artist's conscious design; and one of the most effective means for achieving it, which was to become characteristic of such paintings, was the use of a *repoussoir* figure mediating between the spectator and the epiphany itself. Instead of merely pointing didactically towards it like the donor in a medieval painting, he is himself intimately involved, often a major participant in the drama, caught at the moment of shock. Flung backwards by the force of the vision—almost, as it were, into the arms of the spectator—he lies prostrate, compelling us to share his astonishment, and, at the same time, to gaze at the revelation through his eyes from an impressively new vantage point below. Like Donne's startling first lines, this artistic device demands that we desert any preconceptions and adjust to a fresh way of viewing the world. In Caravaggio's *Conversion of St. Paul* (Plate 10) the canvas is dominated by a very ordinary piebald horse raising one hoof as it carefully steps over a supine figure. Without the lower section of the painting, it would be a pleasant but unremarkable depiction of a natural scene with a peasant patiently holding the horse's head; yet taken as a whole, the canvas vibrates with dramatic force, its energy emanating explosively from the ground where Paul lies stunned by the vision, his arms thrust out, half to ward off and half to welcome the blinding revelation. Technically there is no epiphany to be seen— no miraculous healing, no angelic annunciation, no divine manifestation; only a horse and peasant bathed in a strong but perfectly natural light. The epiphany here is internalized, comprehended emotionally rather than visually as, from the uncustomary angle of the prostrate form, the familiar is made suddenly to appear unfamiliar.[8]

This device of creating a spiritual upheaval by means of a displaced angle of vision is reiterated throughout the religious paintings of the period with sufficient refinement of variation to preserve the sense of shock or surprise. In Tintoretto's *St. Mark Rescuing the Slave* the emotional disturbance is increased by a twofold and interconnected inversion of perspective. The prostrate Christian slave calling for divine aid in the extremity of his torture has been answered by the saint who swoops earthward in a headlong plunge from above, appearing in foreshortened as well as inverted form. Below him the slave lies prone, sloping backwards towards us at an angle to the saint's flight, creating a dizzying spiral of reversals which violate the outward calm of the painting with its curious bystanders oblivious of the vision above their heads. We, like the slave, are caught up in the twisting movement, isolated with him from the ordinary world around, where even the instruments of

physical torture being applied to the slave's head recede into un-
importance beside the revelatory impact of the vision. In both the
Caravaggio and this Tintoretto, the *repoussoir* figure is the central
figure of the scene, but in the latter's *Removal of the Body of St. Mark*
(Plate 3) the same effect is achieved by opposite means. There the
group carrying the body, who together constitute the sacred
element, are completely serene, unhurried, and undisturbed; but
the spectators depicted within the painting—the *Sprecher* drawing
aside the curtain theatrically to reveal the scene, the ghostly shapes
fleeing in terror, and the central figure holding the camel's rope
writhe in spasms of ecstasy or fear as though electrified by the
spiritual charge of the event. We are meant to experience through
them the mingling of joy and terror inspired at the time. Similarly El Greco, in his more complex and symbolically structured
Resurrection splits the canvas across the middle. The inverted soldier
thrown head over heels by the miracle serves as the mortal or
terrestrial reflection of the risen Christ, their feet almost touching
in the centre of the picture. It suggests in pictorial form the literal
'conversion' of the pagan who has in his astonishment been somer-
saulted into a totally new conception of the world by the miraculous
disruption of natural law.

The immediate shock effect of such inversion upon the viewer is
perhaps best exemplified by Zurburan's *Vision of St. Peter Nolasco*
(Plate 11) where the saint is depicted as he kneels before an apparition of the original St. Peter hanging inverted on the cross. There
is nothing original in the subject matter itself—the nailing of St.
Peter head downward is fully in accordance with Christian tradition;
but the pictorial presentation is surprising. Where a Renaissance
artist would have included the apparition in smaller perspective
above, like the angelic visitant in Bellini's *Agony in the Garden*
(Plate 4), or a medieval artist in a larger perspective with a tiny saint
or donor in the foreground, Zurburan has deliberately preserved
an equilibrium of size and positioning between the two figures, one
of which appears to be standing on its head. As a result, the initial
impression as one approaches the picture is a puzzled suspicion that
it has been mistakenly hung upside down, and the viewer must, in
effect adjust himself to the reversed and valid perspective rather

than be gently absorbed into a harmonious scene as he is in the *Noli Me Tangere*. Such paintings, in other words, by their disruption of conventional iconographic order, impose upon the spectator a need to undergo a disturbing spiritual reorientation in order to respond to the artist's unconventional vision of the world. The same holds true of the use of colouring as a means of wresting the viewer out of the mood of calm reverence with which he had been accustomed to approach religious paintings. Rosso's *Descent from the Cross*, an otherwise naturalistic representation of the Deposition, is by its weird hues made strikingly unreal as the livid Jesus hangs drooping against a flat turquoise sky. The garishness of the colours recaptures expressionistically what the Renaissance had chosen to ignore—the supernatural turbulence of the scene as recorded in the Gospels when '. . . the earth did quake, and the rocks rent, and the graves were opened'.

These departures from Renaissance tradition, then, whether in the unexpected angle of vision, the convulsed figures with whom we are compelled to identify, the inversion of perspective, or the shocking hues, together aim at eliciting from the viewer a radical reappraisal of his place in the universe in the light of the specific miracle or revelation which serves as the focal point of the canvas. The serene, universalized Christianity of the Renaissance has been replaced by a striving for personal commitment and introspection, as the individual seeks within the scene for the significance it may offer to his inner self at the moment of enforced identification. There is a new sense of intimacy and urgency, as in the tradition of the Loyolan exercise, whereby the imaginative conjuring up of a holy scene is to be followed at once by its rigorous application to one's self and a questioning how far the responsibilities and duties it implies for the individual have been fulfilled by the meditator:

Imagine Christ our Lord before you, hanging upon the cross. Speak with Him of how, being the Creator He then became man, and how, possessing eternal life, He submitted to temporal death to die for our sins.

Then I shall meditate upon myself, and ask, 'What have I done for Christ? What am I now doing for Christ? What ought I do for Christ?'[9]

Within Donne's devotional poems and most notably within the

holy sonnets, the mannerist practice of assaulting the viewer's preconceptions by forcing him to participate emotionally in the drama of a holy scene is paralleled with remarkable vividness by the brusque opening lines—no longer employed as a device for catching the wandering interest of the reader but as an expression of the poet's personal exercise in meditative self-projection whose intensity irresistibly implicates the reader too. From the opening word of Holy Sonnet XI we are thrust into the full violence and turmoil of the crucifixion, sharply experiencing it from within through the eyes of Jesus himself as he is pierced, buffeted, and scourged:

> Spit in my face yee Jewes, and pierce my side,
> Buffet, and scoffe, scourge, and crucifie mee.

The sharpness of each word fulfils the Ignatian injunction to exploit all five senses in attempting to feel upon one's own flesh the flagellation or torture of the martyr in its full particularity as a prelude to the spiritual elevation or introspective despair at which the exercise is aimed.

However, the shock tactics are more complex than they appear. We are being drawn not merely into a dramatic re-enactment of the scene at Calvary, but almost unaware we have been seduced into accepting a totally new picture of the event, which contradicts the normal assumptions brought to the poem. Instead of the resigned and suffering Jesus of Gospel tradition, humbly bearing the cross upon his back in expiation of the sins of mankind, we are confronted with a bitter, exasperated Christ, taunting his persecutors to redouble his torments. What has happened to the traditional Lamb led willingly to the slaughter? The incident leaps into life as the tinted spectacles of conventional theology are discarded in favour of a direct visualization of Calvary in all its cruelty. Yet there is a further surprise in store, for at the very height of this sharpened actuality, the angle of vision suddenly shifts, and like the magnificent vistas and pillared terraces in the Vatican's Sala Clementina which flatten out to painted mannerist frescoes as one approaches, so here the following phrase proceeds to undermine the carefully created realism of the visualized scene and to return us to this world:

> Spit in my face, yee Jewes, and pierce my side,
> Buffet, and scoffe, scourge and crucifie mee,
> For I have sinn'd, and sinn'd . . .

Where in the Gospels, we ask ourselves in momentary puzzlement, did Jesus *sin*? And as we adjust to the new perspective it transpires that we have been witnessing not Jesus himself, as we had been so obviously led to believe, but the speaker's meditative reliving of the crucifixion in his own person. It is he who has sinned. The scene, in fact, just as in the religious paintings we have examined, is being viewed through the eyes of a speaker (or *Sprecher*) writhing in the foreground of the picture as he visualizes upon his own flesh the agony of the martyr:

> For I have sinn'd, and sinn'd, and onely hee,
> Who could do no iniquitie, hath dyed:

As the Jesuit meditator, after imaginatively re-enacting the crucifixion scene with himself in the central role, subsequently deflects the focus of his thoughts into his real self in order to examine how far he has fallen below the spiritual martyrdom at which he aims, so here, at the moment of the crucifixion our gaze is withdrawn from Jesus to the *repoussoir* figure, flung backwards by the force of the vision as he recognizes its implications for his own life, gazing at it from a markedly new angle and hence compelling us to see it with the full force of his own impassioned response. Within one quatrain, Donne has brilliantly constructed the literary parallel to that mannerist scene. There is the initial shock of revelation with its inversion of traditional values, the sudden dematerialization of actuality as the figure of Jesus merges into that of the speaker, and finally the establishment of a powerful bond between *persona* and reader to create a mood of brooding yet urgent introspection.

The main purpose of this initial shock technique, it will be recalled, is to lure the reader into a world of reversed standards where the Renaissance norms of reason and restraint are discarded in favour of the mystical fervour of the religionist. And here Donne's concern with the interplay of logic and anti-logic, with which we are familiar from his secular poems, reaches its fulfilment within this more solemn setting. In the *Songs and Sonets* it had functioned, in its amused tripping up of the reader, as a witty undermining of Reason's authority and as a means of hinting at spiritual values beyond the physical world. Now the previously tentative belief has been replaced by a firmer conviction that in matters of the spirit, the factual and the rational are nugatory beside the transcendent paradox. Although the tone is muted by a new intensity and the bravado has disappeared, the basic technique remains unchanged. Donne again thrusts at us an apparently impossible or absurdly exaggerated thesis in order to demonstrate by the subsequent validation of that extravagance the ultimate superiority of metaphor over literalism and hence of faith over the pragmatic. The introspective colloquy which follows the opening lines of the holy sonnet we have just been examining illustrates that literary technique at work; but to analyse its movement we shall need to see the sonnet as a whole:

> Spit in my face yee Jewes, and pierce my side,
> Buffet, and scoffe, scourge, and crucifie mee,
> For I have sinn'd, and sinn'd, and onely hee,
> Who could do no iniquitie, hath dyed:
> But by my death can not be satisfied
> My sinnes, which passe the Jewes impiety:
> They kill'd once an inglorious man, but I
> Crucifie him daily, being now glorified.
> Oh let mee then, his strange love still admire:
> Kings pardon, but he bore our punishment.
> And *Jacob* came cloth'd in vile harsh attire
> But to supplant, and with gainfull intent:
> God cloth'd himselfe in vile mans flesh, that so
> Hee might be weake enough to suffer woe.

After so vivid a re-enactment in the opening lines of the brutality and viciousness of Christ's persecutors, there seems a certain perversity in the speaker's new claim that his own sins '. . . passe the Jewes impiety' and hence can never merit atonement even through death. What crime in Christian eyes, we wonder, could possibly exceed the murder of Jesus himself, traditionally attributed to the Jews? The twist of reasoning here, as so often in Donne's writing, appears at first sight to be merely casuistic. At the time of the crucifixion, he seems to argue, Jesus had not yet risen to assume his godly form; technically, therefore, their crime was of lesser magnitude. But the reasoning has deeper implications, echoing as it does a verse from the Christian Bible, which is picked up by the word 'Crucifie'. As the initial word of a strongly enjambed line, it carries a powerful metrical emphasis, so that the latter part of the sonnet seems to hinge upon it. The verse from Hebrews 6: 5 to which it alludes is, in its original context, no more than a passing metaphor, warning against the dangers of backsliding. It is impossible, the verse says, for those who '. . . have tasted the good word of God and the powers of the world to come, if they shall fall away to renew them again unto repentance; seeing they crucify to themselves the Son of God afresh, and put him to an open shame'. For Donne the image has become transformed into fact. To deny the Messiah after his revelation has, in this mood of spiritual self-searching, become an infinitely greater act of betrayal than the slaying of a mere mortal in ignorance of his identity; and within the meditative tradition which has just transcended time and place to create an imaginative reliving of Calvary, the distinction between the actual and the metaphorical crucifixion of Jesus dwindles away to irrelevancy. The hyperbolic self-accusation has been substantiated and hence is, in its final impact, by no means casuistic. And Donne accentuates the relatively greater burden of his own sin by the wry admission that where the Jews transgressed only *once*, his own sin has been *daily*.

We return here to the central theme of the sonnet—his own unremitting or *daily* struggle against unbelief, which he acknowledges as an inseparable part of his stubborn will. From this recognition of his guilt, the sestet moves towards the sole hope in which Donne can ever find consolation—the paradox (as in the stubbornness of his iron will) that his own human weakness may here prove more pertinent to his salvation than his supposed strengths. It is a hope which defies all logical norms. The sonnet had begun with the speaker's longing to scourge his flesh in order to atone for his mortal sins, until he sadly realized that he had '. . . sinn'd and sinn'd' beyond the reach of self-atonement. His position, therefore, is desperate; but he recalls with relief that according to Christian doctrine it was precisely *because* man was weak, sinned in the flesh, and suffered mortal woe that Jesus deigned to join man in that weak, mortal garb and suffer the woe on his behalf. The 'strange love' of Jesus, Donne argues, is strange because of its reversal of human norms. He came not with personal, gainful intent like Jacob, nor as a king condescendingly to pardon the condemned, but in defiance of worldly concepts of justice, in order to take upon himself the punishment for the weakness of men—of those, like the speaker, whose sins cannot be satisfied by their own death. In that illogicality, which reassuringly reverses the otherwise unequivocal evidence of his own damnation, his hope must reside. From the purely poetic viewpoint, this paradoxical conclusion wins credence because the potential opposition or hesitancy of the reader has been so effectively disarmed by the abrupt transmutation of values in the opening quatrain. There we were whirled into the passionate re-enactment of a meditative colloquoy in which the factual world evaporated before the imaginative experience. By the time we reach the final couplet, therefore, the assertion of the Christian mystery which contradicts the dictates of the mind appears not only credible, but even natural. And that, of course, was the primary purpose of the meditative exercises themselves, to move beyond material reality, to identify with the realm of the spirit, and hence to '. . . excitate the will to holy affections and resolutions'.[10]

One need hardly add that, if such was the purpose of the meditative exercise within the religious sphere, it corresponded to the purpose shared by all poetry—to persuade us, by its subtle play upon the mind and the emotions, of the authenticity of an imaginative reality which either transcends or unifies the mundane and disparate elements of human existence. In this respect, the devotional task which Donne set himself in his religious poetry was identical with his task as a poet, and the techniques of persuasion or self-persuasion which he employed are poetic techniques while they yet belong within the historical setting of the meditative tradition. In George Herbert's poetry, for example, perhaps because he is indebted to that milder form of meditation instituted by François de Sales, there is little correlation between the poetic timbre of his verse and the intensity of his religious faith—at least in so far as it is reflected in the poetry. Two of his finest works, 'The Collar' and 'The Pulley', achieve their effects in no small part by their artistic 'distance' from the recorded event. One recounts a past incident to illustrate the invisible strings that tie man's heart to God, the other presents emblematically a universal truth about the restlessness of mankind. In Donne's devotional poems, however, there is a clear relationship between his specific concept of religious commitment and their success as literary artefacts. As he moves away from the intensity of personal experience, so the poetic fire dies down; for both his meditative and his own literary sensibilities coincided in demanding from him an imaginative transference of self into the world of the spirit, a recognition of the irrationality inherent in belief, and a final assertion of the transcendent paradox.

Holy Sonnet XIV provides a particularly apt illustration of this mannerist assault upon the normal patterns of logic or belief. It is obvious enough that the violence of the opening lines performs the same function as 'Spit in my face . . .', plunging the reader into the self-flagellative mood of the meditator:

> Batter my heart, three person'd God; for, you
> As yet but knocke, breathe, shine, and seeke to mend;

But it succeeds also (and almost unnoticed) in impatiently brushing aside the conventional conception of prayer as a plea to God for an alleviation of suffering and for a merciful mitigation of the punishments incurred by sin. Here the longing is not for a remission but for an intensification of torture in the knowledge that suffering must precede forgiveness and frailties be purged painfully away before the hard-won faith can be attained. Once again, the path Donne chooses is tortuous and steep, bypassing any easy roads to penitence and forgiveness. That is why the sonnet invokes the Trinity here—a phenomenon rare in the writings of Donne who, in the Jesuit tradition, tends to address himself almost exclusively to Christ. For the invocation introduces into a position of prominence God the Father, as the symbol of vengeance or retribution, the prerequisite for atonement. In the triplet sequences which correspond to the respective members of the Trinity—'knocke, breathe, shine' and 'breake, blowe, burn'—first place is assigned to the crushing of the human spirit as the necessary prelude for the inspiration of the Holy Ghost and the warming or cleansing benevolence of the Son (here, as elsewhere, identified with the life-giving sun).[11] The vehemence of the opening has served, therefore, not only to subvert the conventional view of prayer but also to presage the violent, searing torture which the speaker demands in place of the shedding of guilt traditionally conferred by the Church upon its prodigal sons.

His rejection of accepted norms now moves forward to a powerful image, which asserts eternal criteria in place of the temporal. On the physical or logical plane, it would be insane to strike a man to the ground in order to ensure that he will stand; but with 'rise' echoing the Christian resurrection, and 'stand' adumbrating the soul taking its place at the right hand of God, the absurdity of the factual meaning serves by inversion to strengthen the validity of the religious ideal:

> That I may rise, and stand, o'erthrow mee, and bend
> Your force to breake, blowe, burn, and make me new.

The image here of being overthrown in order to rise offers in literary form a perfect reflection of the recurrent mannerist theme we have just examined, when the *Sprecher* or saint is flung head over heels by the force of the vision, to see the world afresh from a physically inverted but spiritually more valid viewpoint. In poetry as in painting, the image represents the sovereignty of the inner vision.

It might appear a little strained to read this sonnet as constituting the culmination of Donne's quarrel with the logical principles of empiricism. After all, it is a poem of prayer, not a discourse in philosophical speculation. And yet as we examine the development of the poem, it becomes apparent that the form the prayer takes is in fact the soul's yearning to escape from the confines of the rational or terrestrial, of which it has now despaired. The hint concealed in 'Batter' is now expanded into the fuller image of a soul imprisoned in a captured city and longing for the gate to be battered down by its saviour. In an era so steeped in Neoplatonism, no contemporary reader would have missed the symbol here, whereby the imprisoning city represents the body in which the soul is entombed.[12] Reason, as the main hope of the Renaissance, ought to have elevated the soul above the lusts of the flesh in ascent towards the divine, but

has failed lamentably, leaving the soul captive to Satan in the bonds
of the physical world:

> I, like an usurpt towne, to another due,
> Labour to admit you, but Oh, to no end,
> Reason your viceroy in mee, mee should defend,
> But is captiv'd, and proves weake or untrue,
> Yet dearely I love you, and would be lov'd faine,
> But am betroth'd unto your enemie . . .

'Untrue' here carries a particularly effective ambivalence. In the
setting of the love image, Reason has proved untrue in the sense of
'unfaithful'; but at a more profound level, it has failed to fulfil its
promise of leading the soul to the truth it seeks, and the spirit must
now look elsewhere for its salvation.

In a magnificent peroration, the imprisoned soul pleads for divine
rescue from this subservience to worldly lusts, conjuring up an
image in which the spiritual meaning dwarfs the physical anomaly,
again by inverting normal logical perspective:

> Divorce mee, untie, or breake that knot againe,
> Take me to you, imprison mee, for I
> Except you enthrall mee, never shall be free,
> Nor ever chast, except you ravish mee.

The subtlety here—that serious word-play in Donne's religious
writing—is the double meaning of 'enthrall', which compresses
within itself the polarized elements of the image. On the surface
level, the soul absurdly asks to be 'enslaved' in order to be freed.
But 'enthrall' means also to 'fascinate' or 'entrance'; a man entranced
becomes oblivious of the factual world about him, withdrawn and
totally absorbed in his inner experience or meditation. So here, the
agonized soul recognizes that, since reason has failed, it can achieve
its release from the tyranny of the flesh only by means of a willing
submission to the divine ecstasy which, on breaking the 'knot',
raises the soul from the body. In that sense it must be enthralled in
order to be free. And the image reaches its climax in the concluding
line

> Nor ever chast, except you ravish mee.

where 'ravish' wonderfully consummates the ambivalence. It too means, in addition to the literal sense of 'rape', to fascinate or enthral, underscoring this longing to be snatched from the palpable, terrestrial reality into the world of the spirit. The paradox is absurd only in its sexual setting, achieving in its metaphorical meaning a validity against which the physical impossibility of 'chaste rape' shrinks to triviality.

The sexual image retains none the less a sharp incongruity within the setting of a devotional poem, functioning in much the same way as the opening line to revitalize the tired images of religion. It is intended to jolt us out of that pietistic or celibate frame of mind associated with many poems of Christian faith into a mood of total engagement, in which every aspect of human experience is seen as a rightful and hence potentially sacred part of creation. To perceive in such passages, as some critics have done, an ironic hint that in the midst of his ecclesiastical duties Donne retains some nostalgic or whimsical hankering after the pursuits of his youth is to remove him from the context of his age. For once again Donne was drawing here upon that Counter-Reformation tradition which had moulded so much of his thinking during his formative years. In its attempt to reinvigorate the weakened belief of the time by nurturing a more personal and emotional response, the movement encouraged the worshipper to find within his own most sensual experience the raw material for such fervour which could be refined and purified for rededication on the altar of the Church. Nothing was secular, nothing profane if it could be made to serve the higher purpose of the spiritual life, and this principle was extended, even by the celibate priesthood, to include imaginatively the world of physical love. On the authority of the 'Song of Songs', whose erotic language and imagery had long been interpreted allegorically as a dialogue between Christ and his Church, the most apparently blasphemous comparisons were condoned and welcomed, provided that the spirit in which they were offered remained untainted. In our own day, despite the wide-ranging permissiveness in matters of sex, there is still something unsavoury for the modern reader in Donne's pursuit of the traditional church-spouse image into its more intimate details.

> Betray kind husband thy spouse to our sights,
> And let myne amorous soule court thy mild Dove,
> Who is most trew, and pleasing to thee, then
> When she is embrac'd and open to most men.[13]

It is perhaps of some comfort for us to know that this modern misunderstanding of the Counter-Reformation attitude to physical love was shared in other eras and in other genres. The *Ecstasy of St. Teresa* (Plate 12) which Bernini began in 1645 for the small Cornaro chapel in Rome's S. Maria della Vittoria, is a piece of statuary which even in today's more liberal climate is still treated half apologetically. The saint, idealized as a woman of striking beauty (in contrast to the rather homely, plump figure of contemporary portraiture)[14] lies swooning with head thrown back, and one leg (the foot bare in the new 'discalced' Carmelite tradition) hanging lifelessly over the edge of the cloud on which she floats. Before her stands a young male angel, smiling gently down on her, a spear held poised in his hand. Although the sculptural group was received with general admiration, a pamphlet issued at the time of its unveiling was not slow in identifying the erotic ambience of the scene—for which apparently no knowledge of modern psychology was necessary—and the author roundly attacked Bernini for having blasphemously exploited the religious mysticism of a virgin to portray what he called 'a prostrate, prostituted Venus' within the church.[15] In later years, President Salomon de Brosses was widely quoted for his snide remark that the statuary group reminded him of nothing so much as a bedroom scene. The sensuousness of St. Teresa's swoon is certainly reminiscent of the climactic moment of sexual orgasm, and with a snicker many a spectator has assumed that Bernini, either mischievously or (even worse) unwittingly, has translated a moment of supposed spirituality into an opportunity for erotic voyeurism, the phallic symbolism of the spear being almost impossible to ignore.

However, if we turn to St. Teresa's own account of her vision, on which Bernini based his group in the Cornaro Chapel, the situation becomes very different; for it was she who unabashedly drew upon love in its most human and bodily setting for the terms with which to describe the intensity of her spiritual experience, assuming that only there could she find the closest earthly parallel to celestial ecstasy. She relates that in the hands of the angel who was '. . . not tall, but short, and very beautiful', she saw

. . . a long golden spear, and at the end of an iron tip I seemed to see a point of fire. With this he appeared to pierce my heart several times so that it penetrated into my entrails. When he drew it out, I thought he was drawing them out with it, and he left me completely afire with a great love of God. The pain was so sharp that it made me utter several moans; and so excessive was the sweetness caused me by the intense pain that one can never wish to lose it . . .

In isolation this passage might be read as an unworldly nun's unintentional revelation of her sexual frustrations, a revelation only too obvious to an age such as ours nurtured on Freud. But in the setting of the Loyolan movement—of which she founded the parallel sisterhood, the reformed Carmelite order—it becomes obvious that she was consciously and unembarrassedly following the injunctions formulated by the spiritual leaders of the Counter-Reformation. François de Sales, for example, encouraged the Christian to look to human love as a fainter reflection of the love of God:

. . . as they that be enamoured with humane and natural love, have almost alway their thoughts fixed upon the parson beloved, their hart full of affection towards her, their mouth flowing with her praises; when their beloved is absent, they leese no occasion to testifie their passions by kind letters, and not a tree do they meet with all, but in the barck of it, they engrave the name of their darling: even so such as love God fervently, can never cease thincking upon him, they draw their breath only for him, they sigh and sorrow for their absence from him . . .[16]

and Richard Baxter, who represents the imbibing of this tradition into the Protestant world, suggests to his readers that in those very bodily sensations which normally corrupt man, a source of divine elevation can be perceived. It is, he writes,

. . . a singular help to the furthering of the work of Faith, to call in our Sense to its assistance: If we can make us friends of these usual enemies, and make them instruments of raising us to God, which are the usual means of drawing us from God, I think we shall perform a very excellent work. Sure it is both possible and lawful, yea, and necessary too, to do something in this kind; for God would not have given us either our senses themselves or their usual objects, if they might not have been serviceable to his own Praise, and help to raise us up to the apprehension of higher things.[17]

Teresa, in employing the vocabulary of sexual union as the closest earthly adumbration of divine love, was fully conscious of what she was doing, and her autobiography frequently returns to this theme. She relates in her *Vida* with the simplicity of one anxious to record her experiences accurately and without embellishment, how her early years were dominated by thoughts of her Mystic Marriage to Christ, whom she repeatedly addresses there as 'my bridegroom'. Among her favourite biblical works she numbers the Song of Songs which, as we have noted, was read in Christian exegesis as representing the passionate love between Jesus and his Church. The allegorical interpretation justified its presence in the scriptural canon, but could not disguise the frank sensuousness of the imagery it employed: 'Thy stature is like to a palm tree, and thy breasts to clusters of grapes. I said, I will go up to the palm tree. I will take hold of the boughs thereof: now also thy breasts shall be as clusters of the vine'; or from the female viewpoint, 'His left hand is under my head, and his right hand doth embrace me . . . his belly is as bright ivory overlaid with sapphires. His legs are as pillars of marble.' Teresa, in recording the four stages of ecstasy—the 'four waters' as she termed them metaphorically—described the highest form as a mingling of pleasure and pain where the agony of the envisioned martyrdom blends with the bliss which is a foretaste of heaven; and the account of her own ecstatic epiphany, which served as the source for Bernini's statuary group, concludes with a less frequently quoted passage suggesting that she had not forgotten either the bodily experience from which the vision draws its strength, nor the theme of love linked by its physical and spiritual forms: 'It is not bodily pain, but spiritual, though the body has a share in it—indeed a great share. So sweet are the colloquies of love which pass between the soul and God.'

It was in that context that Bernini had no hesitation in transferring the mystic vision with such astonishing fidelity to the medium of stone. Both the vision itself as St. Teresa recorded it, and the sculptural rendering by Bernini derive, therefore, from the same tradition as inspired Donne's image of the soul longing to be raped by God. No one could accuse Donne of being unaware of the sexual implications of his image, and if there is in that poem a more aggressive desire than in Bernini to shock by the apparent blasphemy, it is a desire to shock into truth. He was removing from the conventional love imagery long authorized by the Church the accumulated patina of generations to reveal in its original vividness the message of the Song of Songs as the church fathers had interpreted it—that only within the immediacy of human experience on earth can be found the materials out of which to construct a concept of the divine.

Whatever charges may be levelled at the Jesuits or the Carmelite sisters, even their bitterest enemies could not accuse them of being cloistered and unworldly. The Society of Jesus had been founded with papal approval as a militant order intended to combat at the highest intellectual level the contemporary challenges to faith, and it attracted to its ranks some of the most brilliant minds of Europe. They exploited poetry and music, painting and architecture, science and philosophy, in order to disseminate at all levels of society, popular as well as aristocratic, the message of Christian faith. The secular masque was converted by Carissimi into an artistic tool for strengthening religion, and the newly founded Jesuit schools and colleges began to rival the established institutions both in their educational techniques and in their scholarly reputation. They did not withdraw from the secular world, but went out to conquer it on its own ground. Even so gentle a figure as St. Teresa was a woman of extraordinary administrative and practical drive who succeeded in refounding and reforming a complete order, travelling all over Castile to open new houses, and urging her fellow nuns never to keep aloof from those they met but to engage them in conversation and win them over to their own way of life. To assume, therefore, that the vein of erotic imagery in Teresa and Donne was either naïvely unintentional or even perversely ribald is to misunderstand the bold extremity to which the love metaphor was taken within those religious circles from which they drew their inspiration. It was a phenomenon of the late sixteenth century which appeared even outside those narrower circles. At precisely the same time, in 1569, that remarkable Jewish mystic, Isaac Luria, had gathered a group of disciples around him in the Galilean town of Safed, dedicating the last three years of his brief life to teaching what was an essentially new and revitalized form of Cabbalistic philosophy. On his own example, he urged his followers to strive for the ecstasy of heavenly ascent by means of a silent, devotional meditation (*kavanah*), employing a symbolism based on erotic, sexual metaphors carried far beyond the milder practice of his predecessors.[18] These were cultural affinities produced by the intellectual sensibility of the age. For in such eras of heightened devotionalism, tending to individualistic rather than corporate faith, the profane world becomes illumined and permeated by the celestial. The risk of blasphemy then seems preferable to a timorous allegiance to orthodox tenet, as the meditator daringly apprehends divine *caritas* in terms of a transfigured and spiritualized *eros*. It is only later generations, judging by more formal, conventional distinctions which are liable to misinterpret the intent.

This recognition of the ultimate unity of mortal and divine love, the awareness that the two forms should be imaginatively merged and interchanged in order to achieve a mutual enrichment through the contact, stands, I think, at the opposite pole to what Louis Martz has called 'sacred parody'. He uses the term (in the positive, non-pejorative sense current in the seventeenth century) to describe the attempt among religious poets to convert the poetry of profane love into the poetry of the divine, and he points to Southwell, Donne, and Herbert as its leading practitioners. Sacred parody (rather like the rock-'n-roll hymn sessions conducted today by more progressive clergymen) hoped to outwit paganism by adopting its more popular fashions and introducing them, after due modification, into the Church itself. Southwell, for example, took a well-known secular lyric by Dyer and rewrote it as a moral piece 'A Phansie turned to a sinners complaint'; and elsewhere he urged his Christian readers to transfer their affections from the baseness of human objects to the divine:

O soule, doe not thy noble thoughts abase,
To lose thy love in any mortall wight,

> Content thine eye at home with native grace,
> Sith God himself is ravisht with thy sight.
> If on thy beautie God enamoured bee,
> Base is thy love of any lesse then hee.[19]

Herbert, a far more sensitive poet than Southwell, shared with him this assumption that human love was degrading and he was particularly perturbed at its domination of poetry which, as the sacred handmaid of religion, he felt should remain the exclusive preserve of devotional themes:

> Let foolish lovers, if they will love dung,
> With canvas, not with arras, clothe their shame:
> Let follie speak in her own native tongue.
> True beautie dwells on high: ours is a flame
> But borrow'd thence to light us thither.
> Beautie and beauteous words should go together.

Accordingly he earned Vaughan's praise for being the first poet '. . . that with an effectual success attempted the diversion of this foul and overflowing stream' from amatory to religious themes.

To place Donne within this group of 'sacred parodists' trying to expunge lasciviousness from poetry and to replace it by Christian *caritas* is to assume that he too deplored the intrusion of secular love into the domain of poetry, regarding it as the rightful home of hymns to spiritual beauty and of exhortations to a life of goodness and virtue.[20] It is true that during the period of his deanship he appears to have made some half-hearted attempts to recall the manuscripts of his love poems, amongst which were some of his more lascivious verses; but it has also been recorded in a letter he wrote to Goodyer immediately before his ordination that he was planning to publish a collection of his earlier poems in order to pay off old debts, even though he recognized the unsuitability of such publication at the time of taking holy orders. Whether he did in fact publish such a collection can only be surmised.[21] What lies beyond conjecture, however, is that in his own devotional poetry, carnal love not only continued to serve as a legitimate source of imagery to convey his striving for divine union, but was presented with a vigour and realism which makes it impossible to regard him as a leader of the sacred parodists, disgusted at the foulness of the flesh. He belongs rather to the Counter-Reformation tradition, with its encouragement to cultivate the bodily senses imaginatively, as a means of glimpsing the celestial.

The disruption of traditional norms characteristic of the meditative and mannerist traditions, and reflected in the explosive openings and aggressive carnality of Donne's religious verse, extends beyond the conventions of Christian belief to include (as in his earlier paralogical poetry) the very conception of time and space. At first sight, Holy Sonnet VI may appear to depart from this pattern, since its opening line lacks any hint of violence or irritability. On the contrary, it is resigned, calm, almost detached. Yet if the first line does not conform to type, the octet taken as a whole produces as powerful an impact as either of the previous instances. Its slow beginning is in fact intended to emphasize by contrast the sudden acceleration which follows, until the imminent terror of death has been conveyed with full vehemence. The closing scene of a full-length tragedy, the last mile of a distant pilgrimage imply that a protracted and somewhat leisurely journey has preceded them; but the swift succession of 'last mile . . . last inch . . . last point' shrinks the gap between man and gluttonous death to present with vivid actuality that dread instant which will determine his fate for ever:

> This is my playes last scene, here heavens appoint
> My pilgrimages last mile; and my race
> Idly, yet quickly runne, hath this last pace,
> My spans last inch, my minutes last point,
> And gluttonous death, will instantly unjoynt
> My bodie and soule, and I shall sleepe a space,
> But my ever-waking part shall see that face,
> Whose fear already shakes my every joynt;

The reader is drawn into a personal confrontation with death; and the elasticity of time which begins stretched out at length and with startling rapidity contracts to nothing, overrides the normal movement of this world to thrust us into a confrontation with that one moment which is the central concern of every meditator, when the subtle knot of body and soul becomes at last *unjointed* and, as the body sinks to rest, the soul rises to offer its final account.

There is in the sestet of this poem a rare instance of that sly wit, the humorous play with specious reasoning, which enlivens the secular verse but almost disappears from the devotional writings except as a serious means of asserting paradoxical truth. It is as though Donne has perceived a narrow crevice of hope through which he knows he cannot escape but which he cannot resist attempting, at least in a verbal gesture. The body, he blandly argues, returns to the earth which bore it, the soul to the heavens in which it had its source; why should not his sins be permitted to follow the same principle and return naturally to the hell in which they were generated, leaving him free from guilt? The plea for so neat a solution is only half-serious, since the argument is obviously untenable—he cannot so easily shrug off responsibility for his sins as if *he* had no part in generating them. But the word 'Impute' restores the graver tone, acknowledging as it does that such a welcome arrangement would be the product not of the 'right' to which he refers, but only of a divine and merciful grace extended to one who belongs justly in hell.

> Then, as my soule, to heaven her first seate, takes flight,
> And earth-borne body, in the earth shall dwell,
> So, fall my sinnes, that all may have their right,
> To where they are bred, and would presse me, to hell.
> Impute me righteous, thus purg'd of evill,
> For thus I leave the world, the flesh, the devill.

Only 'thus', he admits, by the generous intervention of God and not by desert, can he escape the clutches of Satan.

The elongation and compression of time and space which dominated the first part of this sonnet, as it does all mannerist painting, clearly draws its inspiration from medieval sources. There is, however, a fundamental difference; for where the scholiast regarded the transitoriness of the temporal as axiomatic, Donne must argue his case forcefully against a firm Renaissance acceptance of the immutable laws and measurable orbits of a mechanistic universe. As a result, his defiance of ordered time takes on a more passionate note, an insistence upon the imminence of death and the shrinking of life into a span, which creates the urgency of the octet here. It occupies a prominent place in his preaching too, where he often employed similar means to drive home his message. On one occasion he quixotically informed his congregants that he would begin his sermon with its conclusion, on the grounds that neither he nor his auditors knew whether they would live to the end of that hour, and it was therefore incumbent upon him to ensure that the most vital part of his discourse be conveyed to his congregants while there was yet time.[22]

We have often been reminded that Donne's fascination with death forms part of a more general Jacobean concern, ranging from the grave-digger scene in *Hamlet* to the ghoulish kissing of a poisoned skull in Tourneur's *Revengers Tragedie*. The Renaissance, we are told, could not shake off completely the medieval awareness of death's presence within the temporal world—the concept of 'media vita in morte sumus'. In fact, however, Emil Mâle has recently shown that the latter concept was not medieval at all, but formed an integral part of the Renaissance itself.[23] Throughout the thirteenth and most of the fourteenth century, which marks the close of the Middle Ages, sepulchral effigies convey no impression of horror or decay. The sculpted dead lie peacefully upon the tomb, their hands clasped in calm saintliness. Death is the natural end of man, carrying with it not terror but a sweet sadness—a gentle passing from this earth to eternal life. At the turn of the fifteenth century, however, the message of the Church suddenly becomes more strident. Alarmed at the encroachment of secularism and the growing interest in temporal affairs, it began introducing harrowing images of emaciated corpses as chill reminders of the transitoriness of mortal pleasure and worldly success. In the S. Maria Novella of Florence, Masaccio's fresco of the *Holy Trinity*, painted in 1427, created a visual depth of perspective which no earlier painter had achieved and has hence been generally recognized by historians as the first truly Renaissance painting. Less frequently noted is its positioning above a gruesomely realistic skeleton with a text proclaiming in Italian: 'What you are, I once was; what I am, you will become!' The *Dance of Death*, familiar from the woodcuts of Guyot Marchant and Holbein, became a widely disseminated motif, in which a skeleton or mummified figure personifying Death mocks at the pomp of pope and king as it hauls them off to Hell together with lesser mortals—a theme caught to perfection in the passage from Shakespeare's *Richard II*:

> . . . for within the hollow crown
> That rounds the mortal temples of a king
> Keeps Death his court; and there the antic sits,
> Scoffing his state, and grinning at his pomp;
> Allowing him a breath, a little scene,
> To monarchize, be fear'd, and kill with looks;
> Infusing him with self and vain conceit,—
> As if this flesh, which walls about our life,
> Were brass impregnable; and humour'd thus,
> Comes at the last, and with a little pin
> Bores through his castle-wall, and—farewell, king!

In the paintings and woodcuts there is often a macabre humour as Death flirtatiously slips his skinny arm through the fur-lined sleeve of his reluctant victim, or modestly covers with his bony hand the *pudenda* he no longer possesses. Within this 'dance', the skinny figure of Death the Equalizer skips merrily along, ironically throwing into contrast the reluctant, halting pace of the human procession he is escorting.

Such was the phenomenon of the early Renaissance. As one moves into the Jacobean age, however, the tableau changes substantially. Man is no longer the helpless victim of a gleefully triumphant Death, whose eventual victory he ought always to have acknowledged. Instead he has become the dignified, troubled philosopher, contemplating the skull anew as the empty shell of the human mind. He is less perturbed by the loss of fleshly pleasures than by the intellectual implications of the body's decay. For Hamlet, as for so much of the Jacobean stage, death conjures up the nauseating stench of putrefaction which by corrupting the flesh degrades human nobility and retroactively vitiates all human endeavour. His meditation on Yorick's skull forms the culmination of those doubts expressed earlier in his soliloquy on suicide, where his allusions to the bourn from which no traveller returns suggest that the dilemma paralysing his actions derives to no small extent from his uncertainty over the existence of an after-life. Senecan Stoicism had offered the Elizabethan a philosophy ideally suited to the bolstering of his Renaissance self-reliance. He could scorn the gods and determine his own fate in the knowledge that death was merely a dreamless sleep—'. . . to die, to sleep— / No more . . .'Tis a consummation / Devoutly to be wished'. But as he boldly shrugged off his fear of hell, there came the ominous thought that if hell no longer existed, neither did heaven; and the limiting of all human hope to the confines of this material world carried with it the grim corollary that nothing of the human spirit survived the putrid carcase rotting in the tomb:

> *Hamlet*: Dost thou think Alexander look'd o' this fashion i' the earth? . . . And smelt so? pah!

His gorge rises as he handles the decaying skull whose chap-fallen grin makes mockery of the infinite jest and excellent fancy of its erstwhile owner, and nullifies by extension the wit, sensitivity, and nobility of Hamlet himself.

Within the meditative tradition of this same era the contemplation of the skull occupies an equally central position, becoming a recurrent motif in the paintings of Zurburan, El Greco, and de la Tour. Its purpose, however, is almost the reverse of the Yorick scene; for the skull functions in this tradition not as a source of perplexity and disturbance, but as the final and unanswerable proof of the need for religious belief. This more positive attitude to death produces a remarkable and unique effect in Donne's poetry. For the grave is curiously purified there of all gruesome and unpalatable associations. Even in his amatory verse where the religious allusion is subdued or ironical, the grave is neither degrading nor polluting. Donne's lovers are never reduced by death to the unsavoury condition of Polonius—a meal for politic worms whose malodorous presence can be 'nosed' as one goes up the stairs nor, like Ophelia, to a corpse decayed by water more swiftly than the cadaver of a menial tanner. In a sense the grave *is* (for all Marvell's whimsy) a fine and private place, and though Donne's lovers do not embrace there, they can at least preserve with dignity their mutual love, carrying with them the emblems of their fidelity in the poignant hope of a reunion, however brief, on that apocalyptic day when the souls will return to join their bodies and meet for a moment of joyful recognition before being caught up to heaven:

> And thinke that there a loving couple lies,
> Who thought that this device might be some way
> To make their soules, at the last busie day,
> Meet at this grave, and make a little stay.[24]

Donne's corpses seem often to speak from the grave itself, pleading for privacy from the intrusion of prying eyes: 'When my grave is broke up again / Some second ghest to entertaine . . .'; and while the dramatic situation is intended to surprise by its unexpected angle of vision (that viewpoint from ground-level paralleled in Titian and Caravaggio), the final effect is to assume as unquestionable the survival of the spirit not only beyond but even within the grave. The sundials and glittering objects which Donne places so casually within the tomb are, of course, surrealistic in their provocative juxtaposition; but at the same time they serve an additional function by cleansing the grave of its less palatable features, and purifying it from any association with stench and decay. It is, moreover, a poetic technique which grows naturally out of the Catholic tradition in which Donne was reared. The posting of ninety-five propositions on the door of the Castle Church in Wittenberg which marked the formal opening of the Reformation had been prompted specifically by Luther's disgust at the sale of saints' indulgences—the mercenary transfer of superfluous merit-points accumulated by saints and martyrs to those sinners wealthy enough to purchase them; and it was not long before the adoration of saints' relics itself came under attack together with the indulgences. In response, the Catholics defiantly reaffirmed the sanctity of the relics and approved their veneration as a means of encouraging a meditative identification with the martyrs.

Donne's poem 'The Relique' retains a strong affinity to this veneration. Ostensibly it ridicules the superstitious worship of saints' bones which will no doubt prompt some prying grave-digger foolishly to adore the lovers as Jesus and Mary Magdalene. Yet despite the mockery, even the hint of blasphemy in the poem, the sanctity of the religious world is delicately transferred to the lovers themselves in their pathetic attempt to achieve some spiritual meeting, however momentary, on that Judgement Day when souls will gather together the scattered parts of their bodies. Just as the jewelled casket enshrining the sacred relic in the church vicariously endowed with the beauty of its rich ornamentation the otherwise loathsome object it contained, so the bracelet of bright hair about the bone, and the wreath that crowns the dead man's arm serve poetically to illumine the darkness of the tomb and to dispel any hint of morbidity and gloom. In this way death, disinfected from the stench of maggots and putrefaction, becomes the calm, restful sleep of the grave's occupant who hibernates like a chrysalis awaiting the warmth of the summer, while nature slowly transmutes and refines his body into the creature which will take wing on the day of resurrection. As he wrote in his elegy on Lady Marckham:

> In her this sea of death hath made no breach,
>   But as the tide doth wash the slimie beach,
> And leaves embroder'd workes upon the sand,
>   So is her flesh refin'd by deaths cold hand,
> As men of China, after an ages stay,
>   Do take up Porcelane, where they buried Clay;
> So at this grave, her limbecke, which refines
>   The Diamonds, Rubies, Saphires, Pearles, and Mines,
> Of which this flesh was, her soul shall inspire
>   Flesh of such stuffe, as God, when his last fire
> Annuls this world, to recompence it, shall
>   Make and name then, th' Elixar of this All.[25]

There are in Elizabethan and Jacobean literature a few rare instances where the body appears similarly immune to corruption, but even these instances are far removed from the peculiar richness and seriousness of Donne's description. In Ariel's song from the *Tempest*, the drowned king's bones are transformed into coral, his eyes into pearls in much the same way as here; but the song is only a light fantasy set to music, and we know even as we hear it that in fact the king still lives and has reached the shore in safety. In a more sombre setting, Romeo marvels at the beauty of the dead Juliet which she has retained even in the tomb:

> Death that hath suck'd the honey of thy breath
> Hath had no power yet upon thy beauty:
> Thou art not conquer'd; beauty's ensign yet
> Is crimson in thy lips and in thy cheeks,
> And death's pale flag is not advanced there.

But she too is really alive as he gazes at her; and the ominously repeated 'yet' leaves no doubt of the grim transformation that awaits her eventually in what Romeo calls the 'rotten jaws' and 'detestable maw' of the grave. Donne, in fact, has such a remarkable facility for imaginatively imposing his own poetic world upon his reader that it is only on standing back from his verse and comparing it with the more general assumptions of his age that the unique transcendence of fleshly decay and the calm purity of the grave become apparent. In his poetry at least, Donne draws his conception of death from the quiet untroubled confidence of Paul's 'Death, where is thy sting, grave where is thy victory?' rather than the grinning skulls and skeletal figures of the early Renaissance. And what was visible in the love poetry, holds true for the devotional verse too. In the sonnet we were just examining this effect is powerfully conveyed. For the growing urgency and terror of the 'last mile . . . last inch . . . last point' culminates in the horrific image of 'gluttonous' death about to consume the unfortunate mortal like the 'detestable maw' envisaged by Romeo. But at the climax of the terror a sudden hush descends, and instead of the gruesome gnawing of bones which we had been led to expect, we are met by the quiet sleep of the grave:

> My spans last inch, my minutes last point,
> And gluttonous death, will instantly unjoynt
> My body, and soule, and I shall sleepe a space.
> But my ever-waking part shall see that face,
> Whose fear already shakes my every joynt:

His fear is not of death itself, but of the awesome day of reckoning awaiting the soul beyond the grave.

This contempt for physical death becomes the central theme of Holy Sonnet X, but it is treated there with a scornfulness which reduces the fearsome, macabre figure of Death the Equalizer to a pitifully ineffective creature. The sonnet opens with a staunch denial of its supposedly intimidating power:

> Death be not proud, though some have called thee
> Mighty and dreadfull, for, thou art not soe,
> For those whom thou think'st thou dost overthrow,
> Die not, poore death, nor yet canst thou kill mee;

The technique it then employs to substantiate the challenge and to deflate Death's pride is one familiar from the love poems—that spurious logic based upon a literal reading of metaphor, which leads circuitously to an ultimate truth. In fact, it approaches so close to the poems of wit that, despite the obvious solemnity of the theme, there is at times even a touch of overt humour. That very personification of Death which, in Holbein or *Everyman* was intended to terrorize by its dramatization of the ephemerality of life, is suddenly treated here with a sly literalism which transforms it into near-absurdity. The allegory is turned inward upon itself as, with mock compassion, Donne treats this personified Death as a real human being. He lists the unpleasant conditions in which Death must work, the sickrooms in which he is compelled to spend his time, and the subservience with which he must patiently wait for a king to pronounce sentence before he can perform his own part in the execution. In a final triumphant phrase, Donne carries the human personification of Death to its 'logical' conclusion—we are presented, in fact, with the ludicrous picture of Death dying:

> Thou art slave to Fate, chance, kings, and desperate men,
> And dost with poyson, warre, and sicknesse dwell,
> And poppie, or charmes can make us sleepe as well,
> And better then thy stroake; why swell'st thou then?
> One short sleepe past, wee wake eternally,
> And death shall be no more, Death thou shalt die.

In the midst of this playful merging of literal with allegorical death, the message rings true none the less. For beneath the surface exaggeration, the argument itself has been moving relentlessly forward, and the conventional figure of a gruesomely mummified Death coming to claim its terrified victims has dwindled away before the assurance of eternal life at the end of days when, according to Christianity, death shall indeed be no more.

Donne's unique purification of the grave from corruption and the stench of decay holds true throughout his poetry; but a change occurs as we turn to his sermons. For the detailed and deliberately nauseating descriptions of bodily disintegration which they contain have won him a degree of notoriety as suffering from a morbid interest in the physical processes of putrefaction. In fact, such passages are less common in the large body of his prose writings than the general reader has been led to believe; but every now and then one is indeed confronted with a statement such as: 'Between that excremental jelly that the body is made of at first and that jelly which the body dissolves to at last; there is not so noisome, so putrid a thing in nature.' Within their context, such descriptions as this, or as the 'vermiculation' in 'Death's Duell', are nevertheless informed with an extraordinary vigour and light, with a dazzling certainty of faith as they lead towards the climax—that 'ascension into the kingdom which he hath purchased for you'. They fulfil, in fact, the same function as the skull in a Zurbaran painting, to confirm the exclusive significance of the soul and of immortal faith, as the body returns to dust. In the following passage, for example, there is indeed a chilling concern with shattered limbs, worms, and festering sores, but the description is universalized to blunt the horror, and to make it almost scientific in its recounting of anatomical detail. And above all, the jellied, mouldering parts of the body are suddenly transformed (as in the poetry) into pearls and seeds of grain when the glory of the resurrection bids them to rise:

Where be all the splinters of that Bone, which a shot hath shivered and scattered in the Ayre? Where be all the Atoms of that flesh, which a *Corrasive* hath eat away, or a *Consumption* hath breath'd, and exhal'd away from our arms, and other Limbs? In what wrinkle, in what furrow, in what bowel of the earth, ly all the graines of the ashes burnt a thousand years since? In what corner, in what ventricle of the sea, lies all the jelly of a Body drowned in the *generall flood*? What cohaerence, what sympathy, what dependence maintaines any relation, any correspondence, between that arm that was lost in Europe and that legge that was lost in Afrique or Asia, scores of years between?

One humour of our dead body produces worms, and those worms suck and exhaust all other humour, and then all dies, and molders into dust, and that dust is blowen into the River, and that puddled water tumbled into the sea, and that ebs and flows in infinite revolutions, and still, still God knows in what *Cabinet* every *seed-Pearle* lies, in what part of the world every graine of every mans dust lies; and *sibilat populum suum* (as his Prophet speaks in another case) he whispers, he hisses, he beckens for the bodies of his saints and in the twinckling of an eye, that body that was scattered over all the elements, is sate down at the right hand of God in glorious resurrection.[26]

This excited vision of '. . . and still, still God knows in what *Cabinet* every *seed-pearle* lies'; can scarcely be interpreted as a sick fascination with maggots and putrid flesh.

On the other hand, few modern psychiatrists would, I suspect, regard as healthy the incident shortly before his death when (as Walton informs us) he donned his winding sheet and posed, standing upon an urn, for a portrait of himself as he would appear after death.

Upon this urn he then stood with his eyes shut and with so much of the sheet turned aside as might show his lean, pale and death-like face, which was purposely turned towards the East from whence he expected the second coming of his and our Saviour, Jesus. In this posture he was drawn at his just height; and when the picture was fully finished, he caused it to be set by his bedside, where it continued and became his hourly object till his death.[27]

It does, no doubt, require a strong imaginative effort on the part of the twentieth-century reader to comprehend Donne's strange deathbed fancy. But perhaps the problem is broader. In the more sober intellectual climate of our own age it is difficult to recapture even momentarily that mood of mystical fervour which gripped the religionists of sixteenth-century Spain, inspired the missionary orders of the Counter-Reformation Church, and produced a final resurgence of faith before seventeenth-century rationalism settled upon the western world. However distasteful to us Donne's funeral posing may appear, it does serve to underscore the distinction between the Jacobean's gloomy preoccupation with worms and emaciated corpses, and Donne's longing for death as the apogean

moment of transition between the two worlds—a moment that
deserved to be rehearsed, pictorially recorded, and inwardly antici-
pated as he prepared to cross the threshold of immortality. The
rehearsal for death was one he wished recorded in poetic as well as
visual terms:

> Since I am comming to that Holy roome,
>   Where, with thy Quire of Saints for evermore,
> I shall be made thy Musique; As I come
>   I tune the Instrument here at the dore,
>   And what I must doe then, thinke now before.[28]

Donne's conception of mortality has too often been dismissed in
Freudian terms as an obsessional death-wish, as though that explains all that needs to be known. It is the kind of over-simplification
which Hamlet narrowly escaped when Ernest Jones attempted
some years ago to identify his predicament as a classic Oedipal
complex. Perhaps the validity of Donne's attitude, as the literary
expression of a broader cultural phenomenon rather than as a merely
personal psychological problem, may best be seen by relating it to
his most outstanding contemporary. As was noted in an earlier
chapter, Shakespeare's Jacobean phase has been increasingly identified by recent scholars as mannerist in the tortured self-probing of
its central figures, and the tendency to desert clearly defined moral
criteria in favour of a mannerist multiplicity of viewpoint. On the
basis of Hiram Haydn's definition, or Arnold Hauser's, these
Jacobean plays undoubtedly fall within the category of the Counter-
Renaissance. On the other hand, there is almost as much that
excludes them from such classification, not least their predominant
interest in the actuality of this world, with no more than a fearful
glance towards the heaven or hell beyond the grave; and I suggested
in that earlier discussion that they should be compared rather with
Michelangelo's transitional period, of which his *Dying Slave* is an
example, with its muscular realism offset by a serpentine movement
of anguish. If we concentrate for a moment on the changing image
of the human body in this era as representing the physical
elements of this world, it becomes clear that there are in fact three
main stages of development in this period, and not merely Renaissance and mannerist.

The first phase—the resurgence of faith in man's god-like potential and self-reliance—forms the primary motif of the High Renaissance, reflected throughout the art and literature of the period, and as such it requires little comment here. Verrocchio's equestrian statue of Colleone symbolized the mood of the age; the rider's left shoulder is thrust forward in a pose that falls just short of arrogance, the jaw is firmly set, the horse's reins held masterfully in check, and the entire work embodies in stone the spirit of Shakespeare's *Henry V*, urging his men forward to victory on St. Crispin's Day. Man scorns death, if he can die, like Mercutio, with a pun on his lips, having lived and died with honour.

The first flush of confidence, however, was brief, and the shadow that falls across the Jacobean period is a new awareness of the *vulnerability* of man both in body and soul. Man's nakedness before the ravening beasts and the pitiless storm constitutes the central image of *King Lear*. The Fool shivering in the rain, miserably clings to Lear for comfort; Poor Tom whimpers that he's a-cold, and Lear himself strips off the robes of office to become that poor forked animal, unaccommodated man. Hamlet cannot hope even for the peacefulness of death, seeing in the rotting corpse a retrospective disqualification of all human achievement that makes a mockery of life; and Othello, undefeated in battle, succumbs to a more dreadful enemy than the fiercest of Turks—the green-eyed monster that consumes and maddens from within. In this transitional phase of human vulnerability there is no satisfying resolution such as concludes *Romeo and Juliet*, where the heads of the two houses exchange vows henceforth to live in peace. In the tragedies of this phase, the ripeness that marks spiritual maturity is the recognition that human suffering is inevitable—the acknowledgement, in fact, that we must *endure* our going hence even as our coming hither.

The third phase suddenly moves out of the black despair towards a new splendour even in the realm of tragedy itself, and the sombre world of Hamlet gives place to the richness of *Antony and Cleopatra*—the sole Shakespearean play truly belonging within the mannerist tradition. In contrast to the specifically religious colouring of Donne's writing, visible even at its most profane moments, Shakespeare's play is unequivocally pagan, abandoning those Christian, moral assumptions which had served as the underpinning of his earlier plays and were personified by such figures as Cordelia and Desdemona. Yet within its secular setting, it espouses the same spiritual transcendence of reality, and the same dematerialization of the phenomenal world. Its uniqueness in the Shakespearean canon as the sole representative of this third cultural phase accounts, I suspect, for the disquiet it has caused amongst theorists of tragedy who, like Bradley, have tended to shunt it quietly to one side, although recognizing its greatness.[29] For where is that tragic flaw which according to Aristotelian law ought to mark out Antony for death? Only the age of Dryden could be satisfied with a dogmatic condemnation of Antony for failing to fulfil his duties in Rome, and even he had to rewrite the play to make it fit into the rigid theory of his day. For less committed eras, the dramatic excitement of the play has lain in the brilliant manipulation of the audience's emotions, which are buffeted like a needle suspended between two revolving magnets, alternately attracted and repelled by each, and sometimes by both. One magnet, Rome, represents honour and duty, but it represents no less sycophancy, sterility, and parochialism. The other, Egypt, is effete, corrupt, and licentious; but it is also colourful, fertile, and infinitely varied.

To interpret Antony's tragic predicament, then, as a need to choose between Egypt and Rome is to ignore the enormously impressive imagery of the play. For the tragedy both of Antony and of Cleopatra is their transcendent, godlike being—the meeting of Mars and Venus where Cleopatra out-Venuses Venus, so that their love, anger, beauty, and splendour can never be contained in the narrow confines of this world. The petty limitations of corporeal perspective collapse or shimmer away as in an El Greco painting before the cosmic force of their spirit, and the fixed laws of nature fall helplessly aside. Antony is an autumn that grows the more by reaping; Cleopatra, whom age cannot wither nor custom stale, makes hungry where most she satisfies in defiance of all bodily law. Where else in the entire range of Shakespeare's writings is death described in terms of a heart bursting forth from the walls of the body which cannot contain it?

> O cleave, my sides!
> Heart, once be stronger than thy continent,
> Crack thy frail case!

And in their need to soar beyond the restrictive world of physical reality, death takes on a richness and beauty such as it possesses in no other Shakespearean play. Earlier tragic figures had at best scorned death, and more often had shuddered before the loathsome foulness of the tomb; but here death becomes a lover's pinch which hurts but is desired, a baby at the breast that sucks the nurse asleep, a lover's bed into which the bridegroom runs. The warm attraction of death draws its inspiration from the luxuriant world of the spirit that awaits beyond the grave, where the soul, freed from its mortal frame, will rise untrammelled into the infinite spaces.

If we are disturbed today at Donne's rehearsal of his own death, as he solemnly attires himself in the shroud to eternalize the climactic moment of his transition from this world to the next, is the incident so different in quality or intent from Cleopatra's magnificent last scene? There with the help of Charmian and Iris, she arrays herself in her royal vestments to fulfil her longing not for death but for *immortality*, preparing to meet beyond the grave the curled Antony whose kiss it is her heaven to have:

Cleopatra: Give me my robe, put on my crown, I have
Immortal longings in me. Now no more
The juice of Egypt's grape shall moist this lip.
Yare, yare, good Iras; quick: methinks I hear
Antony call. I see him rouse himself
To praise my noble act. I hear him mock
The luck of Caesar, which the gods give men
To excuse their after wrath. Husband, I come:
Now to that name, my courage prove my title!
I am fire and air; my other elements
I give to baser life.

The fire and air of her spirit separate from the earthly components as in the elongating moment of mannerist ecstasy, when death unties 'this knot intrinsicate of life'. And while in the final scene of the play the prosaic Caesar busies himself with the mundane details of her burial, we know that she has soared far beyond his reach, outdistancing death to join her Antony as the cynosure of Olympus. There are no Christian echoes in this pagan scene, but as she willingly applies the asp to her breast in certain expectation of the reunion awaiting her beyond the tomb, she might well have murmured with Donne:

> One short sleepe past, wee wake eternally,
> And death shall be no more. Death thou shalt die.

Such, then, was the final mannerist phase which, having despaired of the flesh, placed its hopes beyond this four-dimensional world. In more general terms, Donne's concept of the pliability of time, where length is determined not by fixed divisions into years or hours but by the subjective or spiritual significance of the events contained within them had, as we have seen, been widely employed in his love poetry too, although there with generally much lighter effect. 'The Sunne Rising' had scorned any attempt to make lovers' hours conform to those rigid measurements of time fit only for schoolboys and sour apprentices, and many of his parodies of the Petrarchan mode banteringly contrasted such unchanging laws of nature as the instantaneous flash of gunpowder or the swift effects of the plague with the astonishing phenomenon of love's unpredictability and its contempt for fixed rules of behaviour:

> He is starke mad, who ever sayes,
>   That he hath beene in love an houre,
> Yet not that love so soone decayes,
>   But that it can tenne in lesse space devour;
> Who will beleeve mee, if I sweare
>   That I have had the plague a yeare?
> Who would not laugh at mee, if I should say,
> I saw a flaske of *powder burne a day*?[30]

Despite their nonchalance, such poems betray some adumbration of the more serious interplay of time, death, and eternity which was in the religious writings to resist so effectively the theory of universal constancy and measurability implicit in the empirical method. The eternity of love treated ironically in these lines can take on an unquestionable solemnity even within the secular poems themselves, as in 'The Canonization', where it functions as a means of transcending the restrictive framework of the new materialistic philosophy. In its fullest expression, however, when Donne writes with the unhesitating commitment of the Christian believer, it becomes the basis for those powerful homilies in which a hundred years shrivel to a minute; and on that last minute of a sermon, when the congregation is restless and anxious to leave, may rest the everlasting future of their souls. The Renaissance perspective of fixed time-patterns melts away before the vision of eternity and the hurried rhythms of the prose reflect the near-desperation of the human predicament:

If there be a minute of patience left, heare me say, This minute that is left, is that eternitie which we speake of; upon this minute dependeth that eternity: And this minute, God is in this Congregation, and puts his eare to every one of your hearts, and hearkens what you will bid him say to your selves: whether he shall blesse you for your acceptation, or curse you for your refusall of him this minute: for this minute makes up your *Century*, your hundred yeares, your eternity, because it may be your last minute.[31]

This process of continuity in Donne's writing whereby the stylistic devices of his secular poems are not discarded but reapplied with deepened effect to the subject matter of his devotional compositions can be discerned even in so apparently casual a usage as the technique of deliberate misdirection employed in more roguish moods. In an earlier chapter I argued that the illusory wit of such lighter poems as 'The Flea' or 'Womens Constancy' which overthrows its own argument in the final lines or alternatively creates a tessellated pattern of successive tergiversations, was aimed, in addition to its humorous purpose, at casting suspicion on the system of ratiocination itself. Yet whatever the ulterior and perhaps only half-conscious motives of these poems, there can be no denying the predominance in their witty setting of a patent desire to amuse. The dialectical ground suddenly gives way beneath our feet and, like the victims of the contemporary wetting-stools, we ruefully discover that we have been duped. It might seem strange to argue that this same technique, whereby words slide from one meaning to another, producing an illusory impression of solidity which retrospectively changes its form as we read on, lies at the core of some of his most moving sermons and meditations, creating that transcendental and, indeed, specifically metaphysical quality which is their most distinguished feature. There is no desire here to tease the intellect nor to provoke even momentary amusement as we realize we have been tricked, but with infinitely heightened effect the mundane is subtly discredited and the criteria of worldly reasoning reduced to triviality as the claims of the spirit are vindicated.

Donne's famous meditation on the tolling of the bell is a case in point. Its central argument, that we should recognize in the ringing of every passing-bell a grim reminder of our own approaching death, is impressive enough to have been made with a firm and simple directness. But he chooses instead to present it, from the literary viewpoint, in a puzzling, labyrinthine form in order to create a more deeply disturbing effect. Again we are surprised into a radical reappraisal of our traditional assumptions, not by an aggressively abrupt opening but by an intricate series of false pointers and verbal elisions whose effect is to make the conventional appear ludicrous and untenable. As in the discussion of 'Loves Growth' I must ask the reader's indulgence for what may appear a fussily microscopic analysis of a magniloquent passage, whose rhythmic flow normally discourages lengthy pauses to ponder the significance of each individual phrase. The cumulative power of the meditation in fact justifies such close analysis; for it is through the subtle movement of thought from phrase to phrase, with its sudden flashes of insight, that the persuasive reversal of standards is achieved.

The quietly philosophical tone with which the passage opens suggests a conventional meditation on death. Accordingly, it takes a moment for the startling implications to be fully grasped:

Perchance hee for whom this *Bell* tolls, may be so ill, as that he knowes not it tolls for him.

The initial phrase had seemed to point unequivocally to the dead man awaiting burial, for whom it would naturally be assumed the bell tolls—until the word 'ill' challenges that assumption and leads us into the preposterous image of an 'ill' corpse anxiously listening out for the knell lest he be late for his own funeral.[32] This is not perversity on Donne's part, but a genuine questioning of the purpose of the funeral bell; and with his usual technique of pretending to brandish before us a mere pun, he compresses this questioning into a single unobtrusive word—the preposition 'for' on which the entire meditation will hinge and which changes its meaning as we gaze at it. The bell may indeed toll for ('in honour of') the dead man, but it is in the most literal sense intended *for* the ears of the living. The grotesque image of a listening corpse compels us to discard as invalid our normal impression that the funeral of an unknown citizen is for him and not for us. And we must therefore ask ourselves afresh for what purpose the bell is really being rung. The bell, Donne now argues, tolls not merely for me but for my own spiritual health and in the word 'better' he ironically blends the clinical metaphor with the deeper moral theme: 'And perchance I may think my selfe so much better than I am, as that they who are about mee and see my state, may have caused it to toll for me, and I know not that.'

The nature of the speaker's sickness (and our own) is at this point left unexplained as Donne moves off, seemingly at a tangent, from his own immediate concerns to the apparent impersonality of the universal Church:

The *Church* is *Catholike, universall*, so are all her *Actions; All* that she does, belongs to *all*. When she *baptizes a child*, that action concernes mee, for that child is thereby connected to that *Head*, which is my *Head* too, and engraffed into that *body*, whereof I am a *member*.

Even out of context, as was noted in an earlier chapter, there is an impressive movement here from the monstrous anatomical image of divers people being engrafted on to the same '*Head*' to the delicate resolution of the image in the concluding word '*member*', which, as it were, chides the reader for having forgotten the original force of the metaphor in Christian history. But within its setting there is an added inconsistency which is also eventually resolved— the strange and seemingly irrelevant shift from solemn funeral obsequies to the baptism of a new-born child. That incongruity is modified here by the term '*universall*', whereby the Church not only demands from its members the intimate relationship of limb to limb, but also creates a new unity out of the various stages and experiences of human life, from the moment when the child has been engrafted on to its body by baptism to that sadder moment when the adult withers from it in death. In that sense too, 'all' the Church does, belongs to 'all'.

Donne's thoughts now turn from the limbs of the Church to its head, the head not only of all Christendom but, by virtue of divine creation, of all mankind. And here too the words seem to disintegrate. For a seventeenth-century reader versed in Latin, the literal and, indeed, primary meaning of 'Author' in this period was still 'Creator' or 'First Cause', and there seems a touch of wilfulness on Donne's part as he slides across to its more specialized meaning of 'writer', distracting attention from the central universal theme of death, as though he cannot resist pursuing an irrelevant pun:

All *mankinde* is of one *Author*, and is one *volume*; when one man dies, one *Chapter* is not *torne* out of the *booke*, but *translated* into a better language, and every *Chapter* must be so *translated*; God emploies several *translators*; some peeces are translated by *age*, some by *sicknesse*, some by *warre*, some by *justice*; but *Gods* hand is in every *translation*; and his hand shall binde up all our scattered leaves againe, for that *Librarie* where every *booke* shall lie open to one another.

The talk of volumes and chapters appears to strain the image and carry us even further away from that death and resurrection which is his central concern. But it is vindicated a moment later by the luminous '*translated*' which returns us immediately to the main theme by its biblical sense of transference from this world to the next. It echoes: 'By faith Enoch was *translated* that he should not see death; and was not found, because God had *translated* him; for before his *translation* he had this testimony, that he pleased God' (Heb. 11: 5)—or even more appropriately: 'Who hath delivered us from the power of darkness and hath *translated* us into the kingdom of his dear son' (Col. 1: 13).[33]

For the third time in this brief passage, then, the elemental or spiritual meaning of a word has thrust aside the colloquial or mundane usage, creating on the linguistic plane the very effect at which the passage as a whole is aiming—the discarding of the transitory in favour of a fundamental and lasting truth. This meditation resembles most great literature in employing surface stylistic devices to reflect the deeper theme, but it is, I believe, unique in employing this specific device, which catches so splendidly the complex idea Donne is attempting to convey. As in that 'transpicuous vision' whereby he perceives the spiritual essence of an object or situation through the actual without losing sight of the external characteristics, so here such everyday words as 'member' and 'translate' are seen at first in a common, everyday setting but, as we watch, they shed their merely contemporary meaning in favour of the elemental or biblical significance containing the spiritual implications which time and worldly activity have obscured. So too, the next ambivalence slides beyond the trivial, localized meaning to the divine. After the grim list of human sufferings which in this world lead agonizingly to death—age, sickness, war, and hanging— the phrase '. . . and his hand shall binde up all our scattered leaves againe . . .' contains beyond its technical reference to bookbinding, the soothing echo of: 'He healeth the broken in heart and *bindeth up* their wounds' (Ps. 147: 3); and the scattered leaves of the book close the phrase with a rich autumnal connotation.

Having reached Judgement Day, when our books will all lie open to each other, Donne returns to his original theme, again exploiting the near-ludicrous to underscore his point. This time it is the idea of a church bell being rung solely to remind the preacher to attend his own sermon. The image, however, takes on an additional force here, since in the context of this meditation the corpse has itself become the preacher, proclaiming by its own condition the ultimate sermon to mankind. At once, as in the Loyolan tradition, Donne deflects the focus inward, from the universal to the intimate self, the 'mee' who at the time he composed this meditation was in fact lying close to death, and in need of the full lesson to be derived from that sermon:

As therefore the *Bell* that rings to a *Sermon*, calls not upon the Preacher onely but upon the *Congregation* to come; so this *Bell* calls us all: but how much more mee, who am brought so neere the *doore* by this sicknesse.

From this point on, the slow-moving meditation gathers momentum, taking on the immediacy of swiftly approaching death. Having

invalidated by his series of grotesque images the selfish unconcern
of the worldly for a distant or unknown parishioner's death, he can
now firmly assert what had at first been suggested only obliquely
and enigmatically, that

The *Bell* doth toll for him that *thinkes* it doth; and though it *intermit*
againe, yet from that *minute* that that occasion wrought upon him,
hee is united to God. Who casts not up his *Eye* to the *Sunne* when it
rises? but who takes off his *Eye* from a *Comet* when that breakes out?
Who bends not his *eare* to any *bell*, which upon any occasion rings?
but who can remove it from that *bell*, which is passing a *peece of himselfe* out of this world?

The bell is no longer tolling for another man, but for 'a *peece of
himselfe*'. In the meditative tradition, the spectator has been drawn
emotionally into the funeral scene, imaginatively projecting himself
into the dead man's coffin in anticipation of the moment of his own
burial. And in the climactic peroration, the scientific concern for
material and measurable size is cast scornfully aside as the single
clod is given its full significance even beside the vast continent or
promontory, when that clod of earth is 'thy friends' or 'thine own'
mansion—the body that houses the human soul:

No man is an *Iland*, intire of it selfe: every man is a peece of the
Continent, a part of the *maine*; if a *Clod* bee washed away by the *Sea*,
Europe is the lesse, as well as if a *Promontorie* were, as well as if a *Mannor*
of thy *friends*, or of *thine owne* were; any mans *death* diminishes *me*,
because I am involved in *Mankinde*; And therefore never send to know
for whom the *bell* tolls; It tolls for *thee*.

If it requires some degree of close reading to identify the stylistic
devices whereby Donne achieves this primacy of the spiritual over
the material—his undermining of reality by extrapolating conventional phraseology or thought, and his mannerist involvement of
the spectator in a personal and vivid experience of death—the
message comes powerfully across even to the reader who is unaware
of the detailed techniques which are used; for the style arises
naturally out of the content, and the illusionist pattern of Donne's
rhetoric is moulded by his consciousness that the measurable, the
haptic, and the verifiable elements of this world are at best no more
than ephemeral.

It may be worth pausing for a moment to remind ourselves that it is precisely this 'serpentine' form of argument with its sudden changes of direction and reversals of perspective which has been described so often by critics as a form of 'nervous indecision' or 'aimless versatility', on the theory that the rejection of any fixed vantage-point in mannerism results in a collapse or weakening of purpose.[34] This is, to my mind, a misreading both of religious mannerism in general, and of Donne's writing in particular. It would be difficult to recall any passage in literature more purposeful in its rhetorical power and more secure in its beliefs than this meditation; and in the world of painting one may well ask in what way El Greco's *Agony in the Garden* appears aimless or indecisive beside Bellini's. On the contrary, El Greco's version vibrates with a sense of personal revelation and of heightened response to a transcendental ideal. The critical error arises from focusing upon only one aspect of the picture—the disintegration of the factual—and ignoring the authentication of the inner or spiritual significance which gives the painting its directional force. So here, in each of the examples we have examined in Donne's poetry and prose, whether in the over-all effect of reaching beyond the temporal to the eternal, or in the small details which contribute to that over-all effect— when conventional ideas are made to collapse into absurdity before an ultimate truth—the final impression is of deep conviction rather than (to use that well-worn phrase) of 'unresolved tension'.

In an age riddled with religious sectarianism and susceptible to millenarian visionaries, it is extraordinary how little Donne cares for celestial epiphanies even in literary form. As love must attain to its initial knowledge of divine love through the earthly form, so the celestial vision interests him only when it is anchored in the flesh. It has often been remarked that we know almost nothing of the mistresses to whom Donne addressed his love poems—whether they were dark or fair, tall or short—for his attention was focused on the experience of the male lover himself, his hopes, musings, disappointments, and joys. And the same holds true for the religious writings. There are no descriptions in his verse either of effulgent heavens or of the gloomy caverns of hell such as abound in the art and literature of the baroque; but, as in mannerist art, his concern is with the Christian worshipper himself, caught at the moment of his personal revelation, insight, or suffering. It is this rooting of religious experience in the troubled, mortal self that separates him so finally from Vaughan. In one of his noblest passages, Vaughan merges the prophetic and the mechanistic cosmologies in a depiction of the ordered orbiting of the spheres, illumined by divine radiance; and in the baroque tradition he remains the wondering but un-involved spectator pointing above to the awesome heavens:

> I saw Eternity the other night
>   Like a great Ring of pure and endless light,
>   All calm as it was bright,
> And round beneath it, Time in hours, days, years
>   Driv'n by the spheres,
> Like a vast shadow mov'd, In which the world
>   And all her train were hurl'd.

There is no moment in Donne's poetry so tranquil in its response to the world of the spirit. In contrast to Vaughan's calm testimony to the universal vision, Donne transforms his own mind and soul into the theatre within which martyrological scenes of the past are re-enacted to test the intensity and validity of his own response. In 'Goodfriday, 1613. Riding Westward', he pointedly inserted the date into the title of the poem to remind us that his subject here is not the Crucifixion itself, but his own ability or inability as a Christian to respond imaginatively to a meditative re-enactment of that event on the anniversary of its original occurrence. Part of the ambivalence of this poem is our knowledge that, even were he able to turn and gaze towards the eastern horizon, he would not see in fact but only in mind the figure of Jesus hanging upon the Cross.

The placing of this vision within a firm temporal and geographi-cal setting creates that initial sense of solidity necessary for Donne's mannerist illusionism; and as the spiritual implications take com-mand and the apparent solidity disintegrates, the reader is gradually seduced into a totally different conception of the world. In a manner reminiscent of his earlier poem 'The Flea', the poem begins with all the confident rationality of a scientific treatise, demonstrating from the astronomical system of the Ptolemaic universe the conflicting forces exerted on the soul in its own movement westward. In an era which still preserved as axiomatic, at least in its literary conventions, the direct relationship between the music of the spheres and the harmony of the soul, there was nothing remarkable or idiosyncratic in the comparison itself; and by adopting the unmistakable format of a geometrical theorem, this opening section lends its final couplet 'Hence is't . . .' the persuasive force of *quod erat demonstrandum*. The analogy of the stars has, as it were, proved conclusively that the soul has accepted pleasure or business as its 'first mover' in place of the devotion which should rightfully impel it.[35] All is clear and eminently reasonable within this empirical setting.

> Let mans Soule be a Spheare, and then, in this,
> The intelligence that moves, devotion is,
> And as the other Spheares, by being growne
> Subject to forraigne motions, lose their owne,
> And being by others hurried every day,
> Scarce in a yeare their naturall forme obey:
> Pleasure or businesse, so, our Soules admit
> For their first mover, and are whirld by it.
> Hence is't, that I am carried towards the West
> This day, when my Soules forme bends towards the East.

The picture of the speaker which emerges from this passage is of a worldly man, unfortunately too preoccupied by his business activities or his pleasure interests to fulfil those religious obligations which in the final line he admits he ought really to be performing. His soul bends in that direction but, after all, the affairs of this world have precedence—hence he is carried towards the west. Just as this realistic setting has been established, however, with each planet completing its orbit precisely within the year assigned by the fixed laws of the universe, those very physical laws are suddenly undercut by the paradoxes of religious faith. The prosaic, mechanistic world of the West is held symbolically in contrast with the rich, imaginative world of the East, where the immutable rules of gravity and the regular, unbroken succession of night and day shrivel away before the supernatural forces of the spiritual experience:

> There I should see a Sunne, by rising set,
> And by that setting endlesse day beget;

But that Christ on this Crosse, did rise and fall,
Sinne had eternally benighted all.

The phrase 'There I should see . . .' reminds us that we are witnessing not the scene itself but a 'meditative' conjuring up of that
scene in the mind of the speaker; yet in contrast to normal Loyolan
practice, and as a means of heightening its dramatic force, the poem
implies throughout that, were the traveller to turn, he would
actually witness with his own eyes the cyclical re-enactment of the
Crucifixion on this solemn anniversary of its original occurrence. At
once the awesomeness of the scene makes him recoil into himself as
he dares almost be glad that he is spared the impact of that vision.
The worldly, nonchalant traveller of the opening scene is becoming
significantly sensitized and we already have reason to suspect that
despite his verbal assertion, it is perhaps not entirely through the
materialistic impulses of the flesh that he has chosen to travel westward on this fateful day. As yet it is no more than a hint, and we
move on to a powerful passage far removed from that cold empirical
demonstration with which we began, and charged instead with the
growing wonder and dread of a meditator reliving with full immediacy the moment of the Crucifixion, this time not in terms of the
physical suffering of Jesus but (as a counterpart to the opening
astronomical section) in terms of its vastness within a cosmic
setting, blinding the sun, cracking the earth, God's footstool, and,
as the wooden poles of the Cross blend into the twin poles of the
universe, spanning the infinite reaches of heaven:

Yet dare I almost be glad, I do not see
That spectacle of too much weight for mee.
Who sees Gods face, that is selfe life, must dye;
What a death were it then to see God dye?
It made his own Lieutenant Nature shrinke,
It made his footstoole crack, and the Sunne winke.
Could I behold those hands which span the Poles,
And tune all spheares at once, peirc'd with those holes?
Could I behold that endlesse height which is
Zenith to us, and to our Antipodes,
Humbled below us? or that blood which is
The seat of all our Soules, if not of his,

> Make durt of dust, or that flesh which was worne
> By God for his apparell, rag'd and torne?
> If on these things I durst not looke, durst I
> Upon his miserable mother cast mine eye,
> Who was Gods partner here, and furnish'd thus
> Halfe of that Sacrifice, which ransom'd us?

Nature, whose immutable laws had appeared to dominate the scientific universe, is recognized now as merely God's lieutenant, subservient to his behests, and shrinking before the divine epiphany. But above all, that supposedly worldly speaker has become the mannerist *Sprecher*, overwhelmed and stunned by the impact of the scene which he has visualized and which we are witnessing through his eyes. He 'durst not' gaze directly at it; and at this point we learn that throughout his journey westward the scene has, in fact, remained ever present in his mind's eye. In one of those masterly twists of direction which lend the dramatic force to Donne's writing, the truth emerges at last:

> Though these things, as I ride, be from mine eye,
> They are present yet unto my memory,
> For that looks towards them; and thou looks towards mee,
> O Saviour, as thou hang'st upon the tree;
> I turne my backe to thee, but to receive
> Corrections, till thy mercies bid thee leave.
> O thinke mee worth thine anger, punish mee,
> Burne off my rusts, and my deformity,
> Restore thine Image, so much, by thy grace,
> That thou may'st know mee, and I'll turne my face.

It transpires in retrospect that it was, in fact, neither business nor pleasure which had earlier drawn him westward, but the tormenting conviction of his own unworthiness, crystallized in the image of his turning his back not in disrespect, but in penitent preparation for the flagellation which may partially expiate his guilt. His 'deformity' (the corruption of that 'naturall forme' alluded to in the opening lines) has tarnished the metal mirror of his soul, and its rusts must be burned away before it can reflect in even faintly recognizable shape the image of God in which it was first created. The almost desperate prayer for its restoration with which the poem concludes contrasts vividly with the apparent nonchalance of the opening. We have once again been led along a seemingly secure, rational path set within the firm dimensions of the Renaissance world, only to be confronted at the first bend with a vision which shatters our confidence in its standards, as the emotional and non-rational criteria of inner faith are asserted in their place.

Donne's keen responsiveness to the latest scientific discoveries of his age has long been regarded as one of his most characteristic features, particularly endearing him to his admirers during the earlier part of this century. It was a rare quality among poets of his time. Shakespeare, for example, despite the enormous breadth and variety of his interests in law, philosophy, music, ship-rigging, and falconry, was always more concerned with the accepted ideas and practices of his age than with its most recent innovations. In the entire range of his writing, one never experiences the excitement aroused by a scientific discovery fresh from the laboratory. Donne, in contrast, displays a sharp curiosity for the novel, a desire to keep up to date with the newest experiments, and to be present at those frontiers where knowledge was being extended. But it would be a mistake to class him even in the most general way with such embryonic empiricists as Francis Bacon or Kepler in their readiness to reassess the settled, authoritative traditions of the past in the light of newly revealed knowledge. For his writing betrays (not always at first sight) a fundamental conservatism. The challenge to convention which he so often offers is a challenge to Renaissance convention, and a harking back to a faith deeply embedded in the past.[36] For in his sympathetic response to scientific thought and experimentation, he is intrigued primarily not by the clear rules and indisputable proofs which such investigation provides, but by the inner contradictions it discloses. He seizes upon such anomalies in order to justify his own belief that, in the final analysis, the answers to man's most pressing problems are not to be found in the neatly organized world of empirical reasoning.

While his love poetry bristles with allusions to the limbecks and flasks of the contemporary laboratory, to the 'sinewie thread' the brain lets fall through the body, to the atoms and elements of which we are composed, there is none the less concealed within these modernistic references a sly disparagement of the limitations inherent in such scientific pursuits. An entire poem, for example, is devoted to 'Loves Alchymie'—a perfect instance, it might appear, of that 'association of sensibility' which T. S. Eliot so admired, the bringing together of love and science in mutual enrichment. On closer inspection, however, the comparison emerges as entirely negative in its intent. The basis for the love–science equation which Donne offers is, in fact, the total failure of the 'chymique' or alchemist to discover that elusive elixir promised for so long, the elixir which supposedly would cure all human ills as well as turn base metals into gold. The connecting filaments, therefore, between love and alchemy are, we discover, merely the frustration and despair they both produce:

> And as no chymique yet th' Elixir got,
> But glorifies his pregnant pot,
> If by the way to him befall
> Some odoriferous thing, or med'cinall,
> So, lovers dreame a rich and long delight,
> But get a winter-seeming summers night.

Moreover, who but Donne would pounce with such triumph upon the anomaly that on a flat map of the world the two points seemingly most distant from each other are in fact adjacent? Ignoring with his usual eclecticism all the achievements of the new empirical method, the genuine search for accuracy and standardization, the testing of hypotheses to produce universal and unarguable truths, he fastens instead upon a contradiction he has exposed within the scientific world itself, asking why, if paradox holds true in science, it should not also hold true for his Christian beliefs:

> As West and East
> In all flatt Maps (and I am one) are one,
> So death doth touch the Resurrection.

On another occasion, he offers reassurance to the despondent Christian, who has recognized the impossibility of ever attaining to full righteousness, by drawing his attention to the newly developed mariners' compass, employed by contemporary seamen as a scientific aid to navigation. Characteristically, however, his comparison is based not on the reliability of the scientific method but on its inaccuracies and errors which, like the human failings present in every Christian soul, do yet not prevent the traveller from reaching his desired haven:

A Compasse is a necessary thing in a Ship, and the helpe of that Compasse brings the Ship home safe, and yet that Compasse hath some variations, it doth not looke directly North; Neither is that starre which we call the North-pole, or by which we know the North-pole, the very Pole it selfe; but we call it so, and we make our uses of it, and our conclusions by it, as if it were so, because it is the nearest starre to that Pole. He that comes as neere uprightnesse as infirmities admit, is an upright man, though he have some obliquities.[37]

This tendency to turn science on its head in order to justify spiritual paradox—or at the very least to pick out only those contradictory elements within it which suited his purpose—is exemplified by his response to an incident in his own life. On rising from his sick-bed in 1623 after a protracted illness, Donne experienced an attack of dizziness. In itself it was nothing remarkable, but with his proclivity for allegorizing the mundane, Donne discovered within this physical dizziness a paradigm for the deceptiveness of all sensory experience—a paradigm which confirmed his own suspicions of scientific reliance on observable phenomena. With a logic of his own which inverts all normal reasoning, he perceives within his vertigo more persuasive evidence for the new solar system of Copernicus than all the demonstrable proof hitherto adduced by Galileo:

I am up, and I seem to stand, and I go round; and I am a new Argument of the new Philosophie, That the Earth moves round; why may I not beleeve, that the whole earth moves in a round motion, though that seeme to mee to stand, when as I seeme to stand to my Company, and yet am carried, in a giddy, and circular motion, as I stand? Man hath no center but misery; there and onely there, hee is fixt, and sure to find himselfe.[38]

He argues quixotically, as though the most convincing element in the new mechanistic universe was the doubt it cast upon the evidence of one's own eyes. We should, in other words, admit the rotation of the earth precisely *because* our senses deny it. He is in effect, applying to science a theological 'Credo quia absurdum', which of course militates against the most fundamental criteria of the scientific method. Here is illusionism employed once again not as a prank, but as a conviction; as, in fact, the cornerstone of fideism. The subjective triumphs over the objective, and any possible impression of caprice in this passage is dissipated by the gloom of the final sentence.

Throughout his life then, Donne's genuine interest in the new discoveries of science was modified by an awareness that at most they affected only a circumscribed area of human experience. The mechanistic explanation of the cosmos may have replaced the symmetrically concentric Ptolemaic universe by an elliptical solar system and hence challenged the religious symbolism of universal harmony which had been read into the older pattern; but in Donne's eyes the mystery and magnificence of Creation remained untouched. Only the Renaissance thinker who had placed his trust in reason and in the physical properties of this world would submit unconditionally to the final authority of such verifiable facts, and Donne was not one of that company. As early as his 'Anatomie of the World' he had written with satirical scorn of the astronomers who imagined that by measuring latitude and longitude they could drag the divine heavens down to human level:

> For of Meridians and Parallels,
> Man hath weav'd out a net, and this net throwne
> Upon the Heavens, and now they are his owne.
> Loth to goe up the hill, or labour thus
> To goe to heaven, we make heaven come to us.
> We spur, we reine the starres, and in their race
> They're diversly content t'obey our pace.

In the same way as twentieth-century man tends to speak confidently of having 'conquered' the moon when he has only set foot precariously upon it, so the scientist, Donne points out, has failed to perceive the enormous gap between merely recording the orbiting of the stars and subjugating them to his will. The cosmographer may learn the laws of their motion, but that is far from a usurpation of divine authority in creating such vast objects, placing them within their courses, and supervising their subsequent movement.

Donne was, in fact, one of the first of his age to recognize and to resist what was so sorely to trouble later generations (particularly the nineteenth century) that the objectivity of science as it accurately measured the circling of the planets and established the unalterable laws of the physical universe implied a silent challenge to the very idea of a Supreme Being. According to the new philosophy, the nature of creation itself might still be arguable, but (to use Paley's image) once the universal clock had been wound up, God himself seemed superfluous. Donne perceived at once that the tendency of the scientific method to strip the universe of its magnificence by means of its prosaic mathematical calculations deprived the beholder of that sense of wonder which each natural movement of the sun and stars should inspire. In a sermon delivered not long after the meditation on his own dizziness, he argued that miracle in the truest sense of the term is not a divine interruption of natural law. Such evidence, he remarks, is required only by those weak in faith and understanding. In the tradition of the Psalmist, who saw the heavens as silently declaring the glory of the Lord in the very regularity of their daily movement,[39] so Donne maintained that true miracle resided in the splendour whereby such massive objects as the stars complete their appointed course with such perfection:

The standing still of the Sun, for *Iosuahs* use, was not, in it selfe, so wonderfull a thing, as that so vast and immense a body as the Sun, should run so many miles, in a minute; The motion of the Sun were a greater wonder than the standing still, if all were to begin againe; And onely the daily doing takes off the admiration. But then God having, as it were, concluded himself in a course of nature, and written downe in the booke of Creatures, Thus and thus all things shall be carried, though he glorifie himselfe sometimes, in doing a miracle, yet there is in every miracle, a silent chiding of the world, and a tacite reprehension of them, who require, or who need miracles.[40]

This contrast between the scientist's exclusive concern with the verifiable or measurable evidence of the physical senses, and the Christian's reaching out beyond the factual to the spiritual experience constitutes the central theme of 'Hymne to God my God, in my sicknesse' from which the map image quoted above was just drawn. That it should form the central theme is the more remarkable as this poem is almost alone among Donne's devotional writings in its freedom from his characteristic inner struggle. There are no traces of the meditative elements we have been examining, no violent assaults on the reader's emotions, no vivid re-enactment of martyrdom or crucifixion, and no desperate admission of personal failings. On the contrary, the mood is calm, the rhythm measured. It is as though, with death itself so near, the need for any imaginative anticipation of mortality was past. Indeed, if the Loyolan exercise had aimed at creating an urgent and passionate response to man's spiritual condition by stimulating a personal awareness of death's significance, Donne's actual encounter with death was, as Walton's account relates, a model of tranquil but devotional resignation.[41] He set his worldly affairs in order, bade farewell to those close to him, and then asked to be disturbed no more as he concentrated his thoughts on the moment for which he had pre-prepared so long. He had not forgotten his past sins nor the weaknesses he still discerned within him, but he had in a very literal sense received intimations of immortality:

... I cannot plead innocency of life, especially of my youth: But I am to be judged by a merciful God, *who is not willing to see what I have done amiss*. And, though of my self I have nothing to present to him but sins and misery; yet I know he looks not upon me now as I am of my selfe, but as I am in my Saviour, and hath given me even at this present time some testimonies by his Holy Spirit, that I am of the number of his Elect: *I am therefore full of unexpressible joy, and shall dye in peace.*

This note of peace permeates the entire 'Hymne'. Yet even here, caught up in the imminence of his bodily dissolution, he remains fascinated by the contrast between the new science and the old faith. Lying mortally ill, and watching with gratitude his physicians' sympathetic examination of his physical condition, he sees in them perfect representatives of scientific inquiry, both in its virtues and its limitations. They are cosmographers sadly and compassionately mapping out on the minor world of the human body the dire straits whereby he is to die. For Donne, however, the word 'straits' has more positive connotations, drawn from its Gospel rather than its geographical setting—'. . . strait is the gate and narrow the way which leadeth unto life'. The scientists grieve because, restricted to somatic symptoms, for them the cessation of bodily functions marks the end of life. He on the other hand, as a Christian believer, rejoices at the corruption of his flesh which will at last release his soul into eternity. Unknown to them, therefore, he is embarking on a new journey.

> Whilst my Physitians by their love are growne
> Cosmographers, and I their Mapp, who lie
> Flat on this bed, that by them may be showne
> That this is my South-west discoverie
> *Per fretum febris*, by these streights to die,
>
> I joy, that in these straits, I see my West;
> For, though theire currants yeeld returne to none,
> What shall my West hurt me? As West and East
> In all flatt Maps (and I am one) are one,
> So death doth touch the Resurrection.

The West–East map image has established, as we have seen, religious paradox on the substructure of scientific anomaly, and after reminding his reader that even geographically all the wealth of the East as well as holy Jerusalem itself can be reached only by passing through narrow straits (which are therefore sources of hope rather than dread), he moves forward to that powerful image in which the entire range of Christian history from the Garden of Eden, through Calvary, and on to the heavenly Paradise is compressed into one brief stanza and, indeed, into one brief moment of time— his own transition from temporal to eternal life. The aeons which chronologically separate the Tree in the Garden of Eden from the Cross at Calvary disappear as the two merge into one;[42] and the meticulous measurements of the map-makers and physicians become meaningless or irrelevant as time and space stretch and shrink once again before the vision of the soul's resurrection:

> We thinke that *Paradise* and *Calvarie*,
> *Christs* Crosse, and *Adams* tree, stood in one place;

> Looke Lord, and finde both *Adams* met in me;
> As the first *Adams* sweat surrounds my face,
> May the last *Adams* blood my soule embrace.

In typically mannerist fashion, instead of the poet finding his baroque comfort by being absorbed into the infinite and eternal as Milton does in the sonnet on his blindness, the infinite and eternal find their validity in Donne's individual predicament. It was, he argues, for the sake of the single human soul trembling before the threat of damnation that Jesus died. As he himself approaches that moment, seeing in the perspiration of his mortal fever the symbolic convergence of the two Adams, the enormous sweep of Christian history from Creation to Doomsday becomes consummated in him. We may appear far removed from the light-hearted, amorous mood of 'The Sunne Rising', but the deeper theme of both poems is remarkably similar—that for all the vastness of the newly mapped heliocentric universe, and the apparent negligibility of man, crawling insect-like on the surface of a minor globe, the individual human remains, in the authenticity of his inner being and the immeasurable significance of his eternal soul, the ultimate purpose of divine creation. The hymn, moreover, concludes with that very image to which we have so often had cause to refer and which, as Donne here acknowledges, had formed a central theme of his preaching, both in poetry and prose. The text he has preached is the mannerist depiction of the saint or penitent flung backwards in order to be raised, and symbolizing in his prostration the Christian paradox of resurrection achieved through the putrefaction of the flesh:

> And as to others soules I preach'd thy word,
> Be this my Text, my Sermon to mine owne,
> Therefore that he may raise, the Lord throws down.

In this period of Donne's life, which marked the final affirmation of themes only hesitatingly suggested before, his rejection of temporal reasoning joins forces with another image recurrent in his earlier years, the eclipsing of the visible world in order to see with the eye of the soul. Within the New Testament, the perfect exemplar for the union of these two themes was the vision of Paul on his way to Damascus. Struck to the earth by a dazzling heavenly light, he rises physically blinded, but spiritually converted to the new faith. He sees with the inner eye. Where Caravaggio had captured that conversion pictorially as the saint is thrown backwards to the ground, Donne sees in the same revelation a paradigm for his own belief (a belief he implemented in his own life with only limited success) that a man should turn away from the 'knowledges of this world' in order to contemplate the truths of the world above. He had always suspected that alchemical inquiry could not answer the deeper spiritual needs of man; and now, with greater certainty than in the past, he joined El Greco in closing the shutters on the sunlit world in order to enjoy those richer visions of the mind which had been, like Marvell's Soul, 'blinded with an eye'. He defends, therefore, what might appear to his age no more than a foolish obscurantism:

Saul was struck blinde, but it was a blindness contracted from light . . . This blindnesse which we speak of, which is a sober and temperate abstinence from the immoderate study, and curious knowledges of this world, this holy simplicity of the soule is not a darknesse, a dimnesse, a stupidity in the understanding, contracted by living in a corner, it is not an idle retiring into a Monastery, or into a Village, or a Country solitude, it is not a lazy affectation of ignorance; not darknesse, but a greater light, must make us blinde . . . *Saul* had such a blindnesse, as that he fell with it. There are birds, that when their eyes are cieled, still soare up, till they have spent all their strength. Men blinded with the lights of this world, soare still into higher places, or higher knowledges, or higher opinions; but the light of heaven humbles us, and layes flat that soule, which the leaven of this world had puffed and swelled up.[43]

As the barbed final phrase suggests, he knew that such withdrawal would appear retrograde to those still caught up by the new confidence in man's conquest of this world, but he saw it as an inevitable step in his search for an inner understanding. The same sentiment prompted him, after taking holy orders, to interpret his journey across the sea to Germany as a symbol of his divorce from all worldly hopes and loves, and he closes the poem once again with the chiaroscuro image of the vision within the darkness:

Churches are best for Prayer, that have least light:
To see God only, I goe out of sight.

There had been a long progression from Donne's *Songs and Sonets* with their teasing undermining of Renaissance perspective and logic to the dedicated writing of his last years, but it was essentially a movement in an unchanging direction. From the literary viewpoint, it was not a process of maturation. Donne had proved as brilliant a poet in paying court to his mistresses as he had in paying court to his God. But only an insensitive reader can be unaware of the bond connecting the two apparently distant poles of his writing —the search for a spiritual reality, whether in the realm of love or faith, which in his eyes could alone give meaning to an otherwise pointless carnality. His wit succeeds because, like all true humour, it touches upon the basic absurdity of the human condition, where man is caught grotesquely between the bestial and the divine. We reach for the stars and trip over a stool; like Falstaff, we talk grandiosely of honour while betraying our gross subservience to the flesh. Donne's lovers amuse us as they consummate their holy matrimony in the entrails of a flea or, like the lady of that poem, pride themselves on the sophistication of their reason which will in a moment collapse beneath them, disproving the very honour and nobility on which their sense of superiority rests. But set against such absurdity is the tremulous assertion of a lasting and sacred love which outreaches all logic and all definition.

In the earliest stages of his specifically religious quest, Donne's suspicion of Reason had been both more limited and more cautious. His *Essays in Divinity* argued concerning the problem of divine *creatio ex nihilo* that '. . . for this point, we are not under the insinuations and mollifyings of perswasion and conveniency; nor under the Spirituall, and peaceable Tyranny, and easie yoke of sudden and present Faith'.[44] The dislodgement of Reason is offset by a hesitancy to accept faith as a final arbiter. However, if we turn to the great sermons of his last days, there logical reasoning is discarded even as a weapon for neutralizing Reason itself, and the scorn he pours on the atheist who refuses to believe merely because he lacks empirical evidence is the scorn not of rational argument nor even of paradoxical proof, but of his own impassioned belief. The strength of his personal conviction throbs through the passage as he challenges the non-believer confident in his own rationality to wait until the silence of the night when the fear of death is upon him, and to *dare* then to deny his God:

Poore intricated soule! Riddling, perplexed, labyrinthicall soule! Thou couldest not say, that thou beleevest not in God, if there were no God; Thou couldest not beleeve in God, if there were no God; If there were no God, thou couldest not speake, thou couldest not thinke, not a word, not a thought, no not against God; Thou couldest not blaspheme the Name of God, thou couldest not sweare, if there were no God; For all thy faculties, how ever depraved, and perverted by thee, are from him; and except thou canst seriously beleeve that thou art nothing, thou canst not beleeve that there is no God . . . Bee as confident as thou canst, in company; for company is the Atheists Sanctuary; I respit thee not till the day of Judgement, when I may see thee upon thy knees, upon thy face, begging of the hills, that they would fall downe and cover thee from the fierce wrath of God, to aske thine own death, Is there a God now? I respit thee not till the day of thine own death, when thou shalt have evidence enough that there is a God, though no other evidence, but to find a Devill, and evidence enough, that there is a Heaven, though no other evidence, but to feele Hell; To aske thee then, Is there a God now? I respit thee but a few houres, but six houres, but till midnight. Wake then; and then darke, and alone, Heare God aske thee then, remember that I asked thee now, Is there a God? and if thou darest, say No.[45]

Here is the final confrontation, as Donne perceives it, between the full implications of the New Philosophy and the faith of the Christian believer. The physical, demonstrable 'evidence' sought by the empiricist is held up to reiterated ridicule as the latter's soul shrinks before a dread realization—that the mechanistic universe of science carries with it the grim cancellation of man's sole hope for the eternity of his soul. In Donne's words, '. . . except thou canst seriously beleeve that thou art nothing, thou canst not beleeve that there is no God'.

Is this, I wonder, the 'insecure', the 'capricious', or the 'hysterical' Donne of whom we have been hearing from the critics; is it even the 'reformed' Dr. Donne who has turned his back on the Jack Donne of the sonnets, when we recall the delicate soulfulness of the lovers hoping that their love will in some way outlast the grave and the Day of Judgement:

> Will he not let us alone,
> And thinke that there a loving couple lies,
> Who thought that this device might be some way
> To make their soules, at the last busie day,
> Meet at this grave, and make a little stay?

Or are these two passages, like the mannerist paintings of El Greco and Tintoretto, unified for all their surface differences by their purposeful reaching out, in defiance of the scientific authority of their day, to values beyond the empirical and the pragmatic?

NOTES

CHAPTER I

1. Jan Kott, *Shakespeare Our Contemporary*, tr. B. Taborski (London, 1964), pp. 48 ff., and Leslie Fiedler, *Love and Death in the American Novel* (New York, 1966), pp. 352 and 405.

2. The growing respect for Donne among scholars during the nineteenth century has been recorded in Joseph E. Duncan, *The Revival of Metaphysical Poetry* (Minneapolis, 1959), and Kathleen Tillotson, 'Donne's Poetry in the Nineteenth Century', *Elizabethan and Jacobean Studies Presented to F. P. Wilson* (Oxford, 1959), pp. 307 ff.

3. *Selected Essays* (London, 1949), p. 287. His partial repudiation in 1931 of the views expressed in this essay did little to stem the interest his original comments had aroused some ten years earlier.

4. Joseph Wood Krutch, *The Modern Temper: a study and a confession* (New York, 1956), p. 7. It was first published in 1929.

5. Aldous Huxley, *Point Counter Point* (New York, 1928), p. 38. The Beethoven section appears on p. 508.

6. In the introduction to her collection of critical essays on Donne published in the 'Twentieth Century Views' series (Englewood Cliffs, N.J., 1962), p. 6.

7. Louis I. Bredvold, 'The Naturalism of Donne in Relation to Some Renaissance Traditions', *Journal of English and Germanic Philology* 22 (1923), 471.

8. J. B. Leishman, *The Monarch of Wit* (New York, 1966).

9. Preface to the *Pseudo-martyr*.

10. In a letter prefacing his 'An Hymne to the Saints, and to Marquesse Hamylton' in Grierson's edition of the poems (Oxford, 1966), i. 288.

11. See the reply to Bishop Morton's offer in Walton's *Life of Donne*, based on Morton's own recollection of the exchange.

12. E. Gosse, *The Life and Letters of John Donne* (Gloucester, Mass., 1959), i. 191. The italics are mine.

13. *The Triple Foole*. All quotations from Donne's poems are drawn from *The Elegies and the Songs and Sonnets*, ed. Helen Gardner (Oxford, 1966), *The*

Satires, Epigrams and Verse Letters, ed. W. Milgate (Oxford, 1967), and *The Divine Poems*, ed. Helen Gardner (Oxford, 1959). Elision marks have, however, been omitted.

14. Cleanth Brooks, *The Well-Wrought Urn* (New York, 1947), pp. 16–17. In his *Modern Poetry and the Tradition* (Oxford, 1965), p. 46, Brooks suggests in passing that both Donne and Yeats create a 'myth' which is for them as valid as truth itself; but he develops the point only in relation to Yeats.

15. N. J. C. Andreasen, for example, has recently described this poem as making '. . . fun of idolatrous lovers who take themselves too seriously', in her *John Donne: Conservative Revolutionary* (Princeton, 1967), p. 160.

16. Clay Hunt, *Donne's Poetry* (New Haven, 1954), p. 92.

17. First Prebend Sermon delivered in 1625, in *The Sermons of John Donne*, ed. Evelyn M. Simpson and George R. Potter (Berkeley and Los Angeles, 1962), vi. 297–8. All subsequent quotations are from this edition, published by the University of California Press and appearing here by kind permission of the Regents of the University.

18. Basil Willey, *The Seventeenth Century Background* (New York, 1955), p. 50.

19. Mario Praz, *Mnemosyne: the Parallel between Literature and the Visual Arts* (Oxford, 1970), p. 55.

20. In 1933, for example, Basil Willey felt it necessary to apologize for 'trespassing so outrageously beyond the supposed limits of literary criticism' in offering his study of the relationship between literature and the philosophical patterns of the age.

CHAPTER II

1. Germain Bazin, *A Concise History of Art* (London, 1962), ii. 273–4. As this study is concerned with art history only tangentially, I have kept bibliographical references to the minimum. Readers may like to consult R. Wellek, 'The Concept of the Baroque' reprinted in his *Concepts of Criticism* (New Haven, 1963), O. D. Mourgues, *Metaphysical Baroque and Precieuse Poetry* (Oxford, 1953), R. Tuve, 'Baroque and Mannerist Milton', *Journal of English and Germanic Philology* 60 (1961), 817, L. Nelson, *Baroque Lyric Poetry* (New Haven, 1961), and Roy Daniells, *Milton, Mannerism and Baroque* (Toronto, 1964).

2. H. Hatzfeld, 'A Clarification of the Baroque Problems in the Romance Literatures', *Comparative Literature* I (1949), 113, M. M. Mahood, *Poetry and Humanism* (London, 1950), pp. 20 and 144, and Wylie Sypher, *Four Stages of Renaissance Style* (New York, 1955), pp. 109 and 139. Sypher does include

phrases here and there nominally acknowledging that mannerism is an authentic art style, but the adjectives he uses to describe the paintings—'sour', 'thin', 'twisted'—and the negative parallels he draws leave no doubt where his sympathies lie.

3. John Keble, *Morning*, 61–4, and Gerard Manley Hopkins, *Thou Art Indeed Just*, 5–7.

4. Arnold Hauser, *Mannerism*, tr. E. Mosbacher (New York, 1965), 2 vols. One of the best introductions to mannerist art, despite its brevity and obviously more popular intent, is Linda Murray, *The Late Renaissance and Mannerism* (London, 1967), which is symptomatic of the growing sympathy for this art form. See also F. Würtenberger, *Mannerism*, tr. M. Heron (New York, 1963). There is a valuable summary of the conflicting views on mannerism in art and literature as well as a useful bibliography in an article by James V. Mirollo, 'The Mannered and the Mannerist in Late Renaissance Literature', published in *The Meaning of Mannerism*, ed. F. W. Robinson and S. G. Nichols Jr. (New Hampshire, 1972).

5. Hiram Haydn, *The Counter Renaissance* (New York, 1950), and E. M. W. Tillyard, *The Elizabethan World Picture* (New York, 1943), especially chapter ii of the latter.

6. H. Jedin, *The History of the Council of Trent*, tr. N. D. Smith (London and Melbourne, 1967).

7. Max Weber's essay 'The Protestant Ethic and the Spirit of Capitalism' later developed in R. H. Tawney's *Religion and the Rise of Capitalism* (London, 1926).

8. For a history of the numerous traditions from which Milton could have chosen, see J. M. Evans, *Paradise Lost and the Genesis Tradition* (Oxford, 1968).

9. M. M. Mahood, *Poetry and Humanism*, p. 200.

10. See D. Saurat, *Milton, Man and Thinker* (London, 1964), pp. 112 ff.

11. Arnold Stein discusses the ridicule implicit in the War in Hell in his *Answerable Style: Essays on Paradise Lost* (Seattle, 1967), pp. 17 ff.

12. It is strange to note Sypher's comment on Milton's hurling down of Satan: 'A titanomachy on this scale was never painted by baroque artists except in Michelangelo's Last Judgement' (p. 209). In fact, Rubens's *Fall of the Damned* is a perfect representation of such a scene.

13. The italics are mine. In his *Spiritual Exercises*, Loyola specifically recommended the closing of shutters against the light as an aid to meditation.

14. Cf. John Shearman, *Mannerism* (Harmondsworth, 1967), p. 130.

15. 'First Anniversarie', 286–9.

16. Marvell, 'On a Drop of Dew', 34 ff.

17. Paul E. Parnell's 'The Sentimental Mask', *Publications of the Modern Language Association of America*, 78 (1963), traces the culmination of this movement in the drama of the eighteenth century, noting how the surface altruism and compassion of the Christian hero or heroine conceal an unquestioning conviction of their own piety, perfection, and superiority to all characters around them. They epitomize the very reverse of Christian humility.

18. Arnold Hauser has argued that mannerism is essentially narcissistic but here too I remained unconvinced, particularly as once again he is attempting to see such 'narcissism' in terms of modern alienation. See his *Mannerism*, i. 112 ff.

19. Mario Praz, *Secentismo e Marinismo in Inghilterra* (Florence, 1925) and H. J. C. Grierson, *Cross Currents in English Literature of the Seventeenth Century* (London, 1958), p. 181. There is actually no foundation for the identification of Mary Magdalene with the anonymous 'sinner' who anoints the feet of Jesus, but the composite image of the penitent Magdalene had become firmly established by this time.

20. Austin Warren, *Richard Crashaw: a study in baroque sensibility* (Ann Arbor, 1957), p. 192. See also Ruth C. Wallerstein, *Richard Crashaw: a study in style and poetic development* (Madison, 1962).

21. Robert M. Adams, 'Taste and Bad Taste in Metaphysical Poetry', *The Hudson Review* 8 (1955), 60.

22. There is a textual variant for the last couplet: 'Where th' milky rivers meet / Thine crawls above and is the Cream'; but the stricture applies equally to 'crawls'.

23. Holy Sonnet IX.

24. Sermon at Lincoln's Inn, delivered during the spring of 1618; in *Sermons* ii. 63.

25. *Meditations upon the Mysteries of our Holie Faith*, tr. John Higham 1619, quoted in Martz, p. 49.

26. I have offered a more detailed and less dogmatic defence of this viewpoint against those who deny the personal elements in the play, in my *Biblical Drama in England* (London, 1968), pp. 152–73, which sees it as part of a broader 'post-figurative' tendency in Protestant writing.

27. *Sermons* ii. 52–3. Lord Faulkland's 'Elegie on Dr. Donne' offers further testimony to his effectiveness as a preacher. For the sense of privacy in Donne's writings, see Earl Miner, *The Metaphysical Mode from Donne to Cowley* (Princeton, 1969).

28. Second Prebend sermon delivered 29 Jan. 1625, in *Sermons* vii. 57.

CHAPTER III

1. Rosemond Tuve, *Elizabethan and Metaphysical Imagery* (Chicago, 1947), p. 345, which was preceded by E. L. Wiggins, 'Logic in the Poetry of John Donne', *Studies in Philology*, 42 (1945), 41. William Empson replied to Miss Tuve in 'Donne and the Rhetorical Tradition', *Kenyon Review*, 11 (1949), 571. See also Norman E. Nelson, 'Peter Ramus and the Confusion of Logic, Rhetoric, and Poetry', in *University of Michigan Contributions in Modern Philology*, No. 2 (April 1947).

2. *A Valediction: of My Name, in the Window*. For 'catachresis', see Tuve, p. 132, and for 'the hardest mathematics', George Williamson, *The Donne Tradition* (New York, 1958), p. 40.

3. J. E. V. Crofts, 'John Donne', in *Essays and Studies by Members of the English Association*, 12 (Oxford, 1937). Cf. also Hardin Craig, *The Enchanted Glass* (Oxford, 1950), p. 157.

4. Baldassare Castiglione, *The Book of the Courtier*, tr. Sir Thomas Hoby, ed. Walter Raleigh (London, 1900), p. 123. Rosalie L. Colie has examined this mode in her *Paradoxia Epidemica* (Princeton, 1966), but she makes little distinction there between the frivolous and serious use of paradox.

5. Letter to Buckingham 1623, in Gosse, *Life and Letters*, ii. 176. S. L. Bethell's 'The Nature of Metaphysical Wit' appeared originally in *The Northern Miscellany of Literary Criticism*, 1 (1953), 19, and has been reprinted in Frank Kermode (ed.), *Discussions of John Donne* (Boston, 1967). J. A. Mazzeo has an article on Gracian and Tesauro in his *Renaissance and Seventeenth Century Studies* (London, 1964) which was originally published in 1951 but of which Bethell seems to have been unaware. In any case, the treatment is fundamentally different. Patrick Cruttwell is correct in pointing out that the Tuve–Bethell approach, at least in the form of its presentation, has minimal relevance to literary analysis, since neither critic works closely with the poems. See his 'Love Poetry of John Donne' in *Metaphysical Poetry*, ed. M. Bradbury and D. Palmer (London, 1970), p. 30.

6. Quoted by Kenneth Muir in his introduction to the Arden edition of *Macbeth* (London, 1957), pp. xviii–xix.

7. Bald, p. 39. Without pressing the point, one may note that Donne's uncle, Jasper Heywood, came to England from the Continent to head the Jesuit mission, and stayed for some time in his home. It is unlikely that he would have missed the opportunity of introducing his own nephew to some of the Jesuit concepts. A. E. Malloch in an article on 'John Donne and the Casuists', *Studies in English Literature*, 2 (1962), 57, examines the attacks on

Jesuit equivocation and casuistical argument in the *Pseudo-martyr, Biathanatos,* and *Ignatius, his Conclave,* but concludes '. . . if he disagreed with their methods, he also appears to have shared with them many of the habits of thought which produced those methods'.

8. *Sermons* iii. 359. William H. Halewood in an interesting essay *The Poetry of Grace* (New Haven, 1970) attributes the anti-rationalism of Donne to Augustinian sources, but he does not suggest what elements in Donne's character or era led him to look to Augustine for guidance rather than to Aquinas.

9. Nikolaus Pevsner, 'The Architecture of Mannerism', *The Mint,* 1946.

10. Letter to Sir Henry Wotton *c.* 1600 in E. M. Simpson, *A Study of the Prose Works of John Donne* (Oxford, 1948), p. 316. It does not appear in the Gosse collection.

11. E. R. Curtius, *European Literature of the Latin Middle Ages,* tr. W. R. Trask (New York, 1953), pp. 273 ff.

12. Paradox i: 'A Defence of Women's Inconstancy'.

13. Helen Gardner provides evidence for the contemporary fashion in her note to the poem. The allusion to the French word *jette* was first noticed by F. L. Lucas, as the editor of the Nonesuch edition records.

14. *Deaths Duell or a Consolation to the Soule, against the Dying Life, and Living Death of the Body,* delivered at Whitehall, Lent 1630, in *Sermons* x. 233. There is a similar image in Herbert's 'Mortification'.

15. Sermon preached at Hanworth, 25 Aug. 1622, in *Sermons* iv. 171. For the porter passage, see Gosse i. 195.

16. Haydn, *Counter-Renaissance,* p. 88. See also Margaret L. Wiley, *The Subtle Knot: creative scepticism in seventeenth century England* (Cambridge, Mass., 1952), pp. 120 ff.

17. Montaigne, *Complete Essays,* tr. Donald M. Frame (Stanford, 1965), p. 438. Louis I. Bredvold, 'The Religious Thought of Donne' in *Studies in Shakespeare, Milton, and Donne* (Michigan, 1925), contains one of the best analyses of the sceptical element in Donne's writings, and George Williamson in his *Seventeenth Century Contexts* (London, 1963), pp. 43 f., suggests his development from scepticism to faith, taking the *Biathanatos* as the primary text.

18. R. Burton, *The Anatomy of Melancholy* (Boston, 1859), ii. 147. For fuller examinations of this theory, see A. O. Lovejoy, *The Great Chain of Being* (Cambridge, Mass., 1936), chapter iv, and Theodore Spencer, *Shakespeare and the Nature of Man* (New York, 1942), pp. 32 ff.

19. Montaigne, *Essays*, p. 331.

20. Francis Bacon, *Descriptio Globi Intellectualis*.

21. Montaigne, *Essays*, pp. 378 and 403.

22. Francis Bacon, *Works*, ed. J. Spedding (London, 1857), ii. 158.

23. Cf. Louis I. Bredvold's article referred to above, on 'The Naturalism of Donne'.

24. Marjorie H. Nicolson gave currency to the term in her *Breaking of the Circle* (New York, 1962).

CHAPTER IV

1. Helen Gardner (ed.), *The Elegies and the Songs and Sonets* (Oxford, 1965), p. 174.

2. Don Cameron Allen, 'John Donne's Knowledge of Renaissance Medicine', *Journal of English and Germanic Philology*, 42 (1943), 334.

3. Donald L. Guss, *John Donne, Petrarchist: Italianate Conceits and Love Theory in the Songs and Sonets* (Detroit, 1966), p. 59.

4. 'Womans Constancy'.

5. Isaiah 40: 7. Cf. Donne's sermon preached at the Spital on 22 Apr. 1622: 'To know, that all the glory of man, is as the flower of the grass: that even the glory, and all the glory, of man, of all mankind, is but a flower, and but as a flower . . .'.

6. Mario Praz, *Secentismo e Marinismo* (Florence, 1925), p. 109.

7. 'The Blossome'.

8. Leonard Unger, *Donne's Poetry and Modern Criticism* (New York, 1962), p. 86. The italics are his.

9. *The Republic*, tr. H. Spens (London, 1906), p. 197.

10. Ibid., p. 88.

11. 'The Litanie', 62–3. The contradictory views of 'fear' are from Holy Sonnet XIX and 'A Hymne to God the Father'.

12. Pierre Legouis, *Donne the Craftsman* (New York, 1928), p. 68. There is a hesitant suspicion of the parodying intent in Wilbur Sanders's recent study *John Donne's Poetry* (Cambridge, 1971), p. 102.

13. Cf. C. S. Lewis, *The Allegory of Love* (Oxford, 1936), M. C. D'Arcy, *The Mind and Heart of Love* (New York, 1967), and Denis de Rougement, *Love in the Western World*, tr. M. Belgion, (New York, 1956). Also A. Nygren, *Agape and Eros*, tr. P. S. Watson (London, 1953).

14. 'Loves Progress', 91 f.

15. 'Loves Alchymie', 18 ff. 'Mummy' here refers, of course, to dead flesh preserved in bitumen for medicinal purposes.

16. A. J. Smith, 'The Metaphysic of Love', in *Review of English Studies*, N.S. 9 (1958), 362, offers a detailed account of the variations within Neoplatonism, although his purpose there is to show the indebtedness of Donne's 'Extasie' to Neoplatonic thought.

17. Mario Praz, 'Donne's Relation to the Poetry of his Time', reprinted in his *The Flaming Heart* (New York, 1958). In an impressive study of the meta-physical poets, Robert Ellrodt has singled out Donne's tendency to absorb the entire world into one point of time and space, and thus to endow his verse with sharp dramatic realism. This is undoubtedly true, but I am more impressed by his ability to expand into the universal again after that moment of contraction, and to hold the double vision in simultaneous focus. See Robert Ellrodt, *Les Poètes métaphysiques anglais*, 2 vols. (Paris, 1960).

18. P. Legouis, *Donne the Craftsman*, p. 50.

19. Miss Elizabeth Sewell has suggested that Eliot employs allusions to the Nonsense literature of Lewis Carroll and G. K. Chesterton, but even she does not seriously argue that his humorous poems are intimately related to his major verse. See her article 'Lewis Carroll and T. S. Eliot as Nonsense Poets' in *T. S. Eliot: A Symposium for his Seventieth Birthday*, ed. N. Braybrooke (New York, 1959).

20. The term had been applied earlier, but not in a strictly literary sense. See A. Alvarez, *The School of Donne* (New York, 1967), p. 117.

CHAPTER V

1. Sermon preached at the funeral of Sir William Cokayne, 12 Dec. 1626; in *Sermons* vii. 264–5.

2. The anthology was published in 1940. For a valuable discussion of their viewpoints, and of religious poetry in general, see Helen Gardner, *Religion and Literature* (London, 1971), pp. 121 ff.

3. Bald, pp. 234 ff. The sick soul is discussed in lectures iv to vii of William James's *Varieties of Religious Experience*.

4. *Sermons* ix. 349, delivered during the last year of his life.

5. *The Crosse*, 19 ff.

6. Their views are presented respectively in Helen Gardner's introduction to her edition of Donne's *Divine Poems*, originally published in 1952, and

Martz, *The Poetry of Meditation*, particularly pp. 49–50. The latter's *Wit of Love* (London, 1969) has since taken further the suggested relationship between the poems and paintings of the time.

7. There is an interesting account of this importation of pagan deities into Christianity in Jean Seznec, *The Survival of the Pagan Gods*, tr. B. F. Sessions (New York, 1953). C. S. Lewis defended the Church against the charge of having itself contributed to the paganizing of the Virgin in his *Allegory of Love*, and Denis de Rougemont has traced the source of the conflict to the Charaist sect, which wished during the Middle Ages to substitute a Church of Love for the established Church. Their founders, justifying the attempt anagrammatically, ingeniously argued that ROMA should be reversed to AMOR. See his *Love in the Western World*, p. 108.

8. Caravaggio, it should be noted, did not normally paint within this more vigorous style of mannerism, usually preferring the quieter naturalism for which he is best known. However, even in such naturalistic painting, he shares with mannerism a desire to resist Renaissance idealization by presenting biblical scenes with shockingly life-like effect, rather like the colloquialism of 'Spit in my face . . .'. His paintings were frequently rejected by those who had commissioned them, on the grounds that the apostles resembled coarse peasants. They alleged (probably with justice) that his *Death of the Virgin* had used as its model the corpse of a drowned prostitute.

9. *The Spiritual Exercises of St. Ignatius*, tr. Anthony Mottola (New York, 1964), p. 56. One of the most illuminating comments on the prose of this period may be applied with equal effectiveness to its poetry. Morris R. Croll, in his 1929 essay on 'The Baroque Style in Prose', pointed out with a glance towards the Italian mannerist painters (at that time still undistinguished from the baroque) that the prose of that era preferred forms expressing '. . . the energy and labor of minds seeking the truth, not without dust and heat, to the forms that express a contented sense of the enjoyment and possession of it . . . Their purpose was to portray, not a thought, but a mind thinking.' The essay is reprinted in *Style, Rhetoric, and Rhythm: Essays by Morris R. Croll*, ed. J. M. Patrick *et al.* (Princeton, 1966).

10. François de Sales, *A Treatise of the Love of God*, tr. Miles Pinkney (Douai, 1630), p. 325.

11. The equation of Jesus with the sun is, of course, common in Donne's poetry, both as a pun on Son and as an allusion to Apollo, the pagan god of male love. Cf. 'Goodfriday', 10–14, and 'Resurrection Imperfect', 1–7. See also Lucio P. Ruotolo, 'The Trinitarian Framework of Donne's Holy Sonnet XIV', *Journal of the History of Ideas*, 27 (1966), 445.

12. Donne uses the same Platonic image 'Else a great Prince in prison lies' in 'The Extasie', 68.

13. Holy Sonnet XVIII.

14. Cf. the painting of her by Fray Juan de la Miseria.

15. Quoted in Robert T. Petersson, *The Art of Ecstasy* (London, 1970), p. 45.

16. François de Sales, *An Introduction to a Devoute Life*, tr. John Yakesley (Rouen, 1614).

17. Richard Baxter, *The Saints Everlasting Rest* (London, 1653), iv; quoted in Martz, p. 171.

18. G. G. Scholem, *Major Trends in Jewish Mysticism* (New York, 1961), especially p. 226.

19. R. Southwell, *At Home in Heaven*, followed by G. Herbert, *The Forerunners*. Both passages are among the quotations offered by Martz as illustrative of the movement; see pp. 186 ff.

20. Taking up this suggestion, Mrs. N. J. C. Andreasen's *John Donne: Conservative Revolutionary* (Princeton, 1967) has argued precisely that. She maintains that the libertine poems were intended to parody or ridicule physical love and lust in order to persuade the reader to adopt the Christian–Platonic ideal instead.

21. See Gosse, ii. 68, and Gardner, *Divine Poems*, lxiii–lxiv.

22. Joan Webber, *Contrary Music: the prose style of John Donne* (Madison, 1963), p. 152.

23. Emil Mâle, *Religious Art from the Twelfth to the Eighteenth Century* (New York, 1965), pp. 140 ff. The phrase itself is, of course, unquestionably medieval, occurring as the opening line of an anonymous sequence within the Gradual; but its use as a central theme in art and literature is a phenomenon of the early Renaissance.

24. 'The Relique'.

25. 'Elegy on the Lady Marckham', 17–28.

26. *Sermons* viii. 98.

27. The resulting portrait served Nicholas Stone as the model for the sepulchral effigy he executed—one of the few figures to survive the Great Fire. It was re-erected almost unharmed in the rebuilt St. Paul's Cathedral. Dame Helen Gardner, in a review of Bald's *Life*, cast doubt on the entire incident of Donne's posing. But quite apart from the confidence with which Walton records it, and the substantiation offered by the statue itself, the event accords so well with Donne's attitude to death (as well as the mannerist's) that I see no reason to reject it as a figment of Walton's imagination merely because it sounds strange to modern ears.

28. 'Hymne to God my God, in my Sicknesse'.

29. A. C. Bradley, for example, devotes his *Shakespearean Tragedy* to *Hamlet*, *Othello*, *Lear*, and *Macbeth*, although his analysis of *Antony and Cleopatra* in his separate Oxford lectures leaves no doubt that he regarded it as one of the five major tragedies '. . . succeeding as triumphantly as *Othello* itself'.

30. 'The Broken Heart'.

31. *Sermons* vii. 368–9.

32. In Donne's day, passing-bells were rung not only for funerals but also for dying men who needed the prayers of well-wishers while they were still alive. Here, however, Donne is clearly speaking of the bell tolled for a dead man. The preceding meditation (of which this is a continuation) had taken as its central theme *From the bells of the Church adjoyning, I am daily remembred of my buriall in the funeralls of others*, and had concluded in the same vein, recalling those hourly bells which tell of 'so many *funerals* of men like me'. There can be no doubt, therefore, that in its context this opening sentence conjures up the grotesque image of a listening corpse.

33. There is no need to determine which version Donne used as the Vulgate itself reads: 'Fide Henoch *translatus* est ne videret mortem et non inveniebatur quia *transtulit* illum Deus . . .'. The same holds true for the second quotation.

34. Even so sensitive a critic as Mario Praz has in his recent *Mnemosyne*, pp. 95–7, reaffirmed his earlier view that Donne reflects in his tortuous line of reasoning the 'caprice' of mannerist art.

35. In fact, Donne reverses here the normal identification of the First Mover with the *motus rationalis*; but the exchange, which suits his analogy better, is clearly meant to pass unnoticed. See Gardner, *Divine Poems*, p. 98.

36. Donne's debt to medieval sources has been examined in detail in Mary P. Ramsay, *Les Doctrines médiévales chez Donne* (Oxford, 1924), and M. F. Moloney attempts to rebut her thesis in *John Donne: his Flight from Medievalism* (New York, 1965).

37. Sermon 'In Vesperis' delivered at St. Paul's, 5 Nov. 1626; in *Sermons* vii. 245.

38. Meditation XXI from *Devotions on Emergent Occasions*.

39. Cf. Psalm 19.

40. From the Easter Sermon delivered at St. Paul's 25 Mar. 1627; in *Sermons* vii. 374.

41. Cf. Bald, p. 525. In view of the difficulties involved in dating Donne's poetry, I have refrained throughout this book from drawing conclusions

based on conjectural chronology. There is, of course, a controversy over the dating of this hymn, some critics accepting Sir Julius Caesar's endorsement of the manuscript as having been written during Donne's earlier sickness in 1623, while others follow Walton in assuming that it was a deathbed composition. The date, in fact, is immaterial to my argument here, as in 1623 he had every reason to believe his death was imminent.

42. The confident statement here that the Tree and the Cross stood at one place is not borne out by Christian sources and Donne may have confused two different traditions. See D. C. Allen, 'John Donne's Paradise and Calvarie', *Modern Language Notes* 60 (1945).

43. Sermon delivered at St. Paul's, 30 Jan. 1624/5; in *Sermons* vi. 215.

44. *Essays in Divinity.*

45. Sermon delivered at St. Paul's, 25 Jan. 1628/9; in *Sermons* viii. 332–3.

INDEX